A Dictionary of Epithets Classified According to Their English Meaning

You are holding a reproduction of an original work that is in the public domain in the United States of America, and possibly other countries.You may freely copy and distribute this work as no entity (individual or corporate) has a copyright on the body of the work.This book may contain prior copyright references, and library stamps (as most of these works were scanned from library copies).These have been scanned and retained as part of the historical artifact.

This book may have occasional imperfections such as missing or blurred pages, poor pictures, errant marks, etc. that were either part of the original artifact, or were introduced by the scanning process. We believe this work is culturally important, and despite the imperfections, have elected to bring it back into print as part of our continuing commitment to the preservation of printed works worldwide. We appreciate your understanding of the imperfections in the preservation process, and hope you enjoy this valuable book.

A

DICTIONARY OF EPITHETS,

CLASSIFIED ACCORDING TO THEIR ENGLISH
MEANING:

BEING

An Appendix

TO

THE "LATIN GRADUS."

BY

C. D. YONGE,

AUTHOR OF THE "LATIN GRADUS;"
ETC. ETC. ETC.

LONDON:

LONGMAN, BROWN, GREEN, AND LONGMANS.

1856.

PREFACE.

THE original idea of the following little work I owe to the Rev. Charles Tarver, Rector of Ilketshall, Suffolk, whose experience, while engaged in preparing pupils for Eton, had shown him the want which beginners felt of some further assistance than was supplied by my Gradus.

The lists of Epithets, as given in the old Gradus, which marked only the quantity, and was silent as to the meaning of the words it gave, had long been seen by every one to be productive of nothing but mischief, as preventing boys from thinking instead of teaching them to think; but my Gradus, which wholly discards them, substituting instead phrases selected from the Augustan poets, requires perhaps, more thought than *very young* beginners are capable of. In this book, therefore, which is only meant for those who are *beginning* to do verses out of their own sense, I have endeavoured not merely to supply them with sufficient help, but, by giving the *meaning* of the Epithets, to lead them to think for themselves, and to consider, not merely the *quantity* of the word, but its *sense,* so that they may judge of each adjective in connection with the subject of which they are writing, and so may select an appropriate one.

As this book does not profess to be a complete Dictionary, but is only meant as a sort of Appendix to my Gradus, I have not thought it necessary either to give every Latin substantive, or even every meaning of those which are to be found in it. But at the same time, while, in order to compress it within the smallest practicable space, I have omitted many words and many meanings, I hope it will be found that I have given all those for which a beginner is likely to require an Epithet.

C. Y.

January 1856.

DICTIONARY OF EPITHETS.

ăbăcus. *A sideboard.*—EP. *Rich, as to the plate on it,* dīves -ĭtis, splendĭdus; *as to the delicacies on it,* lautus, ōpĭmus; *(or, on the other hand,) humble,* hŭmĭlis, mŏdĭcus.

abdōmen, ĭnis, neut. *The belly.*—EP. *Fat,* pinguis. *Lean,* măcer -cra -crum.

ăbies, gen. ăbĭĕtis (trisyll.), fem. 1. *A fir-tree.*—2. *A ship.*—3. *A spear.*—EP. 1. *Tall,* alta, ardua, prōcēra, nōbĭlis. *Evergreen,* vĭrĭdia, vĭrĭdans.—For 2., see navis; 3., see hasta.

ăbĭtus, ûs. *Departure, or passage by which to depart.*—EP. *Easy,* făcĭlis, părātus. *Difficult,* diffĭcĭlis, nullus. *Immediate,* promptus. *Early, seasonable,* mātūrus. *Rapid,* cĭtus, răpĭdus. *Late,* sērus.

ăbolla. *A cloak.* See toga.

ăbortus, ûs. *Miscarriage.* — EP. *Untimely,* immātūrus, intempestīvus. *Sad,* tristis, infēlix, mĭser, flēbĭlis.

ăbrŏtŏnum. *Southernwood.*—EP. *Wholesome,* sălūtāre, sălūtĭfĕrum, sălūbre.

abscessus, ûs. *Departure.* See abitus.

absinthium. *Wormwood.*—EP. *White or grey,* cānum, candĭdum, album, albens. *Bitter,* ăcerbum, aspĕrum.

abundantia. See copia.

ăbūsus, ûs. *Misuse.*—EP. *Wrong, perverse,* prāvus, mălus, perversus. *Foolish,* stultus, insānus.

ăcădēmĭa. *The academy at Athens.*—EP. *Learned, wise,* săpiens, docta. *Celebrated,* clāra, præclāra, insignis, ēgrĕgia.

acceptor. *A receiver.*—EP. *Joyful,* lætus, hĭlăris, fēlix.

accessus, ûs. *Approach, or passage of approach.* — EP. *Easy,* făcĭlis, părātus. *Difficult,* diffĭcĭlis. *Speedy,* cĭtus, răpĭdus. *Slow,* tardus. *Early, seasonable,* mātūrus, tempestīvus. *Late,* sērus.

accĭpĭter, tris, masc. *A hawk.* — EP. *Devouring, greedy,* răpax, ĕdax, vŏrax, ăvĭdus. *Cruel,* crūdēlis, fērus, sævus, immītis. *Swift,* vēlox, răpĭdus, præpes -ĕtis, cĕler -ĕris.

accītus, ûs. *A summons.* — EP. *Welcome,* grātus, acceptus. *Unwelcome,* invīsus, tristis, ŏdiōsus.

accŏla, æ, masc. *One who lives near.* — EP. *Neighbouring,* vīcīnus, fīnĭtĭmus, proxĭmus. *Friendly,* ămīcus. *Beloved,* cārus. *Unfriendly,* inĭmīcus, hostīlis.

accŭbĭtus, ûs. *A lying or sitting down by.* — EP. *Friendly,* ămīcus. *Loving,* ămans. *Joyful,* lætus.

accursus, ûs. *A running towards.*—EP. *Swift,* răpĭdus, cĭtus, cĕler -ĕris, vēlox. *Joyful,* lætus, hĭlăris.

accūsātor. *An accuser.*—EP. *Just,* justus. *Angry, etc.,* īrātus, infensus, implăcābĭlis, inexōrābĭlis, ăcerbus.

ăcer, ăcĕris, neut. *Maple.*—EP. *Worthless,* vīle. *Hard,* dūrum. *Humble (as used by the common people),* hŭmĭle, pauper -ĕris.

ăcerra. *A censer.* — EP. *Full,* plēna. *Pious, pia,* casta, săcra. *Joyful,* fēlix, lætus. (LIT. EP. *properly belonging to the worshippers.*)

ăcervus. *A heap.*—EP. *Collected together,* congestus, cŭmŭlātus. *Large,* magnus, amplus, altus. *Rich,* dīves -ĭtis; *(or, on the other hand,) small,* parvus, hŭmĭlis, mŏdĭcus.

ăcētum. *Vinegar.*—EP. *Sour,* ăcerbum, acre.

Ăchăĭa. *Greece.* See Græcia.

B

2 ACH—ADV

Ăchĕron, ontis, masc. *A river of Hell.* — EP. *Dark*, tĕnĕbrōsus, lūrĭdus, āter. *Pale*, pallens, pallĭdus. *Of Hell*, Tartăreus, infernus. *Hoarse-sounding*, raucus. *Hateful*, invīsus, ŏdiōsus. *Last (as coming after life)*, ultĭmus, sŭprēmus.

Ăchilles. *Brave, active*, fortis, impăvĭdus, audax, strēnuus, impĭger. *Cruel*, fĕrus, fĕrox, immītia, saevus, crūdēlis. *Grecian, etc.*, Lārissaeus, Phthĭus, Ăchīvus, Argīvus.

ăcies, ēi. 1. *An edge.*—2. *Sight, the eye.*—3. *An army.*—EP. 1. *Sharp*, ăcūta, pĕnĕtrăbĭlis; *destructive*, exĭtiālis, exĭtiōsa, lētĭfĕra.—For 2., see oculus.—For 3., see exercitus.

ăcīnăces, is, masc. *A scimetar.*—EP. *Median*, Mēdus. See ensis.

ăcĭnum. *A grapestone.*—EP. *Sweet*, dulcis. *Intoxicating*, ēbriōsus.

ăcĭpenser, ĕris, masc. *A sturgeon.*—EP. *Large*, magnus.

aclis, ĭdis, fem. *A dart.* See jaculum.

ăcŏnītum. *Aconite.* See venenum.

ăcrĕdŭla. *A goldfinch.*—EP. *Sweet*, dulcis, cănōrus. *Singing in the morning*, mătūtīnus.

acta. *Shore.* See littus.

actum. *An exploit.* See factum.

actor. 1. *One who puts in motion, a driver*, etc.—2. *An actor.*—3. *A pleader.* —EP. 1. *Active*, impĭger, indēfessus.—2. *Skilful*, doctus, pĕrītus, callĭdus.— 3. *Eloquent*, făcundus, dīsertus. *Prudent*, prūdens, săpiens, callĭdus. *Learned*, doctus.

actus, ûs. *An act.* See actum.

ăcūleus. *A sting.*—EP. *Painful*, tristis. *Cruel*, dūrus, crūdēlis.

ăcūmen, ĭnis, neut. 1. *A point.*—2. *Cleverness.*—EP. 1. *Sharp*, pĕnĕtrăbĭle. —2. *Shrewd*, argūtum, săpiens, prūdens, săgax, callĭdum.

ăcus, ûs, fem. *A needle.*—EP. *Little*, parva, exĭgua. *Skilful*, pĕrīta, callĭda; *(of the needle of the compass,) true, trustworthy*, vēra, fĭdēlis, fĭda, verax, vērĭdĭca.

ădămas, antis, acc. anta, masc. *Adamant.*—EP. *Hard*, dūrus, ēdūrus, rĭgĭdus. *Unyielding, not to be worn out*, invictus, insŭpĕrābĭlis. *Lasting*, aeternus.

ădauctus, ûs. *Increase.*—EP. *Great*, magnus, grandis. *Continual*, perpĕtuus, assĭduus.

ădeps, ĭpis. *Fat.*—EP. *Gross*, crassus.

ădĭtus, ûs. *Approach.* See accessus.

adjūmentum. *Assistance.* See auxĭlium.

adjūtor, fem. adjūtrix. *An assistant.*—EP. *Friendly, kind*, ămīcus, bĕnignus. *Prompt, willing*, etc., promptus, lĭbens, impĭger. *Useful*, ūtĭlis, ĭdōneus, efficax, pŏtens. *Fearless*, impăvĭdus. *Fearless, or useful*, fortis.

admīrātio. *Admiration.*—EP. *Great*, magna, ingens. *Silent*, tăcĭta. *Eloquent*, făcunda, garrŭla. *Sudden*, sŭbĭta.

admissum. *A fault.* See culpa.

admŏnĭtor. *An admonisher.*—EP. *Prudent*, prūdens, săpiens. *Kind*, ămīcus, bĕnignus. *Gentle*, mītis, hūmānus. *Aged*, sĕnex, cānus. *Earnest*, strēnuus, sollĭcĭtus. *Repeated*, assĭduus, crēber -bra -brum. *Angry*, īrācundus, īrātus.

admŏnĭtus, ûs. *Warning.*—EP. *Prudent*, prūdens, săpiens. *Kind*, ămīcus, bĕnignus. *Gentle*, mītis, tĕner, hūmānus, blandus. *Earnest*, sollĭcĭtus, grăvis. *Angry*, īrācundus. *Repeated*, crēber -bra -brum, assĭduus, rĕpĕtītus. *Seasonable*, tempestīvus, opportūnus. *Unseasonable*, importūnus, intempestīvus. *Too late*, sērus.

ădŏlescens. *A young man.*—EP. *Impetuous*, fervĭdus. *Active, strong*, impĭger, strēnuus, fortis. *Rash*, tĕmĕrārius, praeceps, incautus. *Violent*, vehĕmens, vĭŏlentus. *Foolish*, stultus, imprūdens.

ădor, neut. *(Rare except in nom. and acc. sing.) Wheat.*—EP. *Sacred to Ceres*, Cĕreāle. *Rich*, pingue. *Delicious*, lautum. *White*, album, nĭveum, candens.

ădōrea. *Victory.* See victoria.

Ādria, ae, masc. *The Adriatic sea.*—EP. *Stormy*, prŏcellosus, inquiētus, turbĭdus, implăcĭdus. *Narrow*, angustus, parvus.

advĕna, ae, masc. *A stranger.*—EP. *Unknown, new*, nŏvus, ignōtus. *Arriving suddenly*, sŭbĭtus. *From foreign parts*, pĕrĕgrīnus, externus. *Friendly*, ămīcus. *Grateful*, grātus. *Ungrateful*, ingrātus.

adventus, ûs. *Arrival.*—EP. *Wished for, welcome*, optātus, grātus, jūcundus.

ADV — ÆTA 3

Sudden, unexpected, sŭbĭtus, ĭnŏpīnus, imprŏvīsus, ĭnexpectātus. *Seasonable,* tempestīvus. *Early,* matūrus. *Late, too late,* sērus. *Safe,* tūtus, incŏlŭmis.

adversārius. *Adversary.* See hostis.

ădŭlātor. *A flatterer.*—EP. *Base,* turpis. *Deceitful,* fallax, falsus, perfĭdus, infĭdus, infĭdēlis. *Caressing,* blandus.

ădulter, ĕri, fem. ădultĕra. *An adulterer.*—EP. *Wanton,* lascīvus, prŏtervus, impŭdīcus. *Faithless,* infĭdus, perfĭdus. *Wicked,* impius, scĕlĕrātus, scĕlertus. *Bold,* audax. *Base,* turpis, infāmis. *Beautiful,* pulcher, formōsus. *Effeminate,* mollis, tĕner.

ădultĕrium. *Adultery.* See above.

ădўtum. *A temple.* See templum.

aedes. In sing., *a temple,* in pl., *a house.* See templum, domus.

aedĭficātor. *A builder.* See conditor.

Ægis, ĭdis, fem. *The shield of Minerva, on which she placed Medusa's head.*—EP. *Bearing the head of Medusa,* Gorgŏnea, Mĕdūsaea. *Terrible,* terrĭbĭlis, dīra, horrĭfĭca. *Glittering,* cŏrusca. *Impenetrable,* impĕnĕtrābĭlis, invicta.

aegrĭmōnia. *Melancholy.*—EP. *Sad,* tristis, moesta, lăcrўmōsa, flēbĭlis. *Pale,* pallĭda, pallens. *Fastidious,* fastĭdiōsa.

Ægyptus, ī, fem. *Egypt.*—EP. *Sacred,* săcra, sancta. *Fertile,* fertĭlis, fĕcunda, fĕrax, ūberrĭma. *Celebrated,* illustris, clāra, insignis, cĕlĕberrĭma. *Powerful,* pŏtens, magna. *Beautiful,* pulchra, ēgrĕgia. *Wise, learned,* săpiens, docta, callĭda. *Treacherous,* fallax, falsa, dŏlōsa, perfĭda, infĭda. *Reigned over by Ptolemy,* Ptŏlĕmaeea. *The land of the Nile, of Canopus, of the lake Mareotis, of Pharos, etc.,* Nĭliăca, Cănōpēa, Mărēŏtĭca, Phăria.

aemŭlus, fem. aemŭla. *A rival.*—EP. *Hostile,* adversus. *Envious,* invĭdus. *Treacherous,* infĭdus, perfĭdus. *Hated,* invīsus. *Ancient,* vĕtus –ĕris, vĕtustus, antiquus, priscus.

Æneas, ae. *The son of Anchises.*—EP. *Trojan,* Tros, Trōjānus, Trōjŭgĕna, Dardănĭdes. *The son of Anchises,* Anchīsĭădes. *The son of Venus,* Cўthĕrēius. *Pious,* pius, justus. *Brave,* fortis, impăvĭdus. *Victorious,* victor. *Illustrious,* clārus, insignis, ēgrĕgius. *Having carried his gods on his back,* Pēnătĭger.

aenigma, ătis, neut. *A riddle.*—EP. *Obscure,* obscūrum, ambĭguum. *Hard,* dūrus, diffĭcĭle. *New,* nŏvum, ĭnaudītum. *Celebrated,* nōtum, cĕlĕbre, insigne, clārum.

Æŏlus. *The king of the winds.*—EP. *Turbulent,* turbĭdus, implăcĭdus, inquiētus, prŏcellōsus. *Changeable,* mūtābĭlis, mōbĭlis, vărius. *Mighty,* magnus, pŏtens. *Son of Hippotas,* Hippŏtădes.

aequor, ŏris. *The sea.* See mare.

āër, āĕris, acc. āĕra. *The air, etc.*—EP. *Light,* lĕvis. *Bright, pure, calm,* clārus, pūrus, sĕrēnus. *Cool,* gĕlĭdus, frĭgĭdus. *Cloudy,* nūbĭlus.

aerārium. *The treasury.*—EP. *Full,* plēnum. *Rich,* dīves –ĭtis, lŏcŭples –ētis.

aerumna. *Grief.*—EP. *Sad,* tristis, lūgŭbris, moesta, lăcrўmōsa, flēbĭlis. *Heavy,* grăvis. *New,* nŏva, rĕcens. *Sudden,* sŭbĭter ĭnŏpīna. *Long,* longa. *Continual,* assĭdua, perpĕtua, aeterna.

aes, aeris, neut. *Brass.*—EP. *Yellow,* fulvum, flāvum, flāvens. *Hard,* dūrum. *Corinthian,* Cŏrinthium. *Splendid, glittering, etc.,* pulchrum, splendĭdum, cŏruscum, splendens.

aescŭlus. *A sort of oak.* See quercus.

aestas. *Summer.*—EP. *Hot,* fervĭda, fervens, călĭda, torrĭda. *Dry,* ărĭda, sicca. *Causing dust,* pulvĕrŭlenta. *Fertile,* fertĭlis, fĕcunda, fĕrax. *Golden (as producing golden fruits, crops, etc.),* aurea, flāva. *Returning,* rĕdiens. *About to return,* rĕdĭtūra. *Middle (midsummer),* mĕdia.

aestus, ūs. 1. *Heat.*—2. *The tide.*—3. *Agitation.*—EP. 1. *Burning,* torrĭdus, fervĭdus, călĭdus, fervens. *Dry, causing drought,* ărĭdus, siccus.—2. *Flowing and ebbing,* rĕfluus, rĕfluens. *Rapid,* răpĭdus, viŏlentus. *Deep,* altus, prŏfundus. 3. *Anxious,* anxius, sollĭcĭtus. *Doubtful,* dŭbius, anceps. *Great,* magnus, viŏlentus. *Nervous,* trĕpĭdus.

aetas. 1. *Age, time of life.*—2. *An age.*—3. *Time.*—EP. *The earliest,* prīma. *Youthful,* jŭvĕnīlis. *Manly,* vĭrīlis. *Mature,* mātūra. *Vigorous,* fortis, vĭrīlis (*not of a woman of course*). *Old,* prŏvecta, prŏvectior. See senectus ; 2., see saeculum ; 3., see tempus.

B 2

4 ÆTH—ALL

æther, ěris, æthra. *The air.* See aër.

Ætna. *Mount Ætna.*—EP. *Sicilian,* Sĭcŭla, Sĭcănia, Sĭcăna, Trĭnăcria. *Cyclopean (the Cyclops and Vulcan worked beneath it),* Cӯclōpĕa Vulcānia. *Burning,* torrĭda, flammea, ignea, flammĭfěra. *Furious,* fŭriōsa. *Terrible,* horrĭfĭca, terrĭbĭlis, dīra. *Roaring,* rauca. *Vast,* ingens, magna.

ævum. *Age.* See ætas.

affātus, ûs. *Address.*—EP. *Friendly,* ămīcus. *Courteous,* cōmis, hūmānus. *Gentle,* mītis, blandus.

affectus, ûs. *Emotion of the mind.*—EP. *Friendly,* ămīcus, ămans. *Doubtful,* dŭbius. *Timid,* tĭmĭdus. *Changeable,* vărius.

afflātus, ûs. *A breathing upon.*—EP. *Gentle,* mītis, blandus. *Divine,* dīvīnus, săcer. *Fiery,* igneus.

Africa. *Burnt up, dry, thirsty,* torrĭda, ărĭda, sicca, sĭtiens, sĭtĭcŭlōsa.

Afrīcus. *The south-west wind.*—EP. *Wanton,* prŏtervus. *Stormy,* prŏcellōsus. See ventus.

Ăgămemnon, ŏnis. *The king of Mycenæ.*—EP. *Mycenæan, Greek,* Mӯcēnæus, Argīvus, Pĕlŏpēus, Pĕlŏpēius, Pĕlasgus. *Brave,* fortis, vălĭdus. *Powerful,* pŏtens. *Invincible,* invictus. *Illustrious,* clārus, inclӯtus, insignis, illustris. *Royal,* rēgius.

Ăgāso, ōnis. *A groom.*—EP. *Careful,* cautus, sēdŭlus.—*Skilful,* pĕrītus, doctus. *Active,* impĭger. *Faithful,* fīdus, fĭdēlis.

Ăgellus, ăger, gri. *A field.*—EP. *Fertile,* fertĭlis, fēcundus, fěrax. *Green,* vĭrĭdis, vĭrĭdans. *Golden (with corn, etc.),* flāvus, aureus. *Cultivated,* cultus. *Barren,* stěrĭlis. *Dry,* siccus, ărĭdus. *Wet,* hūmĭdus, ūdus, mădĭdus.

agger, ěris, masc. *A rampart, etc.*—EP. *High,* altus, celsus. *Heaped up,* congestus, structus. *Strong,* vălĭdus, fortis.

ăgĭtātor. *A driver.* See actor.

agmen, ĭnis, neut. 1. *A line (esp. of battle).*—2. *An army.*—EP. 1. *Long,* longum. *Dense,* densum.—2. *Strong,* fortis, vălĭdus. *Armed,* armātum, florens ære, ensĭfěrum, clӯpeātum. *Warlike,* bellĭcum, bellĭcōsum, bellĭgěrum, bellĭpŏtens, armĭpŏtens, martium, mavortium. *Fierce,* fěrum, fěrox, sævum.

agnus, agna. *A lamb.*—EP. *Tender,* těner, těnellus, mollis. *White,* albus, nĭveus, candĭdus. *Weak, timid,* tĭmĭdus, imbellis, plăcĭdus. *Young, newly born,* nŏvellus.

ăgrestis, ăgrĭcŏla, æ, masc. *A countryman, a farmer.*—EP. *Hardy, strong,* dūrus, fortis, vălĭdus. *Rough, unpolished,* rŭdis, incultus. *Contented,* contentus. *Diligent,* sēdŭlus, impĭger, dīlĭgens. *Prudent,* prūdens, săgax. *Skilful,* doctus, pĕrītus.

āla. 1. *A wing.* 2. *A squadron.*—EP. 1. *Light,* lěvis, mōbĭlis. *Swift,* pernix, vēlox, răpĭda, vŏlŭcris. *Borne on high,* sŭblīmis, alta. *Equal (the wings being of equal length),* in plur., pāres. *Making a flapping noise,* strīdens, strīdŭla. *Moving,* mōta. 2. *Swift, impetuous,* vēlox, răpĭda. *Fierce,* fěra, sæva. See agmen.

Alcestis. *The wife of Admetus, who devoted herself for her husband.*—EP. *Faithful,* fīda, fĭdēlis. *Loving,* ămans. *Fearless,* impăvĭda, fortis. *About to die,* mŏrĭtūra.

Alcyon, ŏnis, fem. *A kingfisher, deriving its name from Alcyone, daughter of Æolus, who in grief for the loss of Ceyx, her husband, threw herself into the sea, and was changed into a kingfisher.*—EP. *Haunting the sea,* mărīna, æquŏrea. *Loved by Thetis,* Thetĭdi dilecta. *Sad,* tristis. *Faithful,* fĭda, fĭdēlis.

ālea. 1. *A die.*—2. *A hazard.*—EP. 1. 2. *Uncertain,* incerta, dŭbia. *Changeable,* mŭtābĭlis, văria. *Dangerous,* pĕrĭcŭlōsa. 1. *Deceitful,* fallax, perfĭda.— 2. See periculum.

āleo, ōnis, aleātor. *A dicer, a gambler.*—EP. *Extravagant,* prōdĭgus. *Rash,* tĕmĕrārius, præceps. *Foolish,* stultus, dēmens, ĭneptus.

āles, ĭtis. *A bird.* See avis.

alga. *Seaweed.*—EP. *Lying on, growing near the shore,* lĭttŏrea. *Worthless,* vīlis. *Dripping,* mădĭda, ūvĭda, ūda.

algor. *Cold.* See frigus.

ălĭmentum. *Food.*—EP. *Salutary,* sălūtāre, sălūbre. *Useful,* utile. *Delicate,* lautum, ŏpĭmum.

allapsus, ûs. *A gliding approach.*—EP. *Silent,* tăcĭtus. *Sudden,* sŭbĭtus.

ALL—AMI 5

Unexpected, inŏpīnus, ĭnexpectatus. *Dangerous,* pĕrīcŭlōsus. *Destructive,* damnōsus, exĭtiōsus, lētĭfer.

allium. *Garlic.*—EP. *Strong smelling,* grăveŏlens.

allŏquium. *Address, conversation.* See affatus.

alnus. 1. *An alder tree.*—2. *A ship.*—EP. 1. *Lofty,* alta, ardua. *Easily cut,* sectīlis. *Light,* lēvis.—2. See navis.

Alpis. *An alp, more usu. in plur.* Alpes.—EP. *Lofty,* alta, ardua, sŭblīmis. *Exposed to the wind, stormy,* ventōsa, prŏcellōsa. *Pathless,* invia, ĭnaccessa, diffĭcĭlis. *Snowy,* nīvea, nĭvōsa, nĭvālis. *Cold, frozen,* frīgĭda, gĕlĭda, glăciālis. *Distant,* longinqua, rĕmōta, extrēma.

altāre. *An altar.* See ara.

altor, altrix. *A nourisher.*—EP.—*Kind,* bĕnignus, ămīcus. *Loving,* ămans. *Gentle,* mītis.

alveārium. *A beehive.*—EP. *Of straw,* strămĭneum. *Safe,* tūtum. *Full,* plēnum. *Full of honey,* melleum, mellĭtum.

alveus. 1. *A channel, or river.*—2. *A boat.* 1. See fluvius.—2. See navis.

ălumnus, ălumna. *A fosterchild, a pupil ; in masc., a youth ; in fem., a damsel.* —EP. *Youthful,* jŭvĕnis. *Little,* parvus. *Tender,* tĕner. *Loved,* ămātus, dīlectus, cārus.

ălūta. *Leather, anything made of leather.*—EP. *Soft,* mollis, tĕnĕra. *Hard,* dūra, rĭgĭda. *Lasting,* mansura.

alvus. 1. *The belly.*—2. *The womb.*—EP. 1. *Full,* plēnus. *Fat,* pinguis. *Lean,* măcer. *Round, smooth,* tĕres –ĕtis.—2. See uterus.

ămārăcus. *Marjoram.*—EP. *Soft,* mollis, tĕner. *Sweet,* dulcis, suaveŏlens. *Green,* vĭrĭdis, vĭrĭdans, vĭrens.

ămăranthus. *Amaranth.*—EP. *Sweet,* dulcis, suaveŏlens. *Beautiful,* pulcher, formōsus. *Purple,* purpūreus. *Green,* vĭrĭdis, vĭrĭdans, vĭrens. *Everlasting,* perpĕtuus.

ămārĭties, ămāror. *Bitterness.*—EP. *Sad, disagreeable,* tristis, ingrātus, dūrus.

ămātor. *A lover.*—EP. *Tender,* tĕner. *Welcome, dear,* cārus, grātus, acceptus, dīlectus. *Anxious,* anxius, sollĭcītus. *Fearful,* păvĭdus, tĭmĭdus. *Earnest,* fervĭdus, vehĕmens, instans. *Unwearied,* indēfessus, assĭduus. *Suppliant,* supplex. *Credulous,* crēdŭlus. *Faithful,* fīdus, fĭdēlis, constans. *New,* nŏvus. *Eloquent,* făcundus.

Ămăzon, ŏnis, fem. *An Amazon.*—EP. *Warlike,* bellīca, bellĭcosa, pugnax. *Brave,* fortis, audax, fĕrox, impăvĭda, interrĭta, imperterrĭta. *Thracian,* Thrēĭcia, Thrēissa. *A sister of Hippolyte,* soror Hippolytes. *For the names of some of the principal Amazons,* see Gradus, voc. Amazon.

ambāges, rare in sing. 1. *Any circuitous course.*—2. *An obscure prophecy.*— EP. *Out of the way,* văga, dēvia.—2. *Obscure,* obscūra, incerta, tecta. *Doubtful,* dŭbia, anceps. *Fearful,* dīra, horrenda, horrĭbĭlis.

ambĭtio. *Ambition.*—EP. *Vain, deceitful,* vāna, ĭnānis, fallax. *Foolish,* stulta, insāna, dēmens. *Swelling, proud,* tŭmĭda, sŭperba. *Successful, joyful,* læta. *Diligent, earnest,* assĭdua, sēdŭla, fervĭda, ācris, ŏpĕrōsa, vehĕmens. *Anxious,* anxia, sollĭcīta.

ambĭtus, ûs. See ambages, ambitio.

ambrŏsia. *The food of the gods.*—EP. *Divine, sacred, etc.,* dīvīna, cælestis, immortālis, săcra.

ămentia. *Distraction, madness, ignorant of the future,* cæca, incauta, imprŏvĭda. *Sudden,* sŭbĭta, nŏva. *Furious,* fŭriōsa. *Miserable,* tristis, infēlix, mĭsĕra.

ămentum. *A thing.*—EP. *Flexible,* flexĭle, lentum. *Tenacious,* tĕnax. *Firm,* firmum. *Long,* longum.

ămes, ĭtis, masc. *A fowler's staff.*—EP. *Long,* longus. *Smooth,* lævis.

ămĕthystus. *An amethyst.*—EP. *Purple,* purpūreus. *Bright,* clārus, fulgens, mĭcans. *Hard,* dūrus. *Oriental,* Ŏriens.

ămīca. *A mistress.*—EP. *Tender,* tĕnĕra, mollis. *Dear,* cāra, dīlecta. *Fruitful,* fīda, fĭdēlis. *Deceitful,* perfĭda, fallax, falsa. *Caressing,* blanda. *Beautiful,* formōsa, vĕnusta, pulchra, spectābĭlis, spĕciosa.

ămīcĭtia. *Friendship.*—EP. *Faithful,* fīda, fĭdēlis, constans, tĕnax, firma. *Long, lasting,* longa, perpĕtua, mansūra, vīvax, irrupta. *Unwearied,* indēfessa. *Warm, eager,* fervĭda, strēnua. *Harmonious,* concors, conjuncta, sōcia. *True,*

B 3

6 AMI—ANS

vēra. *Ancient,* vĕtus –ĕris, prisca, vĕtusta, antīqua. *Long accustomed,* sŏlīta, consueta, assueta.

amīcus. *A friend.* See above.

amnis. *A river.* See fluvius.

ămor. 1. *Love.*—2. *The God of love.*—EP. 1. *True, faithful,* vērus, fīdēlis, fīdus, constans. *Bold,* audax. *Inventive,* ingĕniosus. *Earnest,* sēdŭlus, vehĕmens, fervĭdus, ardens. *Concealed,* tectus, dissĭmŭlātus. *Secret,* furtīvus. *Deathless,* æternus, pĕrennis. *Unwearied, unalterable, etc.,* invictus, indēfessus, immūtābĭlis. *Not to be eradicated,* immĕdĭcābĭlis. *Credulous,* crēdŭlus. *Timid,* tĭmĭdus, păvĭdus. *Anxious,* anxius, sollĭcĭtus. *Happy, successful,* fēlix, lætus. *Powerful,* pŏtens, magnus. *Long,* longus. *Ambitious,* ambĭtiōsus. *Tender,* tĕner, mollis. *Caressing,* blandus. *Sweet, delightful,* dulcis. *New,* nŏvus. *Ancient, accustomed,* vĕtus –ĕris, priscus, sŏlĭtus, consuetus.—2. *Son of Venus,* Cȳthĕrēius. *Winged,* ālĭger, ālātus. *Wanton,* lascīvus, prŏtervus. *Cruel,* immītis, crūdēlis, sævus, fĕrus. *Mischievous,* imprŏbus. *Deceitful,* fallax, perfĭdus, infĭdus, infĭdēlis. *Wearing a quiver,* phărētrātus. *Wearing a bow,* arcĭtĕnens. *Golden,* aureus (*an epith. applied to him by* Ov.).

amphŏra. *A bottle.*—EP. *Full,* plēna. *Purple,* i. e. *full of purple wine,* purpūrea.

amplexus, ūs. *An embrace.*—EP. *Loving,* ămans. *Warm,* fervĭdus. *Tender,* tĕner. *Sweet,* dulcis, jŭcundus, ămænus. *Long,* longus. *Close,* arctus.

ănas, ătis, fem. *A duck.*—EP. *Delighting in water, in rivers,* flŭviālis, ăquŏsus.

ancīle. *The sacred shield which fell from heaven.*—EP. *Divine,* dīvīnum, cæleste, sācrum. *Celebrated,* clārum, cĕlĕbre, nōtum.

ancilla. *A handmaid.*—EP. *Diligent,* sēdŭla. *Prudent,* prūdens.

ancŏra. *An anchor.*—EP. *Firm,* firma. *Tenacious,* tĕnax. *Safe,* tūta, incŏlūmis. *Iron,* ferrea, ferrāta. *Crooked,* unca, ădunca, curva, rĕcurva. *Cast out* (*of the ship*), jacta.

ănĕthum. *Anise.*—EP. *Sweet,* dulcis, suavis, suavĕŏlens. *Flourishing,* flōrens. *Green,* vĭrĭde, vĭrens, vĭrĭdans.

anfractus, ūs. *Winding.*—EP. *Crooked,* curvus. *Out of the way,* dēvius.

angor. *Grief.* See dolor.

anguis. *A snake.*—EP. *Cold,* frĭgĭdus. *Scaly,* squāmeus, squāmĭger, squāmōsus. *Hissing,* sĭbĭlans, sĭbĭlus. *Winding,* sĭnuŏsus. *Slippery,* lūbrĭcus. *Gliding,* labens. *Silent,* tăcĭtus. *Poisonous,* vĕnēnātus, vĕnēnĭfer. *Eastern,* Ōriens, Ēŏus.

angŭlus. *A corner.*—EP. *Obscure,* obscūrus. *Sharp,* ācūtus.

ănhēlĭtus, ūs. *Panting.*—EP. *Quick,* răpĭdus. *Frequent,* crēber. *Showing pain,* æger, diffĭcĭlis. *Raised high* (*that is, the man who is panting raises his face*), sŭblīmis.

ănĭma. *The soul.*—EP. *Immortal,* immortālis, æterna, morte cārens. *Pious,* pia. *Happy,* fēlix.

ănĭmal, ālis, neut. *An animal.*—EP. *Living,* vivum. *Brute,* brūtum. *Innocent,* innŏcuum, innoxium. *Mischievous,* perniciŏsus, damnŏsus, nŏcens, noxius.

ănĭmus. 1. *The mind.*—2. *Courage.*—1. *Prudent,* prūdens, săpiens, cautus. *Acute,* ācūtus, subtīlis, săgax, omnia perspĭciens.—2. *Vehement,* fervĭdus, vehĕmens, ācer –cris.

annāles, plur. *Annals.*—EP. *Ancient,* prisci, vĕtĕres, antiqui. *Sacred,* sācri, sancti. *True,* vēri, vērāces, fīdeles. *Well-known,* nōti.

Annĭbal, ălis. *The general in the Second Punic War.*—EP. *Brave,* fortis, impăvĭdus, audax, fĕrox. *Terrible,* dīrus, terrĭbĭlis. *Cruel,* sævus, immītis, crūdēlis, implācābĭlis, illăcrymābĭlis. *Perfidious,* perfĭdus, infĭdus, fallax. *Carthaginian,* Pœnus, Pūnĭcus, Āfer.

annŭlus. *A ring.*—EP. *Golden,* aureus, aurātus. *Jewelled,* gemmeus gemmātus. *Rich,* dives –ĭtis. *Splendid, shining,* splendĭdus, fulgĭdus, cŏruscus, clārus.

annus. *A year.*—EP. *Gliding on, revolving,* lābens, rĕvŏlūbĭlis. *Rapid,* răpĭdus, mōbĭlis. *Passing quickly,* brĕvis, frăgĭlis. *Passing silently,* tăcĭtus, tăcĭte lābens, tăcĭto passu labens.

ansa. *A handle.* 1. *Strong,* firma. *Handy,* hăbĭlis, ĭdōnea, apta.

anser, ĕris, masc. *A goose. Fond of water,* flŭviālis, ăquŏsus. *Watchful* (*in allusion to the goose who saved the Capitol*), vĭgil –ĭlis, pervigil, vĭgĭlax.

ANT—ARA 7

antenna. *The yard of a ship.* *High,* alta, ardua, sŭblīmis. *Long,* longa.

antistes, ĭtis, antistĭta, fem. *A priest, priestess.*—EP. *Pious,* pius, castus. *Holy,* săcer, sanctus. *Venerable,* vĕnĕrābĭlia, vĕnĕrandus.

antrum. *A cave.*—EP. *Vast,* ingens, immāne, magnum. *Deep,* altum, prŏfundum. *Dark,* obscūrum, cæcum. *Ancient,* antiquum, vĕtus. *Eaten away,* exĕsum.

ănus, ûs, fem. *An old woman.*—EP. *Ancient,* antīqua, vĕtŭla. *Weak,* dēbĭlis, infirma. *Trembling,* trĕmŭla, trĕmens. *Chattering,* garrŭla, lŏquax. *Jealous,* invĭda. *Spiteful,* măligna.

Ăpennīnus. *The Apennines.*—EP. *High,* altus, arduus, sŭblīmis. *Supporting the clouds,* nūbĭfer. *Snowcapped,* nĭveus, nĭvōsus, nĭvālis.

ăper, pri. *A wild boar.*—EP. *Fierce,* fĕrus, ferox, sævus. *Bold,* ănĭmōsus, fortis. *Foaming,* spūmans, spūmĭger, spūmeus, spūmōsus. *Bristling,* sĕtōsus, sĕtĭger.

ăpex, ĭcis, masc. *The top.*—EP. *High,* altus, arduus. *Highest,* summus.

ăpis. *A bee.*—EP. *Industrious,* sēdŭla, ŏpĕrōsa, indēfessa. *Prudent,* prŏvĭda, prūdens. *Attic (because Hymettus in Attica was celebrated for its honey),* Cēcrōpia, Attĭca. *Matine (Matinus was a hill in Apulia),* mătīna. *Gathering flowers,* flŏrĭlĕga. *Producing honey,* mellĭfĕra. *Winged,* ălāta, ălĭgĕra, vŏlūcris. *Light,* lĕvis. *Little,* parva.

ăpium. *Parsley.*—EP. *Green,* vĭrĭde. *Growing in damp ground,* ūdum.

Ăpollo. *The son of Jupiter and Latona, God of poetry, music, archery, prophecy, medicine; God of Delos and Delphi.*—EP. *Tuneful,* cănōrus, dulcis, argūtus. *Eloquent,* făcundus, dĭsertus. *Wise,* săpiens, prūdens, prŏvĭdus. *Prophetic,* præscius, fatĭdĭcus, præsāgus. *Unerring,* certus. *Holding the bow,* arcĭtĕnens. *Armed with a quiver,* phărĕtrātus. *Beardless,* imberbis. *Unshaven,* intonsus. *God of Delos, of Delphi, etc.* Dēlius, Pythius. *See* Gradus.

ăpŏthēca. *A repository.*—EP. *Full,* plēna. *Full of different things,* văria.

appărātus, ûs. *Preparation.*—EP. *Plentiful,* amplus, largus. *Rich,* dĭves –ĭtis. *Costly,* prĕtiōsus, sumptuōsus.

applausus, ûs. *See* plausus.

apprŏbātio. *Approbation.*—EP. *Favorable,* dextĕra, syna dextra. *Willing, joyful,* læta, lĭbens. *Deserved,* mĕrĭta, dēbĭta.

Ăprīlis. *April.*—EP. *Vernal,* vernus. *Sacred to Venus,* Cӯthĕrēius.

ăqua. *Water.*—EP. *Liquid,* lĭquĭda. *Pure,* pūra, vĭtrea, argentea. *Running,* jūgis, pĕrennis. *From a fountain,* fontāna. *From a river,* flūviālis. *From the sea,* æquōrea, mărīna. *Descending from a mountain,* montāna.

Ăquārius. *One of the signs of the Zodiac.*—EP. *Light,* lĕvis. *Melancholy,* tristis. *Dark, bringing dark weather,* obscūrus. *Stormy,* prŏcellōsus. *Rainy,* plŭvius.

ăquĭla. *An eagle.*—EP. *Sacred (esp. to Jupiter),* săcra (esp. Jŏvi), dīvīna. *The armour-bearer (of Jove),* armĭgĕra, fulmĭnea *(the arms of Jove being the thunderbolt).* *Swift,* răpĭda, vēlox, præpes –ĕtis. *Fierce,* fĕra, fĕrox, sæva, crūdēlis. *Winged,* ălĭgĕra, ălāta. *Powerful,* pŏtens, magna. *Brown, tawny,* fulva. *With crooked talons,* unca, ădunca.

ăquĭlo. *The north wind.*—EP. *Stormy,* prŏcellōsus. *Cold,* frĭgĭdus, gĕlĭdus. *Violent,* vĭŏlentus, vălĭdus.

ăra. *An altar.*—EP. *Sacred,* săcra, sancta, dīvīna. *Ancient,* vĕtus, antīqua, prisca, pristīna. *Worshipped by one's fathers,* pătria. *Smoking,* fūmĭda. *Reeking with incense,* thūrea, thurĭcrĕma. *Loaded, full,* plena. *Rich,* dĭves –ĭtis. *Votive,* vŏtīva.

Ărābia. *Arabia.*—EP. *Producing perfumes,* ŏdōrāta.

ărānea. 1. *A spider.*—2. *A cobweb.*—EP. *Industrious,* sēdŭla. *Ingenious,* ingĕniōsa. *Unwearied,* indēfessa. *Phrygian (because Arachne, who was changed into a spider, was a Phrygian),* Phrӯgia, Mæōnia, Mæōnis.—2. *Light,* lĕvia, tĕnuis. *Full of holes,* rāra. *Loose,* laxa, sŏlūta. *Made with toil,* lăbōrāta, ŏpĕrōsa.

ărātor. *A ploughman.*—EP. *Industrious,* sēdŭlus, ŏpĕrōsus, lăbōriōsus. *Hard, hardy,* dūrus. *Rough, unpolished,* incultus, rūdis. *Rustic,* rusticus, ăgrestis. *Strong,* fortis, vălĭdus, rōbustus. *Brown,* fuscus. *Sunburnt,* pĕrustus. *Honest,* prŏbus, justus. *Simple,* simplex. *Anxious,* anxius, sollĭcĭtus.

ărātrum. *A plough, sacred to Ceres,* Cĕreāle. *Iron,* ferreum, ferrātum. *Hard,*

B 4

8 ARB—ARI

dūrum. *Heavy*, grăve. *Bent, curved*, curvum, incurvum, inflexum, ădūncum. *Blunt*, obtūsum. *Patient*, pătiens. *Tilling the land*, rūricŏla (*used as epith. of aratrum by Ovid*).

arbĭter –tri, masc. *A judge.*—EP. *Impartial, just*, æquus, justus. *Uncorruptible*, incorruptus. *Faithful*, fĭdēlis, fīdus.

arbĭtrium. *Decision.* See above.

arbŏr, ŏris, fem. *A tree.*—EP. *Tall*, alta, ardua. *Green*, vĭrĭdis, vīrens, vĭrĭdans. *Flourishing*, flŏrens. *Spreading*, pătŭla, lata. *With many branches*, rāmōsa. *Leafy*, frondōsa, frondea. *Shady*, umbrōsa, umbrĭfĕra, ŏpāca. *Aged*, annōsa, antīqua. See quercus, fagus, pinus, etc. *for different sorts of trees.*

arbustum. *A plantation of trees.* See above.

arbŭtus, i, fem. *The arbutus.*—EP. *Red (as to the fruit)*, rŭbens. *Green*, vĭrĭdis, vĭrĭdans, vīrens.

arca. *A chest.*—EP. *Full*, plēna. *Rich*, dives –ĭtis, lŏcŭples –ĕtis.

arctos, i, fem. 1. *The constellation called the Bear.*—2. *The North.*—EP. 1. *Never setting*, æternus, pĕrennis, immunis æquŏris; nunquam cadens.—2. *Cold*, gĕlĭdus, frĭgĭdus. *Icy*, glăciālis. *Snowy*, nĭvōsus, nĭvālis. *Stormy*, prŏcellōsus. *Penetrated by Boreas*, Bŏreālis.

arcus, ûs. *A bow.*—EP. *Sacred to Apollo*, Ăpollĭneus, Ăpollĭnāris. *Used by Parthians*, Parthus. *Cretan*, Cўdōnius, Gnossius. *Syrian*, Ĭtūræus. *Easily bent*, flexĭlis. *Curved*, curvus, sĭnŭōsus. *Bent (in the act of shooting)*, intentus, curvātus, adductus (i. e. *drawn towards the shooter*). *Light*, lĕvis. *Made of yew*, taxeus. *Made of or tipped with horn*, corneus. *Golden (as Apollo's)* aureus. *Silver (as Diana's)*, argenteus. *Strong*, vălĭdus.

Ardea. *A heron.*—EP. *Flying, winged*, vŏlātĭlis, ālāta, ālĭgĕra, præpes –ĕtis, vŏlūcris. *Flying high*, alta, ardua, sŭblīmis. *Bold*, audax. *Undismayed*, impăvĭda, imperterrĭta.

ardor. 1. *Heat.*—2. *Eagerness.*—EP.—1, 2. *Burning*, fervĭdus. *Violent*, vĭŏlentus, vĕhĕmens. *Excessive*, nĭmius. *Fiery*, igneus. 1. *Of summer*, æstīvus. *Of the sun*, sōlāris.

ărea. *A threshing floor.*—EP. *Full, loaded*, plēna, ŏnĕrāta, ŏnusta, grăvis. *Sacred to Ceres*, Cĕreālis. *Smooth*, lēvis, æqua.

ărēna. 1. *Sand.*—2. *The place for contests.*—EP. *Yellow*, flāva. *Light*, lēvis. *Of the shore*, littŏrea. *Of the sea*, æquŏrea, mărīna. *Barren*, stĕrĭlis. *Countless*, innŭmĕra.—2. *Hardy, brave (as the scene of brave contests)*, dūra, vălĭda, fortis. *Well known*, nōta, experta. *Pugnacious (as the scene of contests)* pugnax. *Illustrious*, clāra, inclўta, insignis. *Naked (because combatants were usually naked)*, nūda. *Anointed (because the combatants were anointed)*, uncta.

argentum. *Silver.*—EP. *White*, candĭdum, album. *Bright*, clārum, splendĭdum, splendens. *Valuable*, prĕtiōsum.

argilla. *Clay (esp. potter's clay).*—EP. *Thin, soft*, tĕnuis, mollis. *Easily wrought*, ductĭlis, făcĭlis, lentus. *Moist*, ūda.

Argo, ûs. *The ship in which Jason sailed to seek the golden fleece.*—EP. *First (as the first ship ever launched)*, prīma. *Ancient*, vĕtus –eris, antīqua, prisca. *Celebrated*, inclўta, clāra, præclāra, cĕlĕbris. *Bold*, audax, fortis. *Of which the word came from M. Pelion*, Pēlĭăca, Pēlĭas –ădos, Pelia. *Sailing from Pagasæ*, Păgāsæa. *From Magnesia*, Magnētis –ĭdis. *From Thessaly*, Thessăla, Thessālis –ĭdis. *Commanded by Jason*, Jāsŏnis. See navis.

Argonautæ, arum, masc. See above.

Argos, in sing. neut., in plur. **Argi.** *Argos.*—EP. *Ruled over by Pelops*, Pĕlŏpēum. *By Agamemnon*, Ăgămemnŏnium. *By Abas*, Ăbantēum. *Sacred to Juno*, Jūnōnium. *Ancient*, vĕtus –ĕris; antīquum. *Celebrated*, clārum, insigne, cĕlĕbre. *Grecian*, Ăchīvum, Pĕlasgum. *Warlike*, bellĭcum, bellĭcōsum.

argūmentum. *An argument or proof.*—EP. *Sure*, firmum. *True*, vērum, certum. *Well-known*, nōtum. *Doubtful*, dŭbium, ambĭguum.

Argus. *Appointed by Juno to watch Io.*—EP. *Studded with eyes like stars*, stellātus. *Having a hundred eyes*, centumgĕminus.

Ăriadne. *The daughter of Minos, wife of Theseus.*—EP. *Daughter of Minos*, Mīnōis. *Belonging to Theseus*, Thēsēïa. *Cretan*, Cressa, Gnossis –ĭdos, Gnossias –ados. *Deserted*, dēserta, vĭdua.

Ăries, gen. Ărĭĕtis, trisyll. masc.—1. *A Ram.*—2. *A battering-ram.*—EP.

ARI—ASC 9

1. *Horned*, cornĭger. *Woolly*, lānĭger. *Unwarlike*, imbellis.—2. *Brazen*, iron, ăhēneus, ăhēnus, æreus, ferreus. *Powerful*, vălĭdus, pŏtens. *Giving repeated blows*, crēber, assĭduus. *Hostile*, hostīlis. *Brought against (the walls)*, adductus, admōtus.

Ărĭon, ŏnis, acc. Gr. ŏna. *A poet of Methymna in Lesbos.*—EP. *Lesbian*, Lesbius, Lesbōus, Mēthymnæus. *Celebrated*, inclўtus, clārus, insignis. *Admirable*, ēgrēgius. *Learned*, doctus. *Tuneful*, dulcis, cănōrus, vōcālis. *Betrayed (by the sailors with whom he sailed)*, prōdĭtus.

ărista. *An ear of corn.*—EP. *Sacred to Ceres*, Cĕreālis. *Yellow*, flāva, cŏlōrāta. *Heavy*, grăvis, grăvĭda. *Ripe*, mătūra. *Full*, plēna. *Dense*, in plur. densæ.

arma, ōrum, plur. *Arms.*—EP. *Warlike*, bellĭca, bellĭcōsa, Martia, Māvortia. *Bold*, fortia audācia. *Bloody*, sanguĭnea, cruenta. *Discordant*, discordia. *Deadly*, lētĭfĕra. *Horrible*, dīra, horrenda. *Iron*, *brazen*, ferrea, ăhēnea, ăhēna, ærea. *Flashing*, fulgentia, rŭtĭla, cōrusca, mĭcantia. *Clanging*, strēpĭtantia. *Cruel*, crudēlia, immītia, fēra, fĕrōcia, sæva.

armāmenta, ōrum, pl. *Tackle.*—EP. *Fit*, apta. *Ready*, părāta. *Light*, lēvia.

armentum. *A herd.*—EP. *Fat*, pingue. *Slow*, tardum, grăve. *Horned*, cornĭgĕrum. *Playful*, *wanton*, lascīvum, prŏtervum. *Thirsty*, sĭtiens. *Doomed to die*, mŏrĭtūrum. *Threatening*, mĭnax.

armĭger. *An armour-bearer, a squire.*—EP. *Faithful*, fīdus, fĭdēlis. *Brave*, fortis. *Nobly born*, nōbĭlis, ingĕnuus. *Inexperienced*, rŭdis.

armilla. *A bracelet.*—EP. *Golden*, aurea, aurāta. *Jewelled*, gemmea, gemmāta, gemmans. *Light*, lēvis. *Corrupting*, corruptrix (*because Tarpeia was bribed by bracelets to betray Rome to the Sabines*).

armus. *A shoulder or arm of an animal.*—EP. *Strong*, *muscular*, nervōsus, tŏrōsus, vălĭdus, rōbustus. *Broad*, lātus.

arrŏgantia. *Arrogance.*—EP. *Proud*, sŭperba, tŭmĭda. *Empty*, *groundless*, vāna, ĭnānis. *Odious*, ŏdiōsa, invīsa, dētestābĭlis. *Laughable*, rĭdĭcŭla, rīdenda.

ars, tis, fem. 1. *An art.*—2. *Skill.*—3. *Artifice.*—EP. 1, 2. *Various*, văria. *Ingenious*, ingĕniōsa, callĭda. *Skilful*, pĕrīta, docta. *Industrious*, ŏpĕrōsa, sēdŭla.—1. *Foreign*, pĕrēgrīna.—2. *Grecian*, *French*, etc., Græca, Gallĭca, etc. —3. *Dishonest*, măla, prāva, ĭnīqua. *Deceitful*, fallax, falsa, mendax. *Pernicious*, pernĭciōsa, damnōsa. *Base*, turpis.

artĭcŭlus, i. *A joint.*—EP. *Strong*, vălĭdus, fortis, rōbustus.

artĭfex, ĭcis, masc. *A workman, artist, maker.*—EP. *Skilful*, pĕrītus, doctus. *Ingenious*, ingĕniōsus, văfer -fri, callĭdus. *Laborious*, *industrious*, lăbōriōsus, sēdŭlus, impĭger, ŏpĕrōsus. *Celebrated*, clārus, insignis, inclўtus. *Excellent*, ēgrēgius, præstans.

artus, ûs. *A limb.*—EP. *Strong*, vălĭdus, fortis, rōbustus. *Muscular*, tŏrōsus, nervōsus. *Well-knit*, compactus. *Weary*, fessus, dēfessus. *In pain*, æger -gri.

ărundo, ĭnis, fem. *A reed, or anything made of it, as a flute, an arrow, etc.*—EP. *Hollow*, căva, concăva. *Light*, *thin*, lēvis, tĕnuis. *Smooth*, lævis. *Growing by a river*, flŭviālis. *Growing in a marsh*, pălūdosa, pălustris. *Dry*, sicca, ārĭda. *Moist (as growing in moist places)*, ūda, hŭmĭda. *Knotty*, nōdōsa. *Smooth*, lēvis, tĕres -ĕtis. See tibia, *flute*; sagitta, *arrow.*

arvum. *An arable field.*—EP. *Cultivated*, cultum. *Yellow*, i. e. *bearing corn*, flāvum, aureum. *Bearing ears of corn*, spīceum. *Fertile*, fertĭle, pingue, lætum, fēcundum, fērax. *Sacred to Ceres*, Cĕreāle. *Barren*, stĕrĭle, infēcundum. *Fallow*, incultum, ĭners.

arx, cis, fem. 1. *A height.*—2. *A citadel.*—EP. 2. *Strong*, fortis, vălĭda, pŏtens. *Brazen*, ăhēnea, ăhēna, ærea, ærāta. *Iron*, ferrea. *Fortified*, mūnīta. *Lofty*, alta, ardua, celsa, excelsa. *Inapproachable*, invia, ĭnaccessa. *Ancient*, vĕtus -ĕris, vĕtusta, antīqua. *Royal*, rēgia, rēgālis. *Warlike*, bellĭca, bellĭcōsa. *Unconquered*, invicta. *Safe*, tūta, incŏlŭmis. For 1., see mons.

ăs, assis, neut. *A penny.*—EP. *Of small value*, parvum, vīle. *Of brass*, æreum, ærātum.

ascaules, is, masc. *A bagpiper.*—EP. *Hoarse*, raucus. *Swelling*, tŭmĭdus. *Working hard*, lăbōriōsus, ŏpĕrōsus. *Weary*, fessus, dēfessus. *Scotch*, Cālēdŏnius.

10 ASC—ATL

ascensus, ûs. *An ascent* (1. *the ground*, or 2. *the act*).—EP. 1. *High*, altus, arduus. *Steep*, præceps -ĭpĭtis. *Pathless, scarcely to be surmounted*, invius, inaccessus. 1, 2. *Difficult, hard, laborious*, diffĭcĭlis, dûrus, ŏpĕrōsus, lăbōriōsus.—*Panting, or causing panting*, ănhēlus.

ăsellus, ăsella, ăsĭnus. *An ass.*—EP. *Patient*, pătiens. *Slow*, tardus. *Laborious*, lăbōriōsus, ŏpĕrōsus. *Low, worthless*, turpis. *Quiet, gentle*, quiētus, plăcĭdus. *Strong*, fortis, rŏbustus, vălĭdus. *Little*, parvus, exĭguus. *Long-eared*, aurītus.

Ăsia. *Asia.* *Rich*, dīves -ĭtis, lŏcŭples -ētis, ŏpŭlenta. *Producing gold*, aurea, aurĭfĕra. *Producing frankincense*, thŭrĭfĕra. *Producing perfumes*, ŏdōra, ŏdōrāta, ŏdōrĭfĕra. *Royal*, rēgia. *Proud*, sŭperba. *Powerful*, pŏtens. *Broad*, lāta. *Eastern*, Ŏriens, ˉEōa. *Distant, most distant*, rĕmōta, extrēma, ultīma. *Effeminate*, mollis, imbellis. *Conquered*, victa, dŏmĭta.

aspectus, ûs. 1. *Sight.*—2. *A look.*—EP. 1. *New*, nŏvus. *Sudden, unexpected*, sŭbĭtus, ĭnŏpīnus. *Unusual*, insŏlĭtus, ĭnassuetus.—2. *Steady*, constans. *Joyful*, lætus. *Fearless*, impăvĭdus. *Trembling*, trĕmens, tĭmĭdus. *Unwilling*, invītus.

aspergo, ĭnis, fem. *Spray.*—EP. *Of the sea*, mărīna, æquŏrea. *Salt*, salsa. *Rising high*, alta. *Dripping*, mădĭda. *Foaming*, spūmea, spūmōsa.

aspĕrĭtas. *Roughness, harshness.*—EP. *Hard*, morosa, dūra, trux trŭcis, diffĭcĭlis. *Uncivil*, rustĭca, inculta, ĭnurbāna. *Deserved*, mĕrĭta. *Undeserved*, immĕrĭta, ĭnīqua. *Sudden*, sŭbĭta. *Unusual*, nŏva, insŏlĭta.

aspis, ĭdis, fem. *An asp.*—*Small*, parva, exĭgua, lĕvis. *Poisonous*, vĕnēnāta, vĕnēnĭfĕra. *Causing sleep*, somnĭfĕra. *Deadly*, fătālis, exĭtiālis, exĭtiabĭlis, mortĭfĕra, fūnesta. *Egyptian*, Ægyptia, Phăria, Nĭliăca.

assĕcla, æ, masc. *A slave.* See servus.

assensus, ûs. *Assent.*—EP. *Willing*, lĭbens. *Glad*, lætus. *Unwilling*, invītus, *Unanimous*, ŭnănĭmus.

assentātor, assentātrix. *A flatterer.*—EP. *Base*, turpis. *Deceitful*, fallax, falsus. *Treacherous*, perfĭdus, infĭdus. *Caressing*, blandus. *Assiduous*, sēdŭlus.

assentor. *A liberator.* EP. *Bold*, fortis, audax, impăvĭdus. *Kind*, bĕnignus. *Just*, æquus, justus. *Prompt*, promptus. *Unwearied*, indēfessus. *Suitable*, aptus, ĭdōneus. *Powerful*, pŏtens, effĭcax.

assessus, ûs. *A sitting near.*—EP. *Friendly*, ămīcus, bĕnignus. *Honourable*, hŏnestus.

assuetudo. *Custom.* See mos.

assultus, ûs. *A leaping towards, esp. in attack.*—EP. *Vigorous*, fortis, vălĭdus, vehĕmens. *Repeated*, creber -bri. *Hostile*, hostīlis. *Warlike*, bellīcus. *Fierce*, fĕrus, sævus, fĕrox.

astrum. *A star.*—EP. *Bright*, clārum, splendĭdum, fulgens, rŭtĭlum. *Twinkling*, mĭcans, cŏruscum. *Golden*, aureum. *Shining by night*, nocturnum. *Heavenly*, cæleste. *High*, altum, arduum, sŭblīme. *Fixed (of the fixed stars)*, fixum. *Wandering (of planets)*, văgum, errăbundum. *Rising*, ŏriens, cădens (*used by Virg. of stars as appearing to approach the earth; though Ov. uses* cado *for to set, speaking also of stars*). *Setting (at the approach of morning)*, fŭgiens. *Falling*, lābens. *Natal*, nătāle.

astutia. *Craft.* See ars.

ăsȳlum. *An asylum.*—EP. *Safe*, tūtum, illæsum, incŏlŭme, sēcūrum. *Long*, longum, diūturnum. *For a short time*, brĕve. *Promised*, promissum. *Hoped for*, spērātum. *Known, customary*, nōtum, sŏlĭtum. *Foreign, in a foreign land*, pĕrĕgrīnum. *Distant*, distans, rĕmōtum, ultīmum, extrēmum.

ătāvus. *A greatgrandfather.* See avus.

Ăthēnæ. *Athens.*—EP. *Sacred to Minerva*, Pallădiæ. *Ruled by Cecrops or Pandion*, Cĕcrŏpiæ, Pandĭŏniæ. *Sacred*, săcræ, sanctæ. *Learned*, doctæ. *Polite*, cultæ. *Tuneful*, cănōræ, dulces. *Powerful*, pŏtentes. *Illustrious*, clāræ, insignes, ēgrĕgiæ.

ăthlētes, or ăthlēta, æ, masc. *A wrestler.*—EP. *Brave, strong*, fortis, vălĭdus. *Hardy*, dūrus. *Invincible*, invictus. *Unwearied*, indēfessus. *Firm*, firmus. *Dusty*, pulvĕrŭlentus. *Anointed*, unctus.

Ătlas, antis. *King of Mauritania, father of the Pleiades, who bore the heavens on his shoulders.*—EP. *Moorish*, Maurus. *Mighty*, magnus, pŏtens. *Strong*, vălĭdus, fortis. *Supporting heaven*, cælĭfer.

ATR—AUR 11

ătrāmentum. *Ink.*—EP. *Learned,* doctum. *Conveying words faithfully,* fĭdum, fĭdēle. *Indelible,* indēlēbĭle, æternum.

ătrium. 1. *A hall.*—2. *A house, esp. a palace.*—EP. 1. *High,* altum, arduum. *Long,* longum.—2. *Splendid,* splendĭdum, sŭperbum, nōbĭle, magnĭfĭcum. *Royal,* rēgium, rēgāle, rēgĭfĭcum. *Ancestral,* păternum, pătrium, ăvĭtum.

Attĭca. See Athenæ.

ăvārĭtia. *Avarice.*—EP. *Foolish, blind,* stulta, cæca, insāna, inepta. *Miserable,* mĭsĕra, infēlix. *Anxious,* anxia, sollĭcĭta. *Timid,* tĭmĭda, păvens. *Perpetual,* perpĕtua, assĭdua, æterna.

auceps, cŭpis. *A fowler.*—EP. *Skilful,* pērītus, doctus. *Active,* impĭger ‑gri. *Unwearied,* indēfessus. *Hardy,* dūrus. *Watchful,* vĭgĭl, pervigil, vĭgĭlax. *Crafty,* callĭdus.

auctor. *An author, cause, etc.*—EP. *Primary, original,* prīmus. *Ancient,* prĭscus, vĕtus ‑ĕris, vĕtustus, antīquus. *Honoured,* hŏnōrātus, vĕnĕrābĭlis.

auctus, ûs. *Increase.*—EP. *Greater,* major. *Fortunate, prosperous,* felix, lætus, sēcundus. *Wished for,* optātus. *Hoped, expected,* spērātus. *Yearly,* annuus. *Continual,* perpĕtuus.

aucŭpium. *Fowling.*—EP. *Successful,* felix. See auceps.

audācia. *Boldness.*—EP. *Spirited, manly,* ănĭmosa, vĭrīlis, fortis, gĕnĕrōsa. *Fearless,* impăvĭda, interrĭta, imperterrĭta. *Successful,* fēlix. *Renowned,* clāra. *Eminent,* insignis, ēgrĕgia.

auditor. *A hearer.*—EP. *Docile,* dŏcĭlis. *Willing,* lĭbens. *Not docile,* indŏcĭlis, contŭmax. *Unwilling,* invītus. *Diligent,* assĭduus, sēdŭlus.

ăvēna. 1. *Oats.*—2. *Tares.*—3. *A Flute.*—EP. 1. *Yellow,* flāva, aurea. *Hanging,* pendŭla. *Tender,* tĕnĕra.—2. *Barren, useless,* stĕrĭlis, inūtĭlis. *Worthless,* vīlis.—3. See tilia.

Ăvernus. *Hell.* See Orcus.

augur, ŭris. *A soothsayer.*—EP. *Pious,* pius. *Sacred,* săcer ‑cri, săcrātus, sanctus, dīvīnus. *Prophetic,* præscius, præsāgus, fātĭdĭcus. *Wise,* săgax, săpiens. *True,* vērus, vērax, vērĭdĭcus. *Aged,* sĕnex, annōsus, grandævus. *Experienced,* pērītus, doctus. *Faithful,* fĭdēlis, fĭdus. *Venerable,* vĕnĕrābĭlis.

augurium. *Augury.*—*Sure, true,* certum, vērum. *Sent from heaven,* cæleste, dīvīnum, săcrum. *Obscure,* obscūrum. *Ambiguous,* ambĭguum, dŭbium, anceps. *Deceitful,* fallax, falsum. *Of various kinds,* vărium. See augur.

ăvia. *A grandmother.*—EP. *Aged,* annōsa, vĕtŭla, grandæva. *Credulous,* crēdŭla. *Talkative,* lŏquax, garrŭla. *Kind,* bĕnigna. *Dear,* cāra, ămāta, dīlecta.

ăviārium. *A place for birds.*—EP. *Safe,* tūtum, incŏlŭme.

ăvis. *A bird.*—EP. *Flying, winged,* vŏlūcris, vŏlātĭlis, pennata, ălĭgĕra, ălāta, præpes ‑ĕtis. *Light,* lĕvis. *Swift,* vēlox, răpĭda, cĭta, cĕlĕris. *Chattering,* lŏquax, garrŭla. *Tuneful (of singing birds),* dulcis, argūta, lĭquĭda, cănōra. *Gentle,* mītis. *Fierce (of birds of prey),* fĕra, sæva, crūdēlis, fĕrox. *Greedy,* răpax, ĕdax. *With crooked talons or beak (of eagles, etc.),* unca, ădunca. *Innocent,* innŏcua, innoxia, innŏcens. *Greedy,* ăvĭda, răpax.

aula. *A hall, a palace.* See atrium.

aulæa, orum. *Curtains.*—EP. *Rich, splendid,* dīvĭtia, splendĭda. *Purple,* purpūrea. *Embroidered,* picta.

aura. 1. *The air, sky, esp. the air of day as opp. to the shades below.*—2. *A breeze.*—EP. *Light,* i. e. *not heavy,* lĕvis. *Light, bright,* lūcĭda, clāra. *Pure,* pūra. *Calm,* sĕrēna, plăcĭda, tranquilla. *Vital, of life, etc.,* vītālis. *Of heaven,* cælestis, æthĕria.—2. *Gentle,* lēnis, plăcĭda. *Variable,* vāria, mōbĭlis, mūtābĭlis.—1, 2. *Warm,* tĕpĭda, tĕpens. *Very hot,* călĭda, torrĭda. *Cool, cold,* frĭgĭda, gĕlĭda.

auricŭla, auris. *An ear.*—EP. *Eager to listen, willing,* cŭpĭda, arrecta, lĭbens. *Accessible (of a superior),* făcĭlis. *Kind,* cōmis, ămīca, bĕnigna. *Unwilling,* invīta, āversa. *Deaf (lit. or metaph.),* surda. *Hard, unfriendly,* tarda, ĭnīmica.

auriga, æ, masc. *A charioteer.*—EP. *Bold,* fortis, audax, impăvĭdus. *Active,* impĭger, strenuus. *Skilful,* pērītus, prūdens, săgax. *Faithful,* fĭdus, fĭdēlis. *Impetuous,* vĭŏlentus. *Swift,* răpĭdus, concĭtus.

Aurōra. *The goddess of morning, morning.*—EP. *Rosy,* rŏsea. *Purple,* purpūrea. *Dewy,* roscĭda, prŭīnosa. *Early,* prīma. *Coming from the East,* Ōriens, Eōa. *Wakeful,* vĭgĭl. *Golden,* aurea, flāva, lūtea.

AUR—BAL

aurum. *Gold.*—EP. *Yellow,* flāvum, fulvum. *Ductile,* fūsĭle. *Wished for,* optātum. *Valuable,* prētiōsum. *Rich,* dīves –ĭtis. *Hidden,* abdĭtum, sēcrētum. *Mischievous,* nŏcens, noxium, pernĭciosum, pernĭciale, exĭtiosum, exĭtiāle, fătale. *Wicked,* i. e. *cause of wickedness,* imprŏbum, scĕlestum. *Powerful,* pŏtens.

auspex, auspicium. See augur, augurium.

Auster, tri. *The South Wind.*—EP. *Black,* nĭger –gri, āter –tri. *Wet,* hūmĭdus, ūdus, mădĭdus, plŭvius, pluviālis, ăquātĭcus, āqnōsus. *Cold,* frĭgĭdus, gĕlĭdus. *Stormy,* prŏcellōsus, turbĭdus, inquiĕtus. *Dangerous,* pĕrīcŭlosus. *Treacherous,* insĭdus, perfĭdus.

ausum, ausus, ûs. *A bold deed.*—EP. *Brave,* fortis, ănĭmōsus, impăvĭdus. *Great,* magnus. *Noble, excellent,* nōbĭlis, insignis, gĕnĕrōsus, ēgrēgius. *To be celebrated,* cĕlēbrandus, laudābĭlis. *Youthful,* jŭvĕnīlis. *Manly,* vĭrīlis. *Ancient,* priscus, vĕtus –ĕris, antīquus. *Celebrated, well-known,* clārus, præclarus, nōtus.

Autumnus. *Autumn.*—EP. *Fruitful,* pōmĭfer –ĕri, fertīlis, fĕrax, fēcundus. *Purple (fruit being purple),* purpūreus. *Heavy loaded with fruit,* grăvis, grăvĭdus. *Unhealthy,* grăvis, pestĭfer, pestĭlens. *Late,* sērus.

ăvunculus. *An uncle.*—EP. *Harsh, severe,* rĭgĭdus, dūrus, sĕvērus, diffĭcĭlis, mŏrōsus.

ăvus. 1. *A grandfather.*—2. *Ancestor.*—EP. 1. 2. *Aged,* sĕnex, annōsus, longævus, grandævus, vĕtŭlus.—1. *Wise,* săpiens, prudens. *Kind,* bĕnignus, mitis. *Loved,* cārus, ămātus, dīlectus. 1, 2. *Venerable,* vĕnĕrābĭlis, venerandus. 2. *Ancient,* antīquus, priscus, vĕtus –ĕris. *Most ancient, most remote,* prīmus, ultĭmus.

auxĭlium. *Help.*—EP. *Timely,* opportūnum, tempestīvum. *Prompt,* promptum. *Powerful,* pŏtens, efficax. *Useful,* ūtĭle. *Saving,* sălūtāre. *Friendly,* ămīcum. *Too late,* sērum. *Unwilling,* invĭtum.

axis. *An axletree.*—EP. *Strong, fortis,* vălĭdus. *Revolving,* rĕvŏlūbĭlis. *Glowing hot,* călĭdus. *Made of ash,* fraxĭneus.

B.

Bacca. *A berry.*—EP. *Green,* vĭrĭdis. *Ripe,* mătūra. *Hard,* dūra.

Baccha and Bacche. *A Bacchanalian woman.*—EP. *Excited, frantic,* excĭta, concĭta, fŭriōsa, frĕmens. *Hoarse,* rauca. *Thracian,* Thrēĭcia, Thrācia, Thrāca, Rhŏdŏpēia, Ismāria. *Celebrating her rites by night,* nocturna.

Bacchus. *The God of wine.*—EP. *Son of Semele,* Sĕmēleius. *Youthful,* jŭvĕnis. *Unshorn,* intonsus. *Wearing horns,* cornĭger. *Mirthful,* festīvus, hĭlāris, lætus. *Wearing a crown of ivy berries,* cŏrymbĭfer. *Wearing a crown of grapes,* răcĕmĭfer. *Conqueror,* victor. See Gradus.

băcillum, băcŭlum, băcŭlus. *A staff.*—EP. *Strong,* vălĭdus, firmus. *Of oak,* rŏbōreus, rōbustus. *Customary,* nōtus, sŏlĭtus.

bălæna. *A whale.*—EP. *Vast,* magna, ingens. *British,* Brĭtannĭca, Brĭtanna. *Northern,* arctōa, Hўperbŏrea.

bălănus, i, fem. *A sort of chestnut yielding oil.*—EP. *Fragrant,* frăgrans, ŏdōra, ŏdōrāta, ŏdōrĭfĕra. *Eastern,* Ēōa. *Arabian,* Săbæa.

bălātus, ûs. *Bleating.*—EP. *Soft,* mollis, tĕner –ĕri. *Helpless, timid,* imbellis, tĭmĭdus. *Repeated,* crēber –bri, assĭduus.

bălista. *An engine to hurt stones,* etc.—EP. *Warlike,* bellĭca, Martia, Māvortia. *Vast,* ingens, magna. *Powerful,* pŏtens. *Heavy,* grăvis. *Violent,* vĭŏlenta, vălĭda. *Terrible,* dīra, terrĭbĭlis, mĕtuenda.

balneum. *A bath.*—EP. *Warm,* tĕpĭdum, călĭdum. *Luxurious,* luxŭriōsum. *Marble,* marmōreum. *Cold,* gĕlĭdum, frĭgĭdum. *In the river,* flŭviāle. *In the sea,* æquōreum, mărīnum.

balsămum. *A balsam tree.*—EP. *Fragrant,* frăgrans, ŏdōrum, ŏdōrātum, ŏdōrĭfĕrum. *Arabian,* Săbæum. *Eastern,* Ēōum. *Assyrian,* Assўrium.

balteum, balteus. *A belt, esp. a sword belt.*—EP. *Military,* bellĭcus, Martius, Māvortius, mĭlĭtāris. *Golden,* aureus. *Embossed,* cælātus.

BAR—BOR 13

bărăthro, ŏnis. *A glutton.*—EP. *Greedy,* vŏrax, ăvĭdus. *Shameless,* impŭdens. *Base,* turpis.

bărăthrum. *A pit, a gulf.*—EP. *Deep,* altum, prŏfundum. *Vast,* ingens, immāne. *Devouring,* vŏrax. *Open,* pătens, hians.

barba. *A beard.*—EP. *Long,* longa. *Let down,* dēmissa. *Combed carefully,* prŏpexa. *Manly,* virīlis. *Black,* nĭgra, ātra. *Aged,* sĕnīlis. *White,* cāna, cānens, candĭda.

barbăria, barbăries. 1. *Barbarism, a band of barbarians.*—2. *Cruelty.*—EP. 1. *Uncivilised,* inculta, rŭdis, horrĭda. *Distant,* longinqua, rĕmōta, distans, ultĭma, extrēma. 1, 2. *Fierce,* fĕra, effĕra, fĕrox, sæva. *Impious,* impia.

barbĭtos, i, fem. *A harp.* See cithara.

barrus. *An elephant.* See elephas.

băsium. *A kiss.* See osculum.

bellator, fem. bellātrix. *A warrior.*—EP. *Brave,* fortis, impăvĭdus, audax. *Active,* impĭger -gri, ācer -cris, strēnuus. *Fierce,* fĕrus, effĕrus, fĕrox. *Cruel,* sævus, crūdēlis, immītis. *Martial,* Martius, Māvortius. *Victorious,* victor. *Armed,* armātus. *Bearing a shield,* clўpeātus. *Wearing a sword,* ensĭfer -ĕri. *Illustrious,* clārus, insignis, inclўtus, ēgrĕgius. *Bloody,* sanguĭneus, sanguĭnōlentus, cruentus.

Bellōna. *The Goddess of War.*—EP. *Fierce, cruel,* fĕra, sæva, crūdēlis. *Bloodthirsty,* sanguĭnea. *Furious,* fūriōsa.

bellua. *A beast, a monster.*—EP. *Vast,* vasta, ingens, immānis. *Terrible,* terrĭbĭlis, horrĭbĭlis, horrĭda, trĕmenda, dīra. *Strange,* nŏva, mīra. *Fierce,* fĕra, sæva.

bellum. *War.*—EP. *Fierce, cruel,* fĕrum, sævum, crūdēle, aspĕrum. *Bloody,* sanguĭneum, sanguĭnōlentum, cruentum. *Sacred to Mars,* Martium, Māvortium. *Terrible,* horrĭdum, horrĭbĭle, terrĭbĭle, dīrum. *Hateful,* ŏdiōsum, invīsum. *Long,* longum, diūturnum. *Perpetual,* perpĕtuum. *Avenging,* in plur. ultrīcia. *Tearful, sad,* triste, flēbĭle, lăcrўmōsum, lăcrўmābĭle.

bĕnĕfactum. *A benefit, a kindness.*—EP. *Kind, friendly,* ămīcum, offĭciōsum. *Acceptable,* grātum, jūcundum, acceptum. *Deserved,* mĕrĭtum. *Undeserved,* immĕrĭtum. *Worthy,* dignum. *Unexpected,* inŏpīnum, nĕcŏpīnum, ĭnexpectatum, insprātus.

bestia. *A beast.*—EP. *Tamed,* dŏmĭta, sŭbacta. *Useful,* ūtĭlis, apta (*for any particular purpose*). See bellua.

bĭdens, entis, masc. *A pitchfork.*—EP. *Hard,* dūrus. *Iron,* ferreus, ferrātus. *Belonging to a farmer,* āgrestis, rustĭcus.

bĭdens, entis, fem. *A sheep.* See ovis.

bīga, æ. *A two-horse chariot.*—EP. *Rapid,* răpĭda, admissa. See currus.

bĭpennis. *An axe.*—EP. *Hard,* dūra. *Strong,* vălĭda. *Sharp,* ăcūta. *Iron,* brazen, ferrea, ferrāta, ærea, ahēnea ahēna. *Warlike,* bellĭca, bellĭcōsa, Māvortia. *Belonging to a farmer,* āgrestis, rustĭca.

bĭtūmen, ĭnis, neut. *Pitch.*—EP. *Black,* nĭgrum, ātrum. *Tarry,* pĭceum. *Adhesive,* tĕnax. *Thick,* densus.

blandīmentum, blandītia, usu. in plur. blandītiæ. *A soft speech, a caress.*—EP. *Sweet,* jūcunda, dulcis, suavis, grāta. *Tender,* mollis, tĕnĕra. *Loving,* ămans. *Crafty,* callĭda, dŏlōsa. *Deceitful,* fallax, perfĭda, infĭda. *Customary,* sŏlĭta, assueta, consueta, nōta.

blatta. *A beetle.*—EP. *Vile,* vīlis. *Hateful,* ŏdiōsa, invīsa. *Avoiding the light,* lūcĭfūga.

bombyx, ўcis, masc. 1. *A silkworm.*—2. *Silk.*—EP. 1. *Diligent,* sēdŭlus. *Yellow, spinning yellow silk,* flāvus, aureus. *Changeable,* mūtābĭlis.—2. *Thin,* tĕnuis. *Light,* lĕvis. *Of various colour,* vărius. *Embroidered,* pictus. *Eastern,* Eōus. *Arabian,* Ārăbus, Sābæus.

bŏnĭtas, ătis, fem. *Goodness, kindness.*—EP. *Gentle,* cōmis hūmāna, blanda. *Kind, friendly,* æqua, ămica. *Known, usual,* nōta, sŏlĭta, assueta, consueta. *Delightful,* grāta, jūcunda, ămæna. *Continual,* perpĕtua, assĭdua.

bŏnum. *A good.*—EP. *Fortunate,* faustum, sĕcundum. *Happy, making happy,* fēlix, lætum. *Eternal,* æternum. *Transitory,* brĕve, frăgĭle, cădūcum.

Bŏreas, æ, masc. *The North Wind.*—EP. *Fierce, violent,* fĕrus, trux trŭcis, vĭŏlentus, fūriōsus, immītis. *Cold,* gĕlĭdus, frĭgĭdus, glăciālis. *Stormy,* prŏ-

14 **BOS—CAD**

cellōsus, turbĭdus. *Thracian*, Thrēĭcius, Ēdōnus. *Northern*, Arctōus. *Dry*, siccus. *Penetrating*, pĕnĕtrābĭlis.

bos, bŏvis. *An ox.*—EP. *Patient*, pătiens. *Aiding the farmer*, rūrĭcŏla, agrĭcŏla, ăgrestis, rustĭcus. *Ploughing*, ărātor, ărans. *Strong*, vălĭdus, fortis, rōbustus. *Horned*, cornĭger –ĕri. *Slow*, pĭger –gri, tardus, lentus.

bracca, æ. *Breeches.*—EP. *Persian*, Persĭca. *Loose*, laxa. *Manly*, vĭrīlis.

brāchium. 1. *An arm.*—2. *A branch.*—EP. 1. *Right*, dextĕrum, *sync.* –trum. *Left*, lævum, sĭnistrum. *Muscular*, tŏrōsus, nervōsus. *Strong*, forte, vălĭdum, rōbustum.—2. See ramus.

bractea, æ. *A thin plate of metal.*—EP. *Of gold*, aurea, fulva. *Of silver*, argentia, candĭda. *Thin*, tĕnuis. *Shining*, splendĭda, cōrusca. *Valuable*, prĕtiōsa.

Brĭtannia. *Britain.*—EP. *Distant*, distans, longinqua, rĕmōta, ultĭma. *Brave*, fortis, impăvĭda. *Warlike*, bellĭca, Martia, Māvortia, pugnax. *Invincible*, invicta, indŏmĭta. *Free*, lībĕra. *Insular*, circumflua. *Mistress of the sea*, dŏmĭna æquŏris, classe pŏtens.

brūma, æ. *Winter.*—EP. *Cold*, frĭgĭda, gĕlĭda, glăciālis. *Inactive, making things inactive*, dormant, ĭners, frīgra. *Severe*, imprŏba, dūra, ācris, rĭgĭda. *Hated*, ŏdiōsa, invīsa. *Last (as ending the year)*, ultĭma. *Northern*, Bŏreālis, Hÿperbŏrea.

būbo, ōnis, masc. fem. *An owl.*—EP. *Solitary*, sōlus. *Nightly*, nocturnus. *Sacred to Minerva*, Pallādius. *Mournful, ill-omened*, tristis, fērālis, obscœnus. *Infernal, favoured by the infernal deities.* Stӯgius, infernus. *Slow*, pĭger –gri, tardus. *Inactive*, ignāvus, ĭners. *Howling, hoarse*, ŭlŭlans, raucus.

būbulcus, i. *A cowherd.*—EP. *Slow*, tardus, pĭger –gri. *Rustic*, ăgrestis, rustĭcus. *Hard-working*, ŏpĕrōsus, lăbōriōsus. *Contented*, contentus. *Strong*, fortis, vălĭdus, rōbustus.

bucca. *A cheek.* See gĕna.

buccĭna, æ. *A trumpet.*—EP. *Hollow*, căva, concăvus. *Twisted*, tortĭlis. *Brazen*, ærea, ahĕnea, ahena. *Warlike*, bellĭca, Martia, Māvortia. *Loud*, clāra, cănōra. *Hoarse*, rauca.

būcŭla. *A heifer.* See bos.

būfo, ōnis, masc. *A toad.*—EP. *Brown*, fuscus. *Spotted*, măcŭlōsus. *Slow*, tardus, pĭger. *Long-lived*, longævus.

bulla. *A bubble in water.*—EP. *Bright*, lūcĭda, clāra, vĭtrea. *Transparent*, perlūcĭda. *Sudden, rising suddenly*, sūbĭta. *Frequent*, crēbra.

būris, is. *A ploughtail.* See arātrum.

bustum. *A tomb.*—EP. *Sad*, triste, flēbĭle, mĭsĕrābĭle, miserandum. *Heaped up*, congestum. *Last*, ultĭmum, sūpremum. *Inexorable*, inexōrābĭle. See sepulchrum.

buxum, i. *Box-wood.*—EP. *Easily cut*, sectĭle. *Yellow*, flāvum. *Smooth*, lēve. *From Cytorus (a mountain in Paphlagonia celebrated for box)*, Cӯtōrium, Cӯtōriăcum.

buxus, i, fem. *A box-tree.*—EP. *Leafy*, frondea, frondōsa, frondens. *Green*, vĭrĭdis, vĭrĭdans, vĭrens. *Thick*, densa. *Easily cut*, sectĭlis. *Low*, hŭmĭlis. See buxum.

C.

Căballus. *A horse.* See equus.

căchinnus. *A laugh.* See risus.

căcŭmen, ĭnis, neut. *A top, a summit.*—EP. *Lofty*, altum, arduum, celsum, sūblīme. *Reaching to the stars, to the sky*, sĭdĕreum, ăĕrium. *Snow-clad (of a mountain)*, nĭvōsum. *Cloud-capped*, nūbĭfĕrum. See mons.

cădāver, ĕris, neut. *A carcass.*—EP. *Lifeless*, exănĭmum, exănĭme. *Ill-omened*, obscœnum. *Unsightly*, dēforme. *Bloody*, cruentum, sanguĭneum, sanguĭnŏlentum. *Torn*, lăcĕrum, lăcĕrātum. *Defiled with dust*, pulvĕreum, pulvĕrŭlentum. *Miserable*, mĭsĕrum, mĭsĕrābĭle, triste, flēbĭle.

cădus, i. *A cask.*—EP. *Full*, plēnus. *Sweet*, dulcis, jūcundus. *Of Falernian*,

CÆD—CAN 15

Cœcubian wine, etc., Fălernus, Cæcŭbus, etc. *Old*, antīquus, vĕtus –ĕris.
Smoky, smoke-dried, fūmōsus. *Opened*, versus. See vinum.

cœdes, ĭs, fem. *Slaughter.*—EP. *Miserable*, mĭsĕra, mĭsĕrābĭlis, tristis, flēbĭlis.
Terrible, cruel, dīra, fĕra, sæva, immītis. *Bloody*, cruenta, sanguinea, sanguĭ-
nŏlenta. *In war*, Martia, bellĭca.

cœlāmen, ĭnis, neut. *Carved work.*—EP. *Rich*, dīves –ītis. *Splendid*, splen-
dĭdum, ĕgrēgium. *Elaborate*, lăbōrātum. *Variegated*, pictum. *Skilfully
done*, pĕrītum, doctum.

cœlator. *A carver.* See sculptor.

cœsăries, ĭs. *Hair.* See crinis.

cœstus, ûs. *A boxing-glove.*—EP. *Hard*, dūrus, rĭgĭdus. *Heavy*, grăvis.
Leaden, plumbeus. *Cruel*, crūdus, sæcus, fĕrus.

călămus. 1. *A reed.*—2. *An arrow.*—3. *A flute.*—4. *A pen.*—EP. 1. See
arundo.—2. See sagitta.—3. See tibia.—4. *Easily running, fluent*, făcĭlis.
Learned, doctus. *Eloquent*, făcundus, dīsertus. *Sacred to Apollo, or Mercury
(as the patrons of literary men*, Ăpollīneus, Ăpollīnăris, Mercūriălis.

călăthus. *A basket.*—EP. *Frail*, frăgĭlis. *Made of osier*, vimĭneus. *Light*,
lĕvis. *Full*, plēnus, grăvis.

calcar, ăris, neut. *A spur.*—EP. *Sharp*, ăcūtum. *Sharp, or eager*, ācre.
Eager, vehĕmens, fervĭdum. *Hasty, rapid*, răpĭdum, vēlox, cītum. *Iron*, fer-
reum, ferrātum.

calceus. *A shoe.*—EP. *Fitting well*, aptus. *Double, twofold*, gĕmĭnus. *Soft*,
mollis.

calcŭlus. *A pebble.*—EP. *Small*, parvus, exĭguus. *Hard*, dūrus. *Powerful
(of a pebble when used in voting)*, pŏtens.

călĭga. *A boot.* See calceus.

cālīgo, ĭnis, fem. *Darkness.*—EP. *Black*, ātra, nīgra, pĭcea, fusca. *Such as
cannot be seen in*, cæca. *Obscure*, obscūra, ŏpāca. *Hollow*, căva. *Of night*,
nocturna. *Dense*, densa, multa, crassa. *Sudden*, sŭbĭta.

călix, ĭcis, masc. *A cup.* See poculum.

callĭdĭtas, ātis, fem. *Cunning, craft (in either a good or bad sense).*—EP.
Prudent, prudens, săpiens, săgax. *Provident*, prŏvĭda, cauta. *Ingenious*, in-
gĕniosa. *Artful*, versūta, văfra. *Tricky*, dŏlōsa, subdŏla. *Trying various
schemes*, văria. *Malicious*, măligna. *Perverse, wicked*, prava, măla.

callis, ĭs, masc. *A path.* See via.

călor, ōris, masc. *Heat.*—EP. *Great*, ingens, magnus. *Too great*, nĭmius.
Of summer, æstīvus. *Pleasing*, dulcis, grātus, ămābĭlis, jūcundus.

caltha. *A marigold.*—EP. *Yellow*, flāva, aurea. *Low*, hŭmĭlis.

calva. *The scalp.*—EP. *Covered with hair*, cŏmans.

călumnia. *Calumny.*—EP. *Malignant*, măligna, mordax. *Wicked*, măla,
prava, scĕlĕrāta. *Envious*, invĭda, lĕvĭda. *Undeserved*, immĕrĭta, indigna,
falsa.

calx, cis, fem. *The heel.*—EP. *Heavy*, grăvis. *Tender*, mollis, tĕnĕra. *Iron
(i. e. armed with a spur, as Scott uses it in the Lady of the Lake)*, ferrāta, ferrea.

cămella. *A cup for milk.*—EP. *Of milk*, lactea. *White*, alba, nĭvea, candĭda.
Simple, simplex –ĭcis. *Pure*, pūra. *Rustic*, rustĭca, ăgrestis.

cămēlus. *A camel.*—EP. *Arabian*, Ărăbus, ˇArăbius, Năbăthæus, Săbæus.
Eastern, ˇEōus. *Docile*, dŏcĭlis. *Patient*, pătiens.

cămĕra. *A vaulted roof.*—EP. *Painted*, picta. *With handsome ceiling*, lăqueāta.
Gilded, aurea, aurāta. *Lofty*, alta, ardua. *Inlaid with ivory*, ĕburna, ĕburnea.
Variegated, văria.

cămīnus. *A furnace, a chimney.*—EP. *Glowing*, fervens, fervĭdus. *Shining*,
rŭtĭlus, rŭtĭlans. *Smoking*, fūmōsus, fūmans.

campus. *A field, a plain.*—EP. *Wide*, lātus, spătiōsus. *Green*, vĭrĭdis, vĭrens.
Grassy, grămĭneus. *Level*, plānus, æquus. See ager.

cănālis, ĭs, masc. *A waterpipe.*—EP. *Hollow*, căvus. *Of oak*, īlignus. *Long*,
longus.

cancer, cri, also ăris, masc. *A crab.*—EP. *Ruddy*, rŭbens, rŭber –bri. *Hard*,
dūrus. *Tenacious*, tĕnax.

candēla. *A candle.* See lampas.

candor, ōris, masc. *Whiteness.*—EP. *Pure*, pūrus. *Snowlike*, nĭvālis, nĭveus.
Like ivory, ĕburnus, ĕburneus. *Glossy*, nĭtĭdus.

16 CAN—CAR

cănícŭla. *The dogstar.* See Sirius.

cănis, is, masc. fem. *A dog.*—EP. *Faithful,* fĭdēlis, fĭdus. *Sagacious,* săgax. *With good scent,* ŏdōrus. *Swift,* răpĭdus, vēlox, cĕler -ĕris. *Active, eager,* ācer -cris, impĭger -gri. See the Gradus.

cănistrum. *A basket.* See calathus.

cănĭties, ēi. *Grey hair.*—EP. *Aged,* longæva, vĕtŭla, annōsa. *Thin,* exīlis. *Venerable,* vĕnĕrābĭlis, vĕnĕranda. See senectus.

canna. *A reed.* See arundo.

cănor, ōris, masc. *The sound of music.*—EP. *Tuneful,* argūtus, lĭquĭdus, vōcālis. *Sweet,* dulcis, jūcundus, amœnus. *Divine,* dīvīnus. *Sacred to Apollo (as the god of music),* Ăpollīneus, Ăpollīnāris, Phœbēus, Phœbēius.

cantāmen, cantĭlēna, cantus, ûs. *Song.*—EP. *Tuneful,* cănōrus, lĭquĭdus, argūtus, vōcālis, nŭmĕrōsus. *Sweet,* dulcis, blandus, ămābĭlis ămœnus, jūcundus. *Glad, cheerful,* lætus, hĭlāris. *Plaintive, querulous (like that of the nightingale),* quĕrŭlus, tristis, lūgŭbris.

cantātor, cantor. *A singer.*—EP. *Skilful,* doctus, pĕrītus. *Celebrated,* clārus, inclўtus, nōtus. *Honoured,* hŏnōrātus. See above, cantus.

căper -pri, căpella, căpra. *A goat.*—EP. *Shaggy,* hirtus, hirsūtus. *Wanton,* lascīvus, prōtervus, pĕtulans. *Horned,* cornĭger -ĕri. *Bearded,* barbātus. *With hard feet,* cornĭpes -ĕdis. *Strong smelling,* ŏlens, ŏlĭdus, grăvĕolens (trisyll.), fœdus. *Apt to fight,* pugnax. *Active,* ăgĭlis.

căpillus. *Hair.* See crinis.

căpistrum. *A muzzle.*—EP. *Iron,* ferreum, ferrātum. *Tight,* arctum. *Hard,* dūrum, aspĕrum. *Unpleasant,* ăcerbum.

căprea. *A roe.*—EP. *Timid,* tĭmĭda. *Unwarlike,* imbellis. *With thick coat,* villōsa. *Swift,* velox, răpĭda, cĕlĕris, cĭta.

captīvus. *A captive.*—EP. *Chained, bound,* cătēnātus, vinctus. *Unfortunate,* infēlix, mĭser -ĕri. *Subdued,* dŏmĭtus, sŭbactus, victus. *Abject,* abjectus. *Suppliant,* supplex -ĭcis.

căpŭlus. *A sword hilt.*—EP. *Golden,* aureus, aurātus. *Chased,* cælātus. *Studded with jewels,* gemmeus, gemmātus, gemmans. *Ivory,* ĕburnus, ĕburneus.

căput, ĭtis, neut. *A head.*—EP. *Handsome,* pulchrum, dĕcōrum, bŏnestum. *With long hair,* cŏmans, căpillātus, crīnītus. *Unshorn (i. e. youthful),* intonsus. *Grey (i. e. aged),* cānum, cānens. See crinis.

carbāsus. *A sail.* See velum.

carbo, ōnis, masc.—EP. *Black,* nĭger -gri, āter -tri. *Burning,* flammans, flammĭfer -ĕri. *Smoking,* fūmeus, fūmōsus, fūmĭfer -ĕri.

carcer, ĕris, masc. 1. *A prison.*—2. *The starting post in a race.*—EP. 1. *Iron,* ferreus, ferrātus. *Adamantine,* ădămantīnus. *Hard, cruel,* dūrus, immītis. *Narrow,* angustus, arctus. *Long, perpetual,* longus, perpĕtuus. *Squalid,* squālĭdus, squālens. *Dark,* obscūrus, cæcus, lūrĭdus. 1, 2. *Open,* ŏpertus, laxus. 2. *Equal,* æquus.

carchēsium. *A cup.* See poculum.

cardo, ĭnis, masc. *A hinge.*—EP. *Easy, moving easily,* făcĭlis. *Revolving,* rĕvŏlūbĭlis. *Creaking,* strĭdens, strĭdŭlus. *Brazen,* æreus, ærātus, ahēnus, ahēneus.

carduus. *A thistle.*—EP. *Prickly,* spīnōsus, ăcūtus. *Useless,* segnis, stĕrĭlis, ĭnūtĭlis. *Rough,* hirsūtus. *Scotch,* Călēdŏnius.

cārectum. *A bed of sedge.* See below.

cārex -ĭcis, fem. *Sedge.*—EP. *Sharp,* ăcūta. *Worthless,* vīlis. *Rough,* hirsūta.

cārīca. *A dried fig.*—EP. *Sweet,* dulcis. *Dry,* ārĭda, sicca. *Pressed,* pressa.

cāries, ēi, fem. *Rottenness.*—EP. *Soft,* mollis, tĕnĕra. *Putrid,* pūtris. *Devouring,* ĕdax, vŏrax. *Destructive,* exĭtiōsa, exĭtiālis, māla, pernĭciōsa, damnōsa. *Aged,* vĕtusta.

cărīna. 1. *A keel.*—2. *A ship.*—EP. 1. *Brazen,* ærea, ærāta, ahēna, ahēnea. *Stout,* vălĭda, fortis. *Sharp,* ăcūta. *Curved,* panda, curva, incurva. *Smeared with tar,* uncta. See navis.

carmen, ĭnis, neut. 1. *A verse, a poem.*—2. *A song, etc.*—3. *An incantation.*—EP. 1. *Rhythmical,* nŭmĕrōsum. *Learned,* doctum. *Immortal, undying,* immortāle, æternum. *Epic,* Mæŏnium. *Lyric,* lўrĭcum. *Lesbian,* Lesbōum. *Grand,* grande, sŭblīme. *Sacred to the Muses,* Ăŏnium, Piĕrium. 1, 2. *Sacred to Apollo,* Ăpollīneum, Ăpollīnāre, Phœbēum, Phœbēium. *Sacred,* săcrum. *Divine,*

CAR—CAU 17

dīvīnum. *Sad, pathetic,* triste, flēbĭle, mĭsĕrābĭle. *Joyful,* lætum. *Triumphal,* triumphāle, victrix.—2. *Tuneful,* cănōrum, argūtum, lĭquĭdum, vōcāle, dulce. —3. *Magic,* măgĭcum. *Wicked,* impĭum, prŏfānum, scĕlĕrātum. *Malignant,* mălignum. *Destructive,* exitiōsum, exĭtiāle, fătāle.

carnĭfex, Ĭcis. *An executioner.*—EP. *Cruel,* sævus, fĕrus, immītis. *Infamous,* turpis, infāmis.

carpentum. *A chariot.* See currus.

căsa. *A cottage.*—EP. *Humble,* hŭmĭlis. *Little,* parva, exĭgua. *Thatched or built with straw or reeds,* strāmĭnea, ărundĭnea. *Poor,* pauper -ĕris. *Simple,* simplex, Ĭcis.

căseus. *Cheese.*—EP. *Yellow,* flāvus, crŏceus. *Well-pressed,* pressus. *Fat,* pinguis.

cassis, Ĭdis, fem. *A helmet.*—EP. *Brazen,* ærea, ahēna, ahēnea. *Crested,* cristāta, cŏmans. See galea.

cassis, is, masc. *A net.*—EP. *Cunning,* callĭdus. *Deceitful,* fallax. *Lying concealed,* abdĭtus, lătens.

castellum. *A fort.*—EP. *Strong,* forte, vălĭdum. *Brazen, iron,* æreum, ahēnum, ahēneum, ferreum. *High,* altum, arduum. *Inaccessible,* invium, ĭnaccessum. *Threatening,* mĭnax. *On a mountain,* montānum, aĕrium.

castĭgātor. *A reprover.*—EP. *Wise, judicious,* săpiens, callĭdus, prūdens. *Friendly,* ămīcus, bēnignus. *Honest,* hŏnestus, prŏbus, æquus. *Severe,* sĕvērus, rĭgĭdus, ăcerbus.

castĭtas. *Chastity.*—EP. *White,* alba, candĭda. *Pure,* pūra. *Inviolate,* intĕmĕrāta, invĭŏlāta, invĭŏlābĭlis. *Pious,* pia. *Sacred,* săcra, sancta, săcrāta, dĭvīna.

castor, ŏris, masc. *A beaver.*—EP. *Living in Pontus,* Pontĭcus. *Cunning,* callĭdus, ingĕniosus. *Enduring,* pătiens. *Prudent,* prūdens, săpiens. *Brave,* fortis.

castra, ōrum, neut. plur. *A camp, a tent.*—EP. *Warlike,* bellĭca, Martia, Māvortia. *Strong,* fortia. *Safe,* tūta. *Armed* (i. e. *full of armed men*), armāta. *Pitched,* pŏsĭta. See militia.

căsus, ûs. 1. *A fall.*—2. *An event.*—EP. 1. *Heavy,* grăvis.—1. 2. *Sad,* tristis, flēbĭlis. *Pernicious, fatal, etc.,* pernĭciōsus, exĭtiālis, exĭtiōsus, fătālis.—2. *Sudden, unexpected,* sŭbĭtus, ĭnŏpīnus, nĕcŏpīnus, ĭnexspectātus. *New, fresh,* nŏvus, rĕcens. *Unprecedented,* nŏvus, ĭnaudītus, insŏlītus.

cătăracta, æ, masc. *A cataract.*—EP. *Headlong,* præceps -ĭpĭtis. *Violent,* vĭŏlentus. *Rapid,* răpĭdus. *Vast,* ingens.

cătellus, cătŭlus. *A little dog, etc.* See canis.

cătella, cătēna. *A chain.*—EP. *Heavy,* grăvis. *Severe,* rĭgĭda, sĕvēra. *Cruel,* sæva, fĕra, immītis, crūdēlis. *Iron,* ferrea, ferrāta, ădămantīna. *Tight, confining,* arcta. *Worn as ornament* (in which sense catella is more used than catena). *Golden,* aurea, aurāta. *Jewelled,* gemmea, gemmāta, gemmans. *Bright, splendid,* splendida, fulgens, nĭtens, cŏrusca. *Beautiful,* pulchra, spĕciōsa, spectābĭlis.

cāterva. *A crowd.*—EP. *Numerous, dense,* magna, ingens, frĕquens, densa. *Splendid,* splendĭda. *Eager,* ăvĭda, cŭpĭda, vehĕmens. See turba.

căthĕdra. *A seat.* See sedile.

cauda. *A tail.*—EP. *Long,* longa. *Slender,* grăcĭlis. *Curved,* sĭnuosa, curva, rĕcurva.

caudex, Ĭcis, masc. *A trunk of a tree.* See truncus.

căvea. *A cage.*—EP. *Hard, cruel,* dūra, sæva. *Narrow,* angusta, arcta.

căverna. *A cavern.*—EP. *Deep,* alta, prŏfunda. *Winding,* curva, sĭnuōsa. *Vast,* magna, ingens. See antrum.

caula. *A sheepfold.*—EP. *Full,* plēna. *In the fields,* ăgrestis. See ovis.

caulis, is, masc. *A stalk.*—EP. *Long,* longus. *Straight,* rectus. *Green,* vĭrĭdis. *Prickly,* spīnōsus. *Round and smooth,* tĕres -ĕtis.

caupo, ōnis, masc. *An innkeeper.*—EP. *Knavish,* imprŏbus. *Cheating,* fallax, falsus. *Spiteful,* mălignus.

caupōna. *An inn.*—EP. *Uncomfortable,* măla, ĭnămœna, ĭnămābĭlis. *Dirty,* sordĭda. *Greasy,* uncta. *Splendid,* splendĭda. *Hospitable,* hospĭta.

causa. *A cause.*—EP. *Original,* prīma. *Ancient,* antīqua, vĕtus -ĕris, prisca. *Just,* pia, justa. *Imperious,* impĕriōsa. *Secret,* sĕcrēta, abdĭta, lătens, tăcĭta. *Various,* văria.

c

18   CAU—CHA

causīdīcus. *A lawyer.*—EP. *Learned, skilful,* doctus, pērītus. *Wise,* săpiens. *Eloquent,* făcundus, dīsertus.

cautes, is, fem. *A rock.* See saxum.

cědrus, i, fem. *Cedar (the tree and the wood).*—EP. *Syrian,* Sўra, Sўria. *Fragrant,* frāgrans, ŏdōrăta. *Tall,* prŏcēra, alta, ardŭa. *Green,* vĭrĭdis. *Undecaying,* immortalis, incorrupta, vīvax.

cella. 1. *The cell of a honeycomb.*—2. *A cellar, etc.*—EP. 1, 2. *Full,* plēna. *Sweet (as full of sweet things),* dulcis.—2. *Ancestral,* pătria, păterna, ăvīta. *Deep,* alta, prŏfunda. *Mouldy,* rōbīgīnōsa.

cenchris, ĭdis, fem. *A kestrel hawk.* See accipiter.

censor, ōris, masc. *The censor at Rome.*—1. *A critic, a reprover.*—EP. *Grave, dignified,* grăvis. *Severe,* sĕvērus, rĭgĭdus. *Just,* justus.—2. *Friendly, kind,* ămīcus, bĕnignus. *Acute,* subtīlis, argūtus, doctus.

censūra. *Censorship, criticism.* See above.

census, ûs. *Income, means of livelihood.*—EP. *Ample, rich,* dīves –ĭtis, amplus, *Poor, scanty,* pauper –ĕris, parcus, hūmĭlis.

centaurus, i. *A centaur.*—EP. *Double-formed,* bĭformis. *Thessalian,* Thessălus, Thessălĭcus. See Gradus.

centūrio, ōnis, masc. *A centurion.*—EP. *Great, proud,* magnus, sŭperbus. *Brave,* fortis, impăvĭdus. *Armed,* armātus.

cēra. *Wax.*—EP. *Soft,* mollis. *Easily moulded, yielding,* făcĭlis, lenta. *Frail,* frăgĭlis. *Sticky,* tĕnax. *Brought from Hymettus (as a place celebrated for bees),* Hўmettia ; *(for the same reason one might say,)* Mătīna (see apis). *Fresh,* nŏva, rĕcens.

cĕrastes, æ, masc. *A horned snake.* See anguis.

cĕrăsus, i, fem. 1. *A cherry-tree.*—2. *A cherry.*—EP. 1. *Hard,* dūra, ædūra. —2. *Sweet,* dulcis. *Red,* rŭbens, rōsea. *Ripe* mātūra.

cĕrēbrum. *The brain.*—EP. *Cause of life,* vĭtāle. *Source of invention,* ingĕnĭōsum. *Wounded, torn (of a wounded soldier),* saucium, lăcĕrum. *Dashed out,* effūsum. *Pierced,* trajectum.

Cĕres, ĕris, fem. *The goddess of corn.*—EP. *Golden (from the colour of ripe corn),* aurea, flāva, rŭbĭcunda. *Sicilian (Sicily being the principal place of her worship),* Sĭcŭla, Trĭnăcria ; *so, Eleusinian,* Eleusīna. *The Lawgiver,* Lēgĭfĕra. *Genial, nourishing men,* alma.

certāmen, ĭnis, neut. *A contest.*—EP. *Friendly (in games),* ămĭcum. *Hostile,* hostīle. *Hard,* dūrum, arduum. *Equal, favourable,* æquum. *Unequal, unfavourable,* inīquum. *Martial,* bellĭcum, Martium, Māvortium. See prælium.

cervix, ĭcis, fem. *A neck.* See collum.

cērussa. *White paint used by women.*—EP. *Deceitful,* fallax. *Smeared on,* illĭta.

cervus, cerva. *A stag.*—EP. *Horned,* cornĭger –ĕra. *Horny-footed,* cornĭpes –ĕdis. *Active, swift,* ăgĭlis, vēlox, cĭtus, cĕler –ĕris, ălātus. *Timid, frightened,* tĭmĭdus, terrĭtus, perterrĭtus. *Apt to fear,* fŭgax. *Long-lived,* vīvax. *Helpless,* imbellis. *Living in the woods,* sylvestris.

cespes, ĭtis, masc. *Turf.*—EP. *Green,* vĭrĭdis, vĭrens, vĭrĭdans. *Grassy,* grāmĭneus, herbōsus, herbĭdus. *Soft,* mollis, tĕner –ĕri. *Moist,* ūdus. *Mossy,* muscōsus.

cestus, ûs, masc. *The girdle of Venus.*—EP. *Sacred to Venus,* Cўthĕrēius, Cўthĕrĭăcus, Idālius, Cўprius. *Medicated,* mĕdĭcātus. *Powerful,* pŏtens, *Winning,* ămābĭlis, blandus.

cētus, i. *(For declension,* see Gradus). *A whale.* See balæna.

cētra. *A light leathern shield.*—EP. *Light,* lĕvis. *Spanish,* Ibēra, Ibĕrĭca, Hispāna.

chălybs, ўbis, masc. *Steel.*—EP. *Hard,* dūrus, rĭgĭdus. *Causing wounds (when made into weapons),* vulnĭfĭcus. *Coming from Pontus,* Pontĭcus. *Sacred to Mars,* Martius, Māvortius. *Brittle,* frăgĭlis. *Proved (in the fire, etc.),* spectātus.

chaos (only nom. and acc. sing. neut.). *Chaos.*—EP. *Primeval,* prīmum. *Ancient,* priscum, antīquum, vĕtus –ĕris. *Confused, unmanaged,* rŭde, indĭgestum, incompŏsĭtum, confūsum.

Chărĭtes, um, plur. fem. *The Graces.* See gratia.

Chăron, ontis. *The ferryman of the Styx.*—EP. *Infernal,* Infernus, Stўgius,

CHA—CIT 19

Tartăreus. *Horrible looking*, horrĭbĭlis, horrendus, terrĭbĭlis, dīrus. *Squalid*, aqualĭdus.

charta. *Paper.*—EP. *White*, alba, candĭda, nĭvea. *Faithful (as conveying writing faithfully)*, fīda, fĭdēlis. *Eloquent*, făcunda, dĭserta. *Conveying intelligence*, nuntia.

Chărybdis, is, fem. *A Sicilian whirlpool.*—EP. *Devouring*, vŏrax. *Deep*, alta, prŏfunda. *Black*, ātra, nĭgra. *Hateful*, ŏdiōsa, invīsa. *Hoarse*, rauca, *Sicilian*, Sĭcŭla, Trīnăcria, Zanclæa. *Unquiet*, implăcāta, irrĕquiēta, inquiēta.

chĕlys, yos. *A lyre.* See lyra.

chīrăgra. *Gout in the hand.*—EP. *Painful*, tristis. *Causing lumps*, nōdōsa. *Making one slow*, tarda.

chlămys, ўdis, fem. *A cloak.*—EP. *Embroidered*, picta, văria. *Embroidered with gold*, aurata. *Purple*, purpŭrea. *Syrian*, i. e. *dyed with Syrian purple or scarlet*, Sўria, Sīdŏnia.

chorda. *The string of a musical instrument.*—EP. *Struck*, icta, percussa, impulsa, mōta. *Tuneful*, cănōra, blanda, dulcis, argūta. See lyra.

chŏrēa. *A dance.*—EP. *Active*, ăgĭlis. *Joyful*, hĭlăris, læta. *In tune*, nŭmĕrōsa. *Graceful*, dĕcōra, dĕcens. *Festive*, festa. *Of damsels*, virgĭnea, puellăris. *Of boys and girls mingled*, mista.

chŏrus, i. *A company of dancers or singers.*—EP. *Joyful*, lætus, hĭlăris. *Festive*, festus. *Harmonious*, concors –dis, consŏnus. *Light, lightly moving*, ăgĭlis, lēvis. *Sacred*, săcer –cri.

cĭbōrium. *A cup.* See poculum.

cĭbus, i, cĭbāria, ōrum, plur. neut. *Food.*—EP. *Genial*, nŭtrītĭus, almus. *Useful*, ūtĭlis. *Supporting life*, vītālis. *Sweet, pleasant*, dulcis, jūcundus. *Luxurious, rich*, lautus, dīves –ĭtis.

cĭcāda, æ. *A grasshopper.*—EP. *Living in trees*, arbŏrea. *Tuneful*, cănōra, vōcālis, argūta. *Querulous*, quĕrŭla. *Hoarse*, rauca. *Living on dew*, roscĭda, rōris ămans.

cĭcātrix, īcis, fem.—EP. *Deep*, alta. *Livid*, lĭvĭda. *Purple*, purpŭrea. *Lasting*, longa, mansūra. *Bloody*, sanguĭnea, sanguĭnŏlenta, cruenta. *Old*, vĕtus –ĕris.

cĭcer, ĕris, neut. *A vetch.*—EP. *Worthless*, vīle. *Green*, vĭrĭde, vĭrĭdans. *Springing up again*, Rĕsurgens.

cĭcōnia, æ. *A stork.*—EP. *White*, candĭda. *Foreign, migratory*, pĕrĕgrīna. *Pious*, pia. *Harmless*, innŏcens, innoxia. *With long bill*, rostrāta. *Returning in spring*, verna.

cĭcūta, æ. *Hemlock.*—EP. *Poisonous*, vĕnēnāta. *Deadly*, fătālis. *Producing cold*, gĕlĭda, frīgĭda. *Producing torpor*, ĭners, sĕgnis, pĭgra.

cĭnăra and cĭnăre. *An artichoke.*—EP. *Rough*, hispĭda. *Green*, vĭrĭdis.

cincinnus. *A curl.*—EP. *Carefully combed*, comptus. *Adorned*, ornātus. *Long*, longus, *Twisted*, tortĭlis. *Auburn*, flāvus, aureus.

cingŭla, æ. *A girdle.* See zona.

cĭnis, ĕris, masc. (fem. very rare). *Ashes*, esp. 2. *The ashes of the dead.*—EP. *Black*, āter –tri, nĭger– gri. *White*, candens, albus, candĭdus. *Smoking*, fūmans, fūmĭdus, fūmĭfĭcus.—2. *Sad*, tristis, mĭsĕrābĭlis. *Last*, ultĭmus, sūprēmus. *Lamented*, flētus. *Beloved*, cārus, dīlectus, ămātus.

cinnămum. *Cinnamon.*—EP. *Fragrant*, frāgrans, ŏdōrus, ŏdōrātum, ŏdōrĭfĕrum. *Eastern*, Ŏriens, ´Eōum. *Assyrian*, Assўrium, Panchæum.

cĭrcuītus, ūs. *A circuit.*—EP. *Long*, longus.

cĭrcŭlus. *A circle.*—EP. *Bending*, flexĭlis, obtortus, curvus, rĕcurvus, sĭnuōsus.

cĭrcus. *The circus.*—EP. *Crowded*, cĕlĕber –bris, frĕquens. *Joyful*, lætus. *Applauding*, plaudens, plausu rĕsŏnans.

cĭrrus. *A curl.*—EP. *Long*, longus. *Flowing*, fluĭtans, dēmissus. *Twisted*, flexĭlis, tortus, obtortus. *Delicate*, mollis, tĕner –eri.

cista. *A basket, esp. such as is used in sacred ceremonies.*—EP. *Sacred*, săcra, săcrāta, sancta. *Light*, lēvis. *Of osier*, vīmĭnea. *Wreathed*, cŏrōnāta.

cisterna. *A cistern.*—EP. *Deep*, alta, prŏfunda. *Pure*, pūra, vītrea, intĕmĕrāta.

cĭthăra. *A harp or lyre.*—EP. *Sacred to Apollo*, Ăpollĭnea, Ăpollĭnāris, Phœbēa. *Sacred to the Muses*, Ăŏnia, Pĭĕria. *Thracian (because Orpheus was a Thracian)*, Thrēĭcia, Thrācia. *Lesbian (because Sappho and Alcæus were Lesbians)*, Lesbia,

c 2

20 CIT—CŒL

Lesbōa. *Tuneful,* cănōra, argūta, dulcis, līquĭda. *Golden,* aurea, ĭnaurāti. *Effeminate,* mollis, imbellis. *Crooked,* curva, incurva. *Sportive,* jŏcōsa, festīva, læta.

cĭthărædus. *A harp-player.* See above.

cĭtrus, ĭ, fem. *The citron tree.*—EP. *Perfumed,* ŏdōra, ŏdōrāta. *Easily cut,* sectĭlis. *Assyrian, Phrygian,* Assўria, Phrўgia.

cīvis, is, masc. *A citizen, a fellow citizen.*—EP. *Brave,* fortis, impăvĭdus. *Unanimous,* ŭnănĭmis, concors –dis. *United, friendly,* sŏcius, ămīcus. *Well-known,* nōtus.

cīvĭtas, ātis, fem. *A city, a state.*—EP. *United,* concors –dis, ŭnănĭmis. *Joyful,* læta, fēlix. *Sad,* tristis, mœsta.

clādes. *Defeat, disaster.*—EP. *Sad,* tristis, mĭsĕra, mĭsĕranda, mĭsĕrābĭlis, flēbĭlis. *Bloody,* sanguīnea, sanguĭnŏlenta, cruenta. *Destructive,* exītiōsa, exītiālis, damnōsa. *Unexpected,* ĭnexspectāta. *Sudden,* sŭbĭta. *Unprecedented,* ĭnaudīta, insŏlĭta. *Irremediable,* immĕdĭcābĭlis, insānābĭlis.

clāmor, ōris, masc. *A shout.*—EP. *Loud,* clārus. *Joyful,* lætus, exsultans. *Unanimous, united,* ŭnănĭmis, sŏcius. *Triumphant,* triumphālis. *Grateful,* grātus. *Pious,* pius. *Repeated,* ĭtĕrātus, ingĕmĭnātus. *Sad,* tristis. *Complaining,* quĕrŭlus.

clangor, ōris, masc. *A loud noise, esp. of a trumpet.*—EP. *Brazen (as trumpets are brazen),* æreus, ahēneus, ahēnus. *Warlike,* bellĭcus. See clamor.

classĭcum. *A trumpet.* See tuba.

classis, is, fem. *A fleet.*—EP. *Large,* magna. *United,* juncta. *Allied,* sŏcia. *Sailing,* vēlĭvŏla. *Sailing onwards,* incēdens. *Keeping together,* æquatis procedens velis. *Warlike,* bellĭca, Martia, Māvortia. *Hostile,* hostīlis, hostĭca. *Victorious,* victrix. *Defeated,* victa, dŏmĭta, fūgāta, fŭgiens.

clāva. *A club.*—EP. *Heavy,* grăvis. *Vast,* ingens, magna. *Made of oak,* rŏbŏrea, querna. *Loaded with iron,* ferrea, ferrāta.

clāvis, is, fem. *A key.*—EP. *Faithful,* fīda, fĭdēlis. *Iron,* ferrea, ferrāta. *Powerful,* pŏtens.

claustrum. *A barrier.*—EP. *Firm,* firmum, vălĭdum. *Invincible,* invictum. *Hateful,* invīsum. *Narrow,* arctum, angustum. *Impassable,* invium. *Cruel,* immīte, crūdēle.

clēmentia, æ. *Clemency.*—EP. *Gentle,* mītis, plăcĭda, făcĭlis. *Pious, divine,* pia, săcra, sancta, dīvīna, cælestis. *Golden (as of the golden age),* aurea. *Deserved,* mĕrĭta. *Undeserved,* immĕrĭta. *Unhoped for,* inspērāta, ĭnexspectāta. *Accustomed,* sŏlĭta, assueta, consueta. *Praiseworthy,* laudanda, laudābĭlia. *Known, celebrated,* nōta, clāra, inclўta. *Admirable,* ēgrĕgia.

Cleŏpātra, æ. *The Queen of Egypt.*—EP. *Ægyptian,* Ægyptia, Nīliāca. *Pharia.* *Daughter of the Ptolemies,* Ptŏlĕmœa. *Wanton,* lasciva, prŏterva, incesta, impŭdĭca. *Loving,* ămans. *Fickle,* inconstans, mūtābĭlis, infīda, perfĭda. *Conquered,* victa, sŭbacta, dŏmĭta. *Brave,* fortis, impăvĭda. *Proud,* sŭperba.

cliens, tis, masc. *A client, a dependant.*—EP. *Humble,* hŭmĭlis. *Suppliant,* supplex, ĭcis. *Grateful,* grātus. *Seeking their patron in the morning,* mătŭtīnus.

clīvus. *A hill.* See collis.

clўpeus, ĭ. *A shield.*—EP. *Brazen, iron,* æreus, ærātus, ahēneus, ahēnus, ferreus, ferrātus. *Round,* rŏtundus. *Crescent-shaped,* lūnātus. *Made of triple layers,* trĭplex –ĭcis. *Of seven layers (like that of Ajax),* septemplex. *Made of osier,* sălĭgnus. *Shining,* fulgens, mĭcans. *Handy, easily swayed,* băbĭlis. *Held out against the enemy,* objectus, oppŏsĭtus. *Impenetrable,* impĕnĕtrābĭlis. *Heavy,* grăvis. *Large,* magnus, ingens.

coccum. *Scarlet dye.*—EP. *Red,* rŭber –bri. *Syrian,* Sўrium, Sĭdŏnium.

Cōcўtus. *One of the rivers of Hell.*—EP. *Hellish,* Infernus, Tartāreus, Plūtōnius. *Black,* niger –gri, āter –tri. *Unsightly,* dēformis, turpis. *Ill-omened,* obscœnus. *Hateful,* inămābĭlis, invīsus ŏdiŏsus. *Slow,* tardus, pĭger –gri, languĭdus. *Cruel,* sēverus, immītis, sævus. *Inexorable,* ĭnexōrābĭlis, implācābĭlis, illăcrўmābĭlis.

cœles –ĭtis, cœlĭcŏla. 1. *An inhabitant of heaven, an angel.*—2. *A God.*—EP. 1. *Pious,* pius. *Holy,* săcer –cri, sanctus, dīvīnus. *Happy,* fēlix, beātus.—2. See Deus.

cœlum, plur. cœli. *Heaven.*—EP. *High,* altum, sŭblīme, sŭpĕrum, sŭprēmum,

C CEN — COL 21

summum. *Etherial*, æthērium. *Eternal*, æternum, pĕrenne, immortāle. *Divine*, divīnum. *Sacred*, sācrum, sācrātum, sanctum. *Happy*, fēlix, beātum. *Starry*, sīdēreum. *Hoped for* optātum. *Marvellous*, mīrābile. *To be venerated*, vĕnĕrābīle.

cœna. *Supper, dinner.*—EP. *Luxurious*, lauta, luxŭriōsa, dīves -ītis. *Various*, vāria. *Ample*, ampla. *Late*, sēra. *Simple*, simplex -īcis, munda. *Scanty*, parca. *Wholesome*, sālūtāria, sālūbris.

cœnum. *Mud.*—EP. *Black*, nīgrum, ātrum. *Sticky*, tĕnax. *Deep*, altum. *Unsightly*, dēforme, turpe, obscœnum. *Dirty*, immundum. *Disturbed*, turbātum.

cœptum. *An undertaking, an enterprise.*—EP. *Difficult*, diffīcile, arduum. *Bold*, audax, ātrox, forte, impăvīdum. *Noble*, nōbīle. *Successful*, lætum, fēlix, sēcundum. *New*, nŏvum, inaudītum, inaudītum. *Great*, magnum, ingens. *Ambitious*, ambĭtiōsum. *Manly*, vīrīle.

cœtus, ûs. *An assembly, a crowd.*—EP. *Collected*, collectus, coactus. *Standing around*, circumstans. *Large*, magnus, ingens. *Joyful*, lætus. *Festive*, festus, festīvus. *Exulting*, exsultans. *Contented*, contentus. *Unquiet*, implācīdus, turbĭdus. *Noisy*, clāmōsus, raucus. *Discontented*, æger -gri, tristis.

cohors, tis. *A band of soldiers.*—EP. *Armed*, armāta. *Armed in brass or iron*, ærea, ahēnea, ferrea. *Bearing shields*, clȳpeāta. *Bearing spears*, hastāta, vērūta. *Bearing swords*, ensīfĕra. *Strong*, fīrma, vālĭda. *Undismayed*, impăvīda, interrĭta, impertĕrrĭta. *Bold*, fortis, audax. *Victorious*, victrix -īcis. *Long*, longa. *Arrayed*, instructa, explĭcĭta.

collēga, æ, masc. *A colleague.*—EP. *United as a companion*, sŏcius. *Agreeing with me*, concors -dis, ūnănĭmis, consentiens. *Friendly*, ămīcus. *Faithful*, fīdus, fĭdēlis. *Ancient*, vĕtus -ēris.

collēgium. *A college, a company.*—EP. *Learned*, doctum, săpiens. *Unanimous*, ūnănĭme, or unanimum, concors -dis. *Full*, plēnum. *Ancient*, antīquum, vĕtus -ēris. *Celebrated*, clārum, ēgrĕgium, insigne, nōtum.

collis, is, masc. *A hill.*—EP. *High*, altus, celsus, arduus. *Very high*, sūblīmis. *Steep*, præceps -ĭpĭtis, præruptus, abruptus. *Sloping upwards*, acclīvis, acclīvus, sŭpīnus. *Sloping down*, dēclīvis, dēclīvus. *Inaccessible*, inaccessus. *Pathless*, invius. *Hanging over*, immĭnens. *Sunny*, āprīcus. *Winding*, curvus, incurvus, sĭnuōsus.¶ *Hollow, full of hollows*, căvus. *Woody, shady*, nĕmŏrōsus, umbrōsus, ŏpācus, nĭger -gri. *Flowery*, flōrens, purpūreus. *Pine-bearing*, pinīfer -ĕri, *Grassy*, grāmĭneus, herbīfer -eri, herbōsus.

collŏquium. *Conversation.*—EP. *Social*, sŏcium. *Friendly*, ămīcum. *Courteous*, hūmānum, fācīle. *Jocose*, jŏcōsum, festīvum, lĕpīdum. *Frequent*, crēbrum. *Alternate, mutual*, alternum, alternans, mūtuum.

collum. *The neck.*—EP. *White, fair*, candĭdum, album, nĭveum, lacteum, ĕburneum, ĕburnum, marmŏreum. *Flexible*, molle, lentum. *Tender*, tĕnĕrum. *Rosy*, rōseum. *Dark (of a snake)*, cærūleum, cærūlum. *Swelling*, tŭmĭdum. *Shaggy (of a beast)*, sētōsum, villōsum. *With the hair flowing over it*, cōmans. *Of a maiden*, virgĭneum, puellāre.

collȳrium. *Eyesalve.*—EP. *Black*, nĭgrum. *Wholesome, healing*, sălūtăre, sălūbre, sălūtĭfĕrum.

cŏlōnus, fem. cŏlōna. *A husbandman.*—EP. *Hardy*, dūrus. *Rustic*, rustĭcus, ăgrestis. *Simple*, simplex -īcis. *Contented*, contentus. *Happy*, fēlix, fortūnātus. *Hard-working*, ŏpĕrōsus, lăbōriōsus, impĭger -gri. *Strong*, rŏbustus, vălĭdus. *Anxious*, anxius, sollĭcĭtus.

cŏlōnia. *A colony.*—EP. *New*, nŏva. *Ancient*, prisca, vĕtus -ēris, antīqua, vĕtusta. *Flourishing*, flōrens, felix. *Distant*, distans, longinqua, rĕmōta, ultĭma, extrēma.

cŏlor. *Colour, complexion, etc.*—EP. *Rosy*, rōseus. *Purple*, purpūreus. *White*, nĭveus candĭdus. *Dark*, fuscus. *Changing*, vārius, mūtăbĭlis. *Bright*, nĭtĭdus, splendĭdus, clārus. *Delicate*, tĕner -ĕri. *Feminine*, fœmĭneus, mūlĭĕbris.

cŏlossus, i. *A colossus (esp. the statue of the Sun at Rhodes).*—EP. *Vast*, ingens, vastus. *Brazen*, æreus, ærātus, ahēneus, ahēnus. *Sacred*, săcer -cri. *Rhodean*, Rhŏdius. *Sacred to Apollo*, Apollĭneus.

cŏlŭber -bri, fem. cŏlŭbra. *A snake.* See anguis.

cŏlumba. *A dove.*—EP. *Timid*, tĭmĭda, păvĭda, imbellis. *Frightened*, terrĭta. *Innocent*, innŏcua, innoxia, innŏcens. *Loving*, ămans, blanda. *Tender*, mollis.

C 3

22 COL—CON

tĕnĕra. *Sacred to Venus*, Cýthĕrēïa, Cýthĕrēïäs. *Chaonian*, Chăŏnia. *Winged*, alīgĕra, vŏlūcris. *Flying in the air*, āĕria.

cŏlŭmen, ĭnis, neut. *A prop.*—EP. *Firm, steady*, firmum, stăbĭle, constans. *Solid*, sŏlĭdum. *Perpetual*, perpĕtuum. *Trustworthy*, fīdum, fĭdēle. *Ancient, customary*, priscum, nŏtum, sŏlĭtum, assuetum.

cŏlumna. *A pillar.*—EP. *Marble*, marmŏrea. *Brazen*, ærea, ærāta, ahēnea, ahēna. *Carved*, sculpta. *Cut out*, excīsa. *Lofty*, alta, sūblīmis, celsa, ardua. *Vast*, ingens, vasta. *Beautiful*, pulchra, splendĭda. *Of Tænarian, Phrygian, Carystian, Parian marble, etc.*, Tænăria, Phrýgia, Cărystĕa, Păria, etc.

cŏlus, ĭ (*also more rarely –ūs*, fem.). *A distaff.*—EP. *Feminine*, fœmĭnea, mŭlĭēbris. *Diligent*, assĭdua. *Used daily*, diurna. *Full*, plēna, grăvis. *Lydian* (*because Arachne, a Lydian, was a celebrated spinner*), Lýda. *Sacred to Minerva*, Pallădia.

cŏma. 1. *Hair.*—2. *A leaf.* See 1. crinis; 2. folium.

cŏmes, ĭtis, masc. fem. *A companion.*—EP. *Beloved*, cārus, ămātus, dīlectus. *Faithful*, fīdus, fĭdēlis. *Usual*, sŏlĭtus, assuetus, consuetus. *Ancient*, vĕtus –ĕris, priscus.

cŏmētes, æ, masc. *A comet.*—EP. *Awful*, dīrus, terrĭbĭlis. *Ill-omened*, obscœnus, lævus, sĭnister –tri. *Brilliant*, rŭtĭlus, rŭtĭlans, lūcĭdus, micans, cŏruscus. *Long*, longus. *Fiery*, igneus. *Prophetic*, prænuntius.

cŏmĭtātus, ūs. *A company.* See comes.

commentum. *An invention.*—EP. *False*, fictum, falsum. *Deceitful*, fallax. *Ingenious, cunning*, ingĕnĭōsum, callĭdum, văfrum.

commercium. *Commerce, intercourse.*—EP. *Social*, sŏcium. *Ancient, established*, vĕtus –ĕris, sŏlĭtum, assuetum. *Advantageous, profitable*, ūtĭle, lŭcrōsum, quæstuōsum.

commissum. *A fault.* See culpa.

commŏdum. *Advantage.*—EP. *Useful*, ūtĭle. *Fortunate*, fēlix, faustum. *Wished for*, optātum. *Desirable*, optābĭle. *Unexpected*, ĭnŏpīnum, nĕcŏpīnum, inspērātum, ĭnexspectātum.

cŏmœdia. *Comedy.*—EP. *Mirthful*, jŏcōsa, festīva, lĕpĭda. *Imitative*, ĭmĭtātrix. *Satirical*, mordax.

cŏmœdus. *A comic actor.*—EP. *Skilful*, doctus, pērītus. *Ingenious, clever*, ingĕnĭōsus, callĭdus. *Talkative*, lŏquax, garrŭlus.

compāges, is; compāgo, ĭnis. *A joint.*—EP. *Close*, arcta, bĕnē juncta. *Strong*, firma, vălĭda. *Tenacious*, tĕnax.

compendium. 1. *Gain.*—2. *A short cut.*—EP. 1. See lucrum.—2. *Short*, brĕve, brĕvius. *Easily*, făcĭle. *Rapid*, răpĭdum, cĭtum, cĕlĕre. *Known*, nŏtum, sŏlĭtum, assuetum, consuetum.

compes, ĕdis, fem. *A fetter* (*not found in* nom. sing.).—EP. *Tight*, arcta. *Strong*, firma, vălĭda. *Tenacious*, tĕnax. *Iron*, ferrea, ferrāta. *Hard*, dūra. *Numerous*, multa. *Put around*, circumfūsa.

complĭtum. *A road.* See via.

complexus, ūs. *An embrace.*—EP. *Loving*, ămans, blandus. *Close*, arctus. *Tender*, tĕner –ĕri, mollis. *Eager*, fervĭdus, ardens, ăvĭdus, cŭpĭdus. *Fair, snowy, etc.*, pulcher, nĭveus, ĕburnus, ĕburneus, candĭdus. *Affectionate* (*of children, husband, etc.*), pius.

comptus, ūs. *Carefully dressed hair.*—EP. *Golden*, aureus, flāvus. *Of a damsel*, virgĭneus, puellāris. *Adorned*, ornātus. *Crowned*, cŏrōnātus. *Anointed*, unctus. *Perfumed*, ŏdōrātus.

cŏnāmen, ĭnis, neut. cŏnātus, ūs, cŏnātum. *An attempt.*—EP. *Bold*, audax, fortis. *Successful*, fēlix, sĕcundus, faustus, prospĕrus. *Novel*, nŏvus, ĭnaudītus. *Sudden*, sūbĭtus, rĕpens, rĕpentīnus, ĭnŏpīnus, nĕcŏpīnus.

concentus, ūs. *A singing together.*—EP. *Tuneful*, dulcis, argūtus, lĭquĭdus, cănōrus. *Harmonious*, concors –dis, consŏnus.

concha. *A shell.*—EP. *Thin*, tĕnuis. *Light*, lĕvis. *Found in the sea*, mărīna, æquŏrea. *On the shore*, lĭtŏrea. *Of various colours*, picta. *Bright*, lūcĭda. *Foreign*, pĕrĕgrīna.

concĭlium. *A council.*—EP. *Wise*, săpiens, prūdens, săgax. *Aged*, sĕnex, sĕnĭle, cānum. *Venerable*, vĕnĕrābĭle, vĕnĕrandum augustum. *Attentive*, intentum. *Unanimous*, ūnănĭme, ūnănĭmum, concors –dis.

concordia. *Agreement.*—EP. *Happy*, fēlix. *Social*, sŏcia. *Long, perpetual*,

CON—CON 23

longa, diŭturna, perpĕtua pĕrennis. *Faithful*, fĭda, fĭdēlis. *Inviolate*, in-violāta, inviŏlabĭlis, illæsa, intēgra. *Known*, nōta.

concursus, ûs. *A meeting of people.*—EP. *Dense*, densus. *Rapid*, răpĭdus. *Sudden*, sŭbĭtus, rĕpens, rĕpentīnus. *Wondrous*, mīrus, mīrābĭlis. (*When for the purpose of fighting*) *Fierce*, fĕrus, fĕrox, sævus. *Threatening*, mĭnax. *Armed*, armātus.

condĭtio, ōnis, fem. 1. *Condition (of an agreement).*—2. *Condition (i. e. state).* —EP. 1. *Fair*, æqua, justa. *Agreed upon*, compŏsīta, certa. *Novel*, nŏva, Inandĭta, insŏlĭta. *Severe*, sĕvĕra, immītis, dūra.—2. *Ancient*, prisca, antiqua, vĕtus –ĕris. *Happy*, fēlix, fausta, beāta. *Miserable*, mĭsĕra, tristis. *Lowly*, hŭmĭlis.

condĭtor, ōris, masc. *A builder, a founder.*—EP. *Ancient*, *original*, antīquus, priscus, vĕtus –ĕris, vĕtustus, prīmus. *Wise*, săpiens, prūdens. *Brave*, fortis. *Celebrated*, insignis, clārus, inclỹtus. *Venerable*, vĕnĕrābĭlis, vĕnĕrandus. *Sacred*, săcer –cri, sanctus.

confŭgium. *A place of refuge.*—EP. *Friendly*, ămīcum. *Safe*, tūtum, in-cŏlŭme, sēcūrum. *Desired, desirable*, optātum, optābĭle. *Known*, nōtum, sŏlĭtum, assuetum, consuetum. *Unhoped for*, inspērātum.

conger, gri. *A conger eel.*—EP. *Greedy*, vŏrax, ăvĭdus. *Cruel*, crūdēlis, sævus, fĕrus, immītis.

congĕries, ēi, fem. *A heap.*—EP. *Great, vast*, magna, ingens, vasta. *Piled up*, cŭmŭlāta, accŭmŭlāta. *High*, alta, ardua. *Of various things*, vāria, dīversa.

congressus, ûs. *A meeting.* See concursus.

conjectūra. *A conjecture.*—EP. *Sagacious*, săgax, prūdens, callĭda, subtĭlis. *Prophetic*, præscia. *True*, vēra. *Happy, successful*, fēlix.

conjectus, ûs. *A throw.* See jactus.

conjŭgium. *Marriage.*—EP. *Auspicious*, auspĭcātum, fēlix. *Sacred*, săcrum, săcrātum, dīvinum. *Permanent*, perpĕtuum, mansūrum, stābĭle. *Faithful*, fĭdum, fĭdēle. *Chaste*, castum. *Unpolluted*, intĕmĕrātum. *Prolific*, fēcundum. *Barren*, stĕrĭle. *Delightful*, dulce, jūcundum, ămœnum, ămābĭle.

cōnōpēum. *A canopy or awning.*—EP. *Shady*, umbrōsum, ŏpācum. *Cool*, frīgĭdum, gĕlĭdum.

consanguĭnĭtas. *Relationship.*—EP. *Affectionate*, pia. *Beloved*, dĭlecta, cāra. *Close*, prŏpinqua. *Ancient*, prisca, vĕtus –ĕris.

conscientia. *Conscience.*—EP. *Pure, innocent*, pūra, innŏcua. *Guilty*, impūra, pollūta. *Tender*, tĕnĕra. *Anxious*, sollĭcĭta. *Timid*, păvĭda, tĭmĭda, trĕpĭdans. *Secret*, occulta, lătens. *Powerful*, pŏtens.

consensus, ûs. *Agreement.*—EP. *Unanimous*, ūnănĭmis. *Complete*, plēnus. *Cheerful*, hĭlăris, lætus. *Silent*, tăcĭtus. *Loud*, clāmōsus.

consessus, ûs. *A body of sitters, of spectators.*—EP. *Joyful*, lætus, plaudens. *Numerous*, densus, frēquens.

consĭlium. 1. *Advice.*—2. *Intention.*—EP. 1, 2. *Friendly*, ămīcum, bĕnignum. *Wise*, săpiens, prūdens, săgax. *Honest*, æquum, prŏbum, justum. *Bold*, forte, audax. *Full of foresight*, prŏvĭdum. *Novel*, nŏvum.

consĭtor. *A planter.*—EP. *Provident*, prŏvĭdus, prūdens. *Diligent*, sēdŭlus, assĭduus, ŏpĕrōsus. *Cautious*, cautus. *Anxious*, anxius, sollĭcĭtus. *Mindful*, mĕmor, ōris.

consors, tis, masc. fem. *A partner.*—EP. *Faithful*, fĭdus, fĭdēlis. *Loved*, cārus, ămātus, dĭlectus. *United*, junctus. *Ancient*, vĕtus –ĕris, vĕtustus, priscus.

constantia. *Constancy, firmness.*—EP. *Steady*, stābĭlis, tĕnax. *Firm*, firma, immōta, immōbĭlis, inviŏlāta, inviŏlābĭlis. *Tried*, spectāta, nōta. *Admirable*, ēgrēgia, mīra, mīrābĭlis.

consuetūdo, ĭnis, fem. *Custom.*—EP. *Long*, longa, diŭturna. *Ancient*, prisca, antīqua, vĕtus –ĕris. *Established*, ūsĭtāta, certa. *Pious*, pia. *Pleasant*, dulcis. ămœns, jūcunda, grāta.

consul, ŭlis, masc. *A consul.*—EP. *Double*, gĕmĭnus. *Brave*, fortis. *Wise*, săpiens. *Powerful*, pŏtens. *August*, augustus, vĕnĕrābĭlis, vĕnĕrandus.

consultum. *A decree.*—EP. *Fixed*, certum. *Lasting*, perpĕtuum, pĕrenne. *Wise*, săpiens, săgax. *Provident*, prŏvĭdum. *Unalterable*, immōtum, inviŏlā-bĭle, inviŏlatum.

24 CON—COR

consultus. *A lawyer.*—EP. *Learned,* doctus, pērītus. *Eloquent,* fācundus, dīsertus. *Diligent,* sēdūlus. *Accessible,* fācīlis. *Honest,* prŏbus, incorruptus, justus.

contāges, contagium, neut. *Contagion.*—EP. *Dire,* dīra. *Foul, ill-omened,* fœda, obscœna. *Causing disease,* pestĭlens, pestīfēra. *Causing death,* fătālis, fătĭfēra.

contemplātus, ûs. *Contemplation.*—EP. *Long, diligent,* longus, assĭduus. *Silent,* tăcĭtus. *Deep,* altus, prŏfundus. *Prudent,* prūdens, săgax.

contemptor, fem. **contemptrix.** *A despiser.*—EP. *Bold,* audax. *Impious (of holy things),* impius, prŏfānus. *Noble (of worthless things),* nōbĭlis gĕnĕrōsus.

contemptus, ûs. *Contempt.*—EP. *Deserved,* mĕrĭtus. See above.

contūmācia. *Obstinacy.*—EP. *Pertinacious,* pervĭcax, tĕnax. *Morose,* mōrōsus. *Intractable,* indŏcĭlis, diffĭcĭlis. *Odious,* invīsus, ŏdiōsus.

contūmēlia. *Insult.*—EP. *Intolerable,* intŏlĕrābĭlis. *Undeserved,* immĕrĭta. *Painful,* grăvis, tristis.

contus. *A pole.*—EP. *Long,* longus. *Ashen,* fraxĭneus. *Firm,* firmus, sŏlĭdus. *Hard,* dūrus. *Shod with iron,* ferrātus. *Sharpened at the end,* ăcūtus, præăcūtus.

convallis. *A valley.* See vallis.

conventus, ûs. *An assembly.* See cœtus.

convīcium. *A reproach.*—EP. *Angry,* īrātum, īrācundum. *Bitter,* ăcerbum, aspĕrum, acre. *Deserved,* mĕrĭtum, dignum. *Undeserved,* immĕrĭtum, indignum. *Grievous,* triste, grăve.

convictor. *A companion.* See comes.

convictus, ûs. *Intimacy.*—EP. *Friendly,* ămīcus. *Ancient,* vĕtus -ĕris, antiquus, priscus. *Long,* longus, diŭturnus. *Social,* sŏcius. *Unbroken,* irruptus, invĭŏlātus.

convīva, æ, masc. *A guest.*—EP. *Merry,* hĭlāris, lætus. *Crowned,* cŏrōnātus. *Sated,* sătur -ūri. *Temperate,* mŏdĕrātus, sŏbrius.

convīvium. *A banquet.*—EP. *Rich, luxurious,* dīves -ĭtis, lautum, ŏpīmum, luxŭriōsum. *Magnificent,* magnĭfĭcum, splendĭdum. *Joyful,* lætum, festīvum.

cŏmus. *A cone, crest of a helmet.*—EP. *Adorned with hair,* cŏmans. *Waving,* nūtans. See crista.

cōpia. *Plenty.*—EP. *Golden,* aurea. *Rich,* dīves -ĭtis, lŏcŭples -ētis, ŏpŭlenta. *Welcome,* grăta, accepta. *Joyful, prosperous,* læta, fēlix.

cŏpŭla. *A tie.*—EP. *Close,* arcta. *Indissoluble,* invĭŏlābĭlis, irrupta, invĭŏlāta, intĕgra. *Dear,* cāra. *Perpetual,* perpĕtua.

cŏquus, fem. **cŏqua.** *A cook.*—EP. *Skilful,* doctus, pērītus.

cor, dis, neut. *The heart.*—EP. *Soft,* molle, tĕnĕrum. *Easily penetrated, easily influenced,* pĕnĕtrābĭle, mōbĭle. *Friendly,* ămīcum. *The inmost heart.* cor intīmum īmum. *Hard, cruel,* dūrum, sĕvērum, ferreum. *Implacable,* inexŏrābĭle, implăcābĭle, illăcrўmābĭle.

cŏrālium. *Coral.*—EP. *Red,* rŭbrum, rōseum. *Hard,* dūrum, rĭgĭdum. *Found in the sea,* æquŏreum, mărīnum. *Eastern,* Ĕrўthræum, Ēoum.

corbis, is, fem. *A basket.*—EP. *Of osier,* vīmĭnea. *Yielding, flexible,* lenta. *Full,* plēna. *Heavy,* grăvis.

cornicen. *A trumpeter.* See tūbicen.

cornīcŭla, cornix, īcis, fem. *A jackdaw, a crow.*—EP. *Black,* nĭgra, ātra. *Hoarse,* rauca. *Ill-omened,* sĭnistra, obscœna, imprŏba. *Prophetic,* prænuntia. *Aged,* vĕtŭla. *Long-lived,* longæva, vīvax, annōsa.

cornu. *A horn.*—EP. *Crooked,* curvum, incurvum, rĕcurvum, curvātum, cămūrum. *Hard,* dūrum, aspĕrum. *Branching,* arbŏreum. See tuba.

cornus, i, fem. *The cornel-tree.*—EP. *Hard, strong,* dūra, vălĭda. *Fit for warlike uses,* bellĭca, bellĭcōsa.

cŏrolla, cŏrōna. *A chaplet, a garland, a crown.*—EP. *Of flowers,* flōrea, flōrĭda. *Of roses,* rŏsea. *Of myrtle, etc.,* myrtea, etc. *Green,* vĭrĭdis. *Royal,* rēgia. *Golden,* aurea. *Jewelled,* gemmea. *Sacred,* săcra, sancta. *Well-woven,* nexa. *Sown together,* sūtĭlis. *Emblem of victory,* victrix -īcis. *Festive,* festa. *Proud,* sŭperba. *Simple,* simplex -ĭcis.

corpus, ŏris, neut. *A body.*—EP. *Large,* ingens, magnum. *Strong,* vălĭdum, rōbustum. *Living,* vīvum. *Dead,* mortuum, exănĭmum. *Lacerated,* lăcĕrum, lăcĕrātum.

COR—CRO 25

corrector. *A corrector.*—EP. *Friendly,* ămīcus. *Kind, gentle,* bĕnignus, mītis, tĕner –ĕri. *Wise,* prūdens, săgax. *Harsh,* ācerbus, asper –ĕri.

corruptor. *A corruptor.*—EP. *Base,* turpis, infāmis. *Shameless,* impŭdens. *Immodest,* impŭdīcus, lascīvus. *Impious,* impius.

cortex, īcis, masc. 1. *Bark.*—2. *Cork.*—EP. 1. *Green,* vīrīdis. *Wrinkled,* rūgōsus. *External,* externus.—2. *Light,* lĕvis. *Not to be sunk,* immersăbĭlis.

cortīna. *The sacred tripod.* See oraculum.

corvus, i. *A crow.* See cornix.

cŏrўlus, i, fem. *A hazel-tree.*—EP. *Hard,* dūra, ēdūra, rĭgĭda.

cŏrymbus. *A bunch of ivy-berries.*—EP. *Pale,* pallĭdus, pallens. *Sacred to Bacchus,* Bacchēus, Bacchēius, Bacchĭcus. *Thick,* densus. *Hanging,* pendŭlus, pendens.

cŏrўtus. *A quiver.* See pharetra.

cos, cŏtis, fem. *A whetstone.*—EP. *Soft,* mollis. *Wet,* ūda, mādĭda, mădens.

costum. *Spikenard.*—EP. *Persian,* Persĭcum, Ăchæmĕnium. *Eastern,* Eōum. *Fragrant,* ŏdōrātum, frāgrans. *Unctuous,* pingue.

cŏthurnus. *A buskin.*—EP. *High,* altus. *Tragic,* trăgĭcus. *Attic, Sophoclean,* Æschylean, Sŏphŏclēus, Æschŭlēus, Cĕcrŏpius, Attĭcus. *Hardy (when worn by hunters),* dūrus.

cŏturnix, īcis, fem. *A quail.*—EP. *Quarrelsome,* pugnax, bellĭca. *Little,* parva. *Brave, fearless,* impăvĭda, fortis.

crābro, ōnis. *A hornet.*—EP. *Fierce,* fĕrus, sævus. *Rough,* asper –ĕri. *Of golden colour,* aureus. *Striped,* vārius.

crāter, ēris. *A goblet.* See poculum.

crātes, is, fem. *A wattled hurdle.*—EP. *Made of twigs,* arbŭtea, vīmīnea. *Frail,* frăgĭlis. *Light,* lĕvis. *Woven, plaited,* implīcĭta.

creātor. *A creator, maker.*—EP. *Great,* magnus. *Powerful,* pŏtens. *Original,* prīmus. *Wise,* săpiens. *Foreseeing,* prŏvīdus.

crēdĭtor. *A creditor.*—EP. *Severe, harsh,* sĕvērus, dūrus, asper –ĕri, rĭgĭdus, immītis. *Inexorable,* ĭnexōrābĭlis. *Rich,* dīves –ĭtis, lŏcūples –ĕtis, ŏpŭlentus. *Ancient, of long standing,* vĕtus –ĕris, vĕtustus.

crēdŭlĭtas. *Credulity.*—EP. *Simple,* simplex –ĭcis. *Foolish,* stulta, dēmens, imprūdens. *Rash,* incauta, tĕmĕrāria, præceps –ĭpĭtis. *Unfortunate,* infēlix.

crĕpīda. *A slipper.*—EP. *Greek,* Graia. *Low,* hŭmĭlis. *Soft,* mollis. *Loose,* laxa.

crĕpīdo, ĭnis, fem. *The edge or brow (of a cliff).*—EP. *Precipitous,* præceps –ĭpĭtis, ăbrupta, prærupta. *Lofty,* alta, ardua. *Eaten away,* exēsa. *Rough,* aspĕra.

crĕpĭtus, ûs. *A rattling noise.*—EP. *Sudden,* sŭbĭtus, rĕpens, rĕpentīnus. *Loud,* clārus. *Sharp,* ācer –cris.

crĕpuscŭlum. *Twilight.*—EP. *Late,* sērum. *Dim,* ŏpācum, dūbium. *Cool,* gĕlĭdum, frĭgĭdum. *Pale,* pallĭdum, pallens.

Crēta, Crēte. *Crete.*—EP. *Sacred (esp. to Jupiter),* săcra. *Reigned over by Minos,* Mĭnōia. *Ancient,* antīqua, vĕtus –ĕris.

crēta. *Chalk.*—EP. *White,* alba, candĭda, nĭvea. *Soft,* mollis.

crībrum. *A sieve.*—EP. *Full of holes,* rārum. *Thin,* tĕnue. *Light,* lĕve.

crīmen, ĭnis, neut. 1. *A crime.*—2. *An accusation.*—EP. *Wicked,* impium, scĕlĕrātum, scĕlestum. *Unprecedented,* nŏvum, ĭnaudītum. *Cruel,* sævum, immīte. *Ineffaceable,* indēlēbĭle.—2. *Bitter, malignant,* ācerbum, mālignum. —1. 2. *Disgraceful,* infāme, prŏbrōsum. *Ancient,* vĕtus –ĕris, vĕtustum, antīquum.

crīnis, is, masc. *Hair.*—EP. *Black,* nĭger –gri. *Golden,* aureus, flāvus, flāvens, crŏceus. *White, hoary,* cānus, cānens. *Flowing,* fluens. *Dishevelled,* passus (*only in plur.*), fūsus, effūsus. *Dressed,* comptus, ornātus, compŏsĭtus. *Anointed,* unctus, ŏdōrātus. *Crowned,* cŏrōnātus; (*with a sacred fillet,*) vittātus. *Glossy,* nĭtens. *Unadorned,* ĭnornātus.

crista. *A crest.*—EP. *Waving,* nūtans. *Proud,* sŭperba. *Made of horsehair,* ĕquīna, cŏmans. *Glittering,* cŏrusca.

crŏcŏdīlus, acc. um and on, masc. *A crocodile.*—EP. *Of Egypt, of the Nile,* Ægyptus, Nĭlĭăcus. *Devouring,* vŏrax. *Living in the rivers,* flūmĭneus, flŭviālis. *Savage,* sævus, ferus. *Savage, large,* immānis.

crŏcus, acc. um and on, masc. *Saffron.*—EP. *Golden, yellow* aureus, flāvus,

CRO—CUP

flāvens. *Of orange colour,* rŭber –bri, rŭbens. *Lowly,* hŭmĭlis. *Liquid (of the dye),* lĭquĭdus.

crŏtălum. *A castanet.*—EP. *Rattling,* crĕpĭtans. *Sounding in time,* nŭmĕrōsum.

crŭciātus, ûs. *Torment.* See dolor.

crūmēna. *A purse.*—EP. *Full,* plēna, grăvis. *Gives* –ītis, lŏcŭples, ĕtia. *Silken,* sērica.

cruor, ōris, masc. *Blood when shed.*—EP. *Poured out,* fūsus, effūsus. *Purple,* ruddy, purpūreus. *Dark,* ăter –tri. *Sad,* tristis, miser –ĕri. *From a deadly wound,* fătālis.

crus, ūris, neut. *A leg.*—EP. *Strong,* nervōsum, vălĭdum. *Active,* ăgĭle.

crusta. *A crust or external covering.*—EP. *Forming the top,* summa.

crustŭlum. *A cheesecake.*—EP. *Sweet,* nice, dulce, lautum.

crux, crŭcis, fem. *A cross, a gibbet.*—EP. *Fatal,* fătālis. *Vile,* infamous, infāmis, vīlis. *Cruel,* sæva, fĕra, immītis. *Terrible,* dīra, terrĭbĭlis, horrĭbĭlis, horrenda. *Hateful,* ŏdiōsa, invīsa.

crystallus, i, fem. *Crystal.*—EP. *Clear,* perlūcĭda, vītrea, ăquōsa. *Bright,* splendĭda. *Brittle,* frăgĭlis.

cŭbīle, is, neut. *A bed.*—EP. *Soft,* molle, tĕnĕrum. *Accustomed,* sŏlĭtum, assuetum, consuetum. See lectus.

cŭcullus, i. *A hood.*—EP. *Large,* magnus. *Let down,* dēmissus.

cŭcŭmis, is, masc. *A cucumber.*—EP. *Low, lying on the ground,* hŭmĭlis.

cūlex, ĭcis, masc. *A gnat.*—EP. *Disagreeable,* mălus, invīsus. *Hostile,* hostĭlis. *Numerous,* multus, innŭmĕrus. *Attacking in the summer,* æstīvus. *In the evening,* vespertīnus.

culmen, ĭnis, neut. *The roof of a house* (*esp. if thatched*).—EP. *High,* altum, arduum. *Low,* hŭmĭle. *Thatched with straw or reeds,* strāmĭneum, ărundĭneum.

culmus, i. *The stalk or straw of corn ; thatch.*—EP. *Green* (i. e. *unripe*), vĭrĭdis, *Yellow* (i. e. *ripe*), flāvus, aureus. *Thin,* tĕnuis. *Light,* lĕvis. *Weighed down, beaten down,* dējectus.

culpa. *A fault.*—EP. *Impious,* impia, scĕlĕrāta. *Heavy,* grăvis. *Base,* turpis. *Slight, pardonable,* lĕvis, excūsăbĭlis.

culter –tri. *A knife.*—EP. *Sharp,* ăcūtus. *Fatal,* fătālis, lētĭfer –ĕri. *Wounding,* vulnĭfĭcus. *Sacred* (*of a sacrificial knife*), săcer –cri.

cultor, ōris, masc., **cultrix,** fem. 1. *A cultivator.*—2. *An inhabitant.*—3. *A worshipper.*—EP. 1. 3. *Diligent,* assĭduus, sēdŭlus. *Humble,* hŭmĭlis. 1, 2, 3. *Ancient,* priscus, vĕtus –ĕris, antīquus. 1. *Rustic,* ăgrestis, rustĭcus. *Hardy,* dūrus. *Hard-working,* ŏpĕrōsus, lăbōriōsus, strēnuus. 3. *Pious,* pius. *Suppliant,* supplex –ĭcis. *Offering incense,* thūrĭfer –ĕri.

cultūra. *Cultivation.*—EP. *Diligent,* sēdŭla, assĭdua. *Laborious,* lăbōriōsa, ŏpĕrōsa. *Difficult,* diffĭcĭlis. *Repeated each year,* annua. *Fortunate, productive,* fēlix –īcis, fausta.

cultus, ûs. 1. *Cultivation.*—2. *Worship.*—3. *Dress.*—EP. 2. *Pious,* pius. *Holy,* săcer –cri, săcrātus, sanctus. *Diligent,* sēdŭlus, assĭduus. *Acceptable,* grātus, acceptus. *Due,* mĕrĭtus, dēbĭtus. *Customary,* sŏlĭtus, assuetus, consuetus. *Pure,* pūrus. 2, 3. *Simple,* simplex –ĭcis.—3. *Handsome,* splendĭdus, dīves –ĭtis. *Neat,* nĭtĭdus.

cŭlullus. *A cup.* See poculum.

cŭmŭlus. 1. *A heap.*—2. *A crowning addition.*—EP. 1. *Large,* magnus. *High,* altus. *Piled up,* congestus.— 2. *Complete,* summus. *Wished for,* optātus.

cŭnābŭla, ōrum, plur. neut., **cunæ, ārum,** plur. fem. *A cradle.*—EP. *Early, original,* prīmæ. *Tender* (*as holding tender children*), tĕnĕræ.

cŭneus. *A wedge.*—EP. *Narrow,* angustus. *Sharp,* ăcūtus. *Dense* (*when used metaph. for a wedge-shaped crowd*), densus.

cŭpīdo, ĭnis, fem., *more rarely* masc. *Desire, wish.*—EP. *Vehement, eager,* ăvĭda, vehĕmens, dīra, fervĭda. *Foolish,* stulta, insāna. *Foolish and vehement,* fŭriōsa. *Ignorant* (*of the future*), ignāra, dēmens, imprŏvĭda, imprūdens. *Rash,* præceps –ĭpĭtis, tĕmĕrāria. *Anxious,* anxia, sollĭcĭta. *Wakeful,* vĭgil –ĭlis. *Unhappy,* infēlix –īcis, mĭsĕra. *Sudden,* nŏva, sŭbĭta. *Unsatisfied,* ĭnexplēta. *Unrestrained,* impŏtens.

cŭpressus, i, fem. *A cypress-tree.*—EP. *Funereal,* fūnĕbris, fūnĕrea, fĕrālis.

CUR—DAT   **27**

Ill-omened, obscœna. *Hated*, invīsa, ŏdiōsa. *Black*, ātra, nīgra, cærūlea. *Undecaying*, incorrupta, vīvax. *Bearing cones*, cōnīfĕra. *With sharp points*, ăcūta.

cūra. *Care.*—EP. *Unavoidable*, ĭnēvītābĭlia, indēvītāta. *Anxious*, anxia, sol-līcīta. *Doubtful*, dūbia, incerta, anceps –ĭpĭtis. *Long*, longa, assīdua. *Perpetual*, perpĕtua. *Severe*, grăvis, dūra. *Hateful*, invīsa, ŏdiōsa. *Injurious*, damnōsa, măla, pernĭciōsa, exĭtiōsa, exĭtiālis. *Devouring*, mordax, ĕdax.

curcŭlio, ōnis, masc. *A weevil.*—EP. *Devouring*, ĕdax, vŏrax. *Mischievous*, mălus, pernĭciōsus, exĭtiōsus, exĭtiālis, damnōsus.

cūria. *The senate-house.*—EP. *Noble*, nōbĭlis. *Proud*, sŭperba. *Sacred*, săcra, săcrāta. See senator.

currĭcŭlum, currus, ūs. *A chariot.*—EP. *With two or four horses*, bījŭgus, quădrījŭgus. *Swift*, răpĭdus, cĕler –ĕris, vēlox, admissus. *Armed*, armātus. *Armed with a scythe (of the ancient British war-chariots)*, falcĭfer –ĕri. *Light*, lĕvis, hăbĭlis. *Painted*, pictus. *Dusty*, pulvĕrens, pulvĕrŭlentus.

cursor, ōris, masc. *A runner.*—EP. *Swift*, răpĭdus, vēlox, cĕler –ĕris. *Painting*, ănhēlus.

cursus, ūs. *A course, a race, etc.*—EP. *Swift*, răpĭdus, vēlox, cītus. *Customary*, sŏlĭtus, assuetus, consuetus. *Long*, longua.

curvāmen, ĭnis, neut., curvātūra. *A curve.*—EP. *Winding*, sĭnuōsa, ōblīqua. *Sudden*, sŭbīta.

cuspis, ĭdis, fem. 1. *A point.*—2. *A spear.*—EP. 1, 2. *Sharp*, ăcūta. See hasta.

custōdia. *Guard.*—EP. *Careful*, prūdens, prōvĭda, cauta. *Watchful*, vĭgil –īlis, pervigil. *Safe*, tūta, incŏlŭmis. *Strong, powerful*, vălĭda, fortis, pŏtens.

custos, ōdis, masc. fem. *A guardian, a keeper, a sentinel.*—EP. *Watchful, wakeful*, vĭgil –īlis, pervigil, insomnis. *Prudent, cautious*, cautus, prūdens, prōvĭdus. *Brave*, fortis. *Faithful*, fīdēlis, fīdus. *Watching by night*, nocturnus. *Armed*, armātus.

cŭtis, is, fem., cŭtĭcŭla. *The skin.*—EP. *Thin*, tĕnuis. *Fair*, alba, candĭda, nĭvea.

cyăthus. *A cup.* See poculum.

Cyclops, ōpis, masc. *A Cyclops.*—EP. *Huge*, vastus, ingens. *Cruel, fierce*, sævus, fĕrus, immītis, immānis, immansuetus. *Dwelling under Ætna*, Ætnæus. *Servant of Vulcan*, Vulcānius. *One-eyed*, luscus.

cygnus. *A swan.*—EP. *White*, albus, nĭveus, candĭdus. *Tuneful*, vōcālis, cānōrus, argūtus, dulcis.—*Sad*, tristis, flēbĭlis, lŭgūbris. *Living on the Mæander or Cayster, rivers in Asia Minor, or near the Asian Marsh*, Mæandrius, Caystrius, Asius. *Winged*, ālĭger –ĕri, ālātus. *Flying high*, sŭblīmis, altus.

cylindrus. *A round roller.*—EP. *Large*, magnus, ingens. *Heavy*, grăvis. *Round and smooth*, tĕres –ĕtis.

cymba. *A boat.* See navis.

cymbălum. *A cymbal.*—EP. *Brazen*, æreum, ærātum, ahēnum, ahĕneum. *Hollow*, căvum, concăvum. *Hoarse*, raucum. *Used in Crete*, Crētæum, Crētĭcum, Cŏrȳbantium.

cytĭsus, i, fem. *Trefoil.*—EP. *Flourishing*, flōrens. *Low*, hŭmĭlis. *Green*, vĭridis.

D.

Dāma, masc. fem. *A deer.* See cervus.

damnātio, onis, fem. *Condemnation.*—EP. *Just, deserved*, justa, mĕrīta, dēbĭta. *Severe*, sĕvēra, rĭgĭda.

damnum. *Loss, injury.*—EP. *Sad*, triste, flēbĭle, mĭsĕrābĭle. *Unfortunate*, infēlix, infaustum. *Ill-omened*, obscœnum, sĭnistrum. *Unexpected*, ĭnŏpīnum, nĕcŏpīnum, imprōvīsum. *Recent*, rŏcens.

daps, dăpis, fem. (not used in nom. sing., most usu. in plur.). *A feast.* See epulæ.

dător, ōris, masc. *A giver.*—EP. *Rich*, dīves –ĭtis, lŏcŭples, ētis, ŏpŭlentus.

28 DEA—DES

Liberal, largus. *Friendly, kind*, ămīcus, bĕnignus. *Accustomed*, sŏlĭtus, assuetus, consuetus. *Unknown*, ignōtus.

Dĕa. *A goddess.* See Deus, Juno, Minerva, Venus, etc.

Dĕcember, bris, masc. *December.*—EP. *Wintry*, hyĕmālis, hўbernus, brūmālis. *Cold*, frigĭdus, gĕlĭdus, glācĭālis. *Bringing the north wind*, Bŏreālis. *Stormy*, prŏcellōsus, ventōsus. *Rainy*, plŭvius, plŭvĭālis, āquōsus, ūvĭdus, imbrĭfer -ĕri, nimbĭfer -ĕri. *Smoky (as bringing fires)*, fūmōsus.

dĕcoctor, ōris, masc. *A spendthrift.*—EP. *Prodigal*, prŏdĭgus, prŏfūsus. *Needy*, ĕgens, ĕgēnus. *Foolish*, stultus, insānus, dēmens.

dĕcor, ōris, masc. *Grace, beauty.*—EP. *Pretty*, pulcher -chri, vĕnustus, formōsus, spĕcĭosus, spectābĭlis. *Juvenile*, jŭvĕnīlis. *Feminine*, fœmĭneus, mŭlĭĕbris, *Lovely*, ămābĭlis, ămœnus. *Admirable*, mīrābĭlis, ēgrĕgĭus. *Divine*, dīvīnus. *Unusual*, insŏlĭtus, inassuetus.

dĕcrētum. *A decree.*—EP. *Just*, justum, æquum. *Wise*, săpĭens, prūdens. *Firm, lasting*, stăbĭle, mansūrum, perpĕtuum. *Rash*, præceps -ĭpĭtis, inconsultum.

dĕcursus, ūs. *A running down (of a river*, etc.).—EP. *Rapid*, răpĭdus. *Gentle*, lēnis. *Sudden*, sŭbĭtus.

dĕcus, ōris, neut. 1. *Beauty.*—2. *Glory.*—3. *Ornament.*—EP. 1. See decor. —2. *Everlasting*, immortāle, æternum, pĕrenne, perpĕtuum. *Deserved*, mĕrĭtum, dēbĭtum, dignum. *Desired*, optātum, optābĭle. See gloria.—3. *Splendid*, splendĭdum, magnĭfĭcum, nōbĭle. *Conspicuous*, spĕcĭōsum, conspĭcuum, conspĭcĭendum. *Royal*, rēgĭum.

dēdĕcus, ōris, neut. *Disgrace.*—EP. *Shameful*, turpe, prŏbrōsum, infāme. *Sad*, triste, infēlix, mĭsĕrum, mĭsĕrābĭle. *Eternal*, æternum, perpĕtuum. *Wicked*, *Unspeakable*, nĕfandum.

dēfectus, ūs. *A failure, an eclipse.*—EP. *Terrible*, terrĭbĭlis, dīrus. *Marvellous*, mīrābĭlis. *Ominous*, præsāgus, prænuntĭus, ōmĭnātus.

dēfensor, ōris, masc. *A defender.*—EP. *Brave, strong*, fortis, vălĭdus. *Powerful*, pŏtens. *Ready*, præsens, promptus. *Friendly, kind*, ămīcus, bĕnignus.

dejectus, ūs, masc. *A throwing down.*—EP. *Heavy*, grăvis. *Sudden*, sŭbĭtus.

dēlātor, ōris, masc. *An informer.*—EP. *Malignant*, mălus, mălignus. *False*, falsus, mendax. *Unjust, wicked*, ĭnīquus, imprŏbus.

dēlectus, ūs, masc. *A choice.*—EP. *Careful*, cautus. *Prudent*, prūdens, callĭdus, săpĭens. *Various*, vărĭus. *Anxious*, sollĭcĭtus, anxĭus. *Doubtful*, dŭbĭus, incertus.

dēlĭcĭæ, arum, plur. fem. *Delight.*—EP. *Great*, magnæ, ingentes. *Sweet*, dulces, grātæ, jūcundæ, ămœnæ. *Customary*, sŏlĭtæ, assuetæ, consuetæ, nōtæ. *Lasting*, dĭūturnæ, stăbĭles. *New*, nŏvæ.

dēlictum. *A sin.*—EP. *Grave*, grăve, magnum, ingens. *Sad*, triste, flēbĭle, mĭsĕrum, mĭsĕrābĭle. *Unfortunate*, infēlix, infaustum. *Excusable*, excūsābĭle. *Light*, lēve. *Injurious, destructive*, damnōsum, pernĭcĭōsum, exĭtĭāle, exĭtĭōsum, noxium.

Dēlos, i, acc. on, fem. *Delos.*—EP. *Sacred*, săcra, săcrāta. *Sacred to Apollo*, Ăpollĭnea, Ăpollĭnāris, Phœbēa, Phœbēia. *Sacred to Latona*, Lătōnia. *Fixed*, fixa, stăbĭlis. *Wandering*, errātĭca (*the fable being that it was a floating island, till it was rendered stationary that Apollo and Diana might be born on it*).

delphin, īnis, plur. **ĭnēs,** masc.—EP. *Crooked, with crooked back*, pandus, curvus, rĕcurvus. *Bright-coloured*, clārus, rŭtĭlus, cŏruscus, splendĭdus. *Living in the sea*, æquŏreus. *Swift*, răpĭdus, vēlox, cĭtus, cĕler -ĕris. *Variegated*, pictus, vărĭus. *Sportive*, lūdens.

dēlŭbrum. *A temple.* See templum.

dēmentia. *Madness, folly.*—EP. *Silly*, stulta, ĭnepta. *Imprudent, incautious*, rash, imprūdens, imprŏvĭda, incauta, tĕmĕrārĭa, præceps -ĭpĭtis. *Marvellous*, mīra, mīrābĭlis. *Insane*, insāna, fŭrĭōsa.

dens, tis, masc. *A tooth.*—EP. *Devouring*, ĕdax, vŏrax. *Greedy*, ăvĭdus. *Fierce, cruel*, fĕrus, sævus, immītis. *White*, nĭveus. *Ivory*, ĕburnus, ĕburneus.

dērīsor, ōris, masc. *A laugher, a derider.*—EP. *Malignant*, mălignus. *Unjust*, imprŏbus, ĭnīquus. See risor.

descensus, ūs. *A descent.*—EP. *Easy, gentle*, făcĭlis, lēvis, lēnis. *Downward*, dēclīvis. *Steep*, præceps -ĭpĭtis. *Rapid*, răpĭdus.

desertor, ōris, masc. *A desertcr.*—EP. *Faithless*, perfĭdus, infĭdus. *Timid*,

DES — DIR 29

frightened, tĭmĭdus, păvĭdus, terrĭtus, conterrĭtus. *Fleeing, apt to flee,* fŭgax. *Unwarlike,* imbellis. *Base,* turpis, infămis.

dēsertum. *A desert.*—EP. *Pathless,* invium. *Inaccessible,* ĭnaccessum. *Distant,* extrēmum, longinquum, rēmōtum, distans. *Unknown,* ignōtum. *In foreign lands,* pĕrĕgrīnum. *Uncultivated,* incultum. *Desolate,* sōlum. *Odious,* invīsum, ŏdiōsum, ĭnāmābĭle, ĭnāmœnum.

dēsĭdĕrium. *Regret for what is lost or absent.*—EP. *Mindful,* mĕmor –ŏris, tĕnax. *Faithful,* fīdum, fīdēle. *Sad,* triste, lūgŭbre, mœstum. *Long, lasting,* longum, diŭturnum. *Everlasting,* perpĕtuum, pĕrenne, æternum.

dēsĭdia. *Sloth.*—EP. *Sluggish, idle,* ĭners, ignāva, segnis. *Worthless,* imprŏba, măla, ĭnīqua. *Inglorious, shameful,* inglōria, turpis. prōbrōsa. *Incurable,* immĕdĭcābĭlis, insānābĭlis. *Useless,* ĭnûtĭlis.

despectus, ûs. *A view from an elevated place.*—EP. *Extensive,* lātus, spătiōsus. *Pleasant,* grātus, jūcundus, ămœnus.

dēsuetudo, ĭnis, fem. *Desuetude.*—EP. *Long,* longa. . *Indolent,* segnis, ĭners.

dēsultor, ōris, masc. *One who leaps from one horse to another, a skirmisher.*—EP. *Light,* lĕvis. *Active,* ăgĭlis, cĕler –ĕris.

dētestātio. *A curse.*—EP. *Terrible,* dīra, terrĭbĭlis, horrenda. *Cruel,* sæva, immītis. *Impious,* impia, scĕlĕrāta, infanda.

Deus. *God.*—EP. *Almighty,* omnĭpŏtens. *Eternal,* æternus. *Thundering,* tŏnans. *Supreme,* summus. *Genial, who nourishes all things,* almus. *Great, powerful,* magnus, pŏtens. *Kind,* bŏnus, bĕnignus. *Unforgetting,* mĕmor –ŏris. *Just,* æquus, justus. *Merciful,* mītis, clēmens. *Angry, offended,* īrātus, offensus. *Avenging, chastising,* vindex –ĭcis. *To be worshipped,* vĕnĕrābĭlis, vĕnĕrandus, vĕrendus. *To be feared,* mĕtuendus, tĭmendus.

dextĕra, *sync.* **dextra.** *The right hand.*—EP. *Strong, brave,* fortis, vălĭda. *Armed,* armāta. *Faithful (when given in making a promise),* fīda, fĭdēlis. *Given (in making a promise),* dăta, juncta (c. dat. *of the hand to which it is joined*).

diădema, ătis, neut. *A crown.* See corona.

Dīāna, æ. *The Goddess of hunting, the same as Luna in Heaven, and Hecate in Hell.*—EP. *Daughter of Latona,* Lātōia. *Hunting,* vēnātrix –ĭcis. *Wearing a quiver,* phărētrāta. *Bearing a bow,* arcĭtĕnens. *Bearing arrows,* săgittĭfĕra. *Virgin,* virgo –ĭnis. *Modest, chaste,* pŭdīca, vĕrēcunda, casta. *Of triple form,* trĭformis, tergĕmĭna. *Born at Delos,* Dēlia, Cynthia.

dictātor, ōris, masc. *A dictator.*—EP. *Great, powerful,* magnus, pŏtens. *Supreme,* summus.

dictum. *A saying, a word.*—EP. *Powerful, authoritative,* pŏtens. *Joyful,* lætum. *Sad,* triste. *Of doubtful import,* dŭbium, ambĭguum, incertum. *Prophetic,* præsagum, prænuntium, fātĭdīcum. *Kind, friendly,* ămīcum, bĕnignum. *Of good omen,* bŏnum. *Of ill omen,* mălum, obscœnum, sĭnistrum. *Irrevocable,* irrĕvōcābĭle.

dies, ēi, masc. fem. in sing. more usu. fem. masc. in plur. *A day.*—EP. *Bright,* clāra, splendĭda. *Genial,* alma. *Lovely,* ămābĭlis, ămœna, grāta, jūcunda, dulcis. *Festive,* festa. *Sacred,* săcra, sancta. *Wished for,* optāta, optābĭlis. See the Gradus.

diffĭdentia. *Diffidence, distrust.*—EP. *Modest, humble,* vĕrēcunda, pŭdībunda, pŭdīca, hūmĭlis. *Simple,* simplex –ĭcis. *Ignorant,* ignāra.

dĭgĭtus. *A finger.*—EP. *Taper,* tĕres –ĕtis. *Skilful, ingenious,* doctus, pĕrītus, callĭdus. *Soft, tender,* mollis, tĕner –ĕri. *Of a woman,* fœmĭneus.

dignĭtas. *Dignity.*—EP. *High,* alta. *Supreme,* summa. *Lasting,* longa, diŭturna. *Sacred,* săcra, sancta. *Venerable,* vĕnĕrābĭlis, vĕnĕranda, augusta. *Royal,* rēgia.

dĭlātor, ōris, masc. *A procrastinator.*—EP. *Slow, lazy, segnis,* tardus, ĭners, ignāvus. *Foolish,* stultus, ĭneptus. *Imprudent,* imprūdens.

dĭlŭvies, ēi, **dĭlŭvium.** *A flood.*—EP. *Terrible,* horrenda, terrĭbĭlis, dīra. *Cruel,* fĕra, sæva, immītis. *Carrying everything away,* răpax. *Sudden, unexpected,* sŭbĭta, ĭnŏpīna, nĕcŏpīna. *Destructive,* exĭtiōsa, exĭtiālis. *Proceeding headlong,* præceps –ĭpĭtis.

diōta. *A cask.* See cadus.

dīræ. *Curses.* See detestatio.

30   DIS—DOM

discessus, ûs. *Departure.*—EP. *Sudden,* sŭbĭtus, rĕpentīnus, rĕpens. *Sad,* tristis, flēbĭlis. *Desired, desirable,* optātus, optābĭlis. *Future,* fŭtûrus.

discĭdium. *A separation.*—EP. *Long,* longum, diŭturnum. *Perpetual,* perpĕtuum, æternum. *Short,* brĕva. *Sad, triste,* flēbĭle. *Sudden,* sŭbĭtum, rĕpentīnum, rĕpens. *Expected,* prōvīsum, exspectatum.

disciplīna. *Discipline.*—EP. *Rigid,* sĕvēra, rĭgĭda. *Irksome,* grăvis, mŏlesta. *Customary,* sŏlĭta, consueta, assueta.

discĭpŭlus, discĭpŭlu. *A pupil.*—EP. *Tender,* tĕner –ĕri. *Docile,* dŏcĭlis, tractābĭlis. *Youthful,* jŭvĕnis. *Mindful,* mĕmor –ŏris. *Industrious,* sēdŭlus, *Clever,* subtĭlis, acer –cris.

discordia. *Discord, disagreement.*—EP. *Ill-omened, unfortunate,* măla, infēlix, obscœna. *Miserable,* tristis, mĭsĕra. *Foul, shameful,* fœda, imprŏba, tĕtra, turpia. *Foolish, mad,* stulta, insāna, dēmens, fŭriōsa. *Implacable,* implācābĭlis, ĭnexōrābĭlis, indŏmĭta. *Long,* longa, diŭturna. *Perpetual,* perpĕtua, æterna.

discrimen, ĭnis, neut. 1. *Division, difference.*—2. *Danger.*—EP. *Much, great,* multum, longum. *Ancient,* vĕtus –ĕris, antĭquum.—2. See periculum.

discursus, ûs. *A running to and fro.*—EP. *Over an extensive space,* lătus. *In various directions,* vărius. *Rapid,* răpĭdus, vēlox, cĕler –ĕris.

dispendium. *Loss.* See damnum.

dissensus, ûs, dissidium. *Disagreement.* See discordia.

dissĭmŭlātor, ōris *A dissembler, a concealer.*—EP. *Close,* tectus. *Deceitful,* fallax, falsus. *Crafty,* dŏlōsus, subdŏlus, văfer –fri.

distantia. *Distance.*—EP. *Long, great,* longa, longinqua, lāta. *Short,* brĕvia, exĭgua, parva, augusta.

dītio, ōnis, fem. *Dominion, extensive,* ampla, lāta, magna. *Powerful,* pŏtens. *Ancient,* antĭqua, vĕtus –ĕris.

dīva. *A goddess.* See Deus.

dīvĭtiæ, plur. fem. *Riches.*—EP. *Yellow, golden-coloured,* flāvæ. *Great,* magna, ingentes. *Heaped up, stored up,* congestæ. *Happy, making happy,* fēlīces, beātæ. *New,* nŏvæ. *Sudden, unexpected,* sŭbĭtæ, rĕpentīnæ, ĭnŏpīnæ, nĕcŏpīnæ, inspērātæ. *Transitory, short-lived,* brĕves, frăgĭles, instābĭles, cădūcæ, fŭgāces. *Worthless, vain,* vānæ, ĭnānes. *Wicked, acquired by wickedness,* imprŏbæ, scĕlērātæ.

dīvus. *A god.* See Deus.

doctor, ōris, masc. *A teacher.*—EP. *Wise,* săpiens, prūdens. *Skilful,* pĕrītus, callĭdus. *Gentle, kind,* mītis, bĕnignus. *Aged,* sĕnex, cānus (i. e. grey-headed).

doctrīna. *Instruction, learning.*—EP. *Useful,* ūtĭlis, apta. *Various,* văria, dīversa. *Desirable,* optābĭlia, optāta. *Divine,* dīvīna.

dŏcŭmentum. *A proof.*—EP. *Sure,* certum, firmum. *Useful,* ūtĭle. *Known,* nōtum. *Credible,* crēdĭbĭle.

dŏlābra. *A pickaxe.* See securis.

dōlium. *A cask.*—EP. *Hollow,* căvum. *Full,* plēnum. *Old,* antĭquum, vĕtus –ĕris.

dŏlo, ōnis, masc. *A spear.* See hasta.

dŏlor, ōris, masc. *Grief, pain.*—EP. *Severe,* grăvis, dūrus, sĕvērus, ăcūtus. *Cruel,* sævus, fĕrus, immītis. *Sad,* tristis, mĭser –ĕri, mĭsĕrābĭlis. *Causing tears,* lăcrÿmōsus, lăcrÿmābĭlis, flēbĭlia. *Inconsolable,* inconsōlābĭlis. *Causing complaints,* quĕrŭlus. *Deep,* altus. *Silent,* tăcĭtus. *Felt by woman,* fœmĭneus, mŭliĕbris. *Unspeakable,* infandus. *Unprecedented,* inaudītus.

dŏlus. *Cunning, a trick.*—EP. *Crafty, artful,* văfer –fri, callĭdus, versūtus, *Deceitful,* fallax. *Novel,* nŏvus. *Secret,* occultus, cæcus, tăcĭtus. *Wicked,* imprŏbus, scĕlērātus, nefandus. *Base, unworthy,* turpis, indignus.

dŏmātor, dŏmĭtor. *A conqueror.* See victor.

dŏmĭna. *A mistress.*—EP. *Imperious,* impĕriōsa. *Fickle,* lĕvis, inconstans, văria, mūtābĭlis. *Faithless,* infīda, perfĭda, fallax, falsa. *Beautiful,* pulchra, vĕnusta, spĕciōsa, formōsa. *Amiable,* ămābĭlis. *Dear,* căra. *Disengaged, loving no one else,* văcua. *Arrogant,* insŏlens.

dŏmĭnus. *A master, a lord, a ruler.*—EP. *Powerful, great,* pŏtens, magnus. *Ancient,* priscus, antĭquus, vĕtus –ĕris. *Merciful,* mītis, mansuetus. *Affable,* făcĭlis, affābĭlis. *Cruel,* sævus, fĕrus, immītis, immansuetus. *Severe, stern,* sĕvērus, dūrus, rĭgĭdus. *Hated,* invīsus. *Proud,* sŭperbus.

dŏmus, ûs. 1. *A house, a home.*—2. *A family.*—EP. 1. *Lofty,* alta. *Marble,*

DON—EGE 31

marmŏrea. *Splendid,* splendĭda. *Happy,* fĕlix, beāta. *Hereditary,* pātria, pāterna, āvīta. 1, 2. *Rich,* dives -ĭtis, lŏcūples -ētis, ŏpŭlenta. *Proud,* sŭperba.—2. *Ancient,* antīqua, vĕtus -ĕris. *Noble,* nōbĭlis, gĕnĕrōsa. *Illustrious,* clāra, præclāra, inclўta.

dōnārium. *An altar on which to offer gifts, a temple.* See templum.

dōnātor, ōris, masc. *A giver.* See dator.

dōnum. *A gift.*—EP. *Grateful,* grātum. *Pleasing,* grātum, jūcundum, acceptum, dulce, ămābĭle. *Liberal, abundant,* largum. *Rich,* dives -ĭtis. *Kind, friendly,* bĕnignum, ămīcum. *Expected,* spĕrātum, exspectātum. *Customary,* sŏlĭtum, assuetum, consuetum. *Pious,* pium. *Sacred,* săcrum, săcrātum. *Frequent,* crēbrum, multum, plūrĭmum (all usu. in plur.).

dorca, æ, masc. fem., and dorcas, ădis, fem. *A roe.* See cervus.

dos, dōtis, fem. *A dowry, large, rich,* magna, ampla, dives -ĭtis. *Splendid,* splendĭda. *Connubial (of marriage),* nuptiālis, conjŭgiālis.

drăco, ōnis, masc. *A dragon.* See anguis.

Druĭdæ. *Priests of Britain and Gaul.*—EP. *Pious,* pii. *Sacred, holy,* săcri, sancti, săcrati. *Bearded,* barbāti. *Venerable,* vĕnĕrandi, vĕrendi. *Ancient,* prisci, vĕtĕres, antīqui.

ductus, ūs. *Leading.*—EP. *Prudent,* prūdens, cautus. *Skilful,* pĕrītus.

dulcēdo, ĭnis. *Sweetness.*—EP. *Winning,* blanda. *Unaccustomed,* insŏlīta, · īnassueta. *Ancient,* vĕtus -ĕris, prisca. *Known,* nōta.

dūmētum. *A thicket.*—EP. *Thick,* densum. *Thorny, bristling,* spīnōsum, horrĭdum, horrens. *Green,* virĭde, virĭdans. *Leafy,* frondōsum, frondeum.

dūmus. *A briar.* See above.

dūrĭtia. *Hardness.*—EP. *Invincible,* invicta, indŏmĭta. *Rigid,* rigĭda. *Fierce,* fera, fĕrox, trux -ūcis. *Iron,* ferrea, ădămantīna. *Unlovely,* inămābĭlis, inămœna, ingrāta.

dux, dŭcis; ductor, ōris, masc. *A guide, a leader, a general.*—EP. *Skilful,* pĕrītus, callīdus. *Brave, fortis,* impāvidus. *Faithful,* fīdus, fīdēlis. *Invincible,* invictus, indŏmĭtus. *Watchful, vigilant,* vigil -ĭlis. *Prudent,* prūdens, cautus, prōvĭdus. *Celebrated, illustrious,* insignis, clārus, inclўtus. *Excellent,* ĕgrĕgius, optĭmus.

E.

Ĕbĕnus, i, fem. and ĕbĕnum. *Ebony.*—EP. *Black,* nĭgra, ātra. *Hard,* dura. *Indian,* Inda, Indĭca, ˘Eōa.

ĕbriĕtas. *Drunkenness.*—EP. *Mad, maddening,* āmens, fŭriōsa. *Wanton,* lascīva, prōterva. *Unrestrained,* impŏtens.

ĕbur, ŏris, neut. *Ivory.*—EP. *Indian, Eastern,* Indum, Indĭcum, ˘Eōum. *White,* album, candĭdum, candens, nĭveum. *Smooth,* lēve. *Easily cut,* sectĭle, sculptĭle. *Shining,* nitĭdum, nĭtens. *Pure,* pūrum.

ĕchidna. *A serpent.* See anguis.

Ēcho, ūs, fem. *Echo.*—EP. *Aonian,* Āŏnia. *Dwelling in the Cephisus,* Cēphĭsĭăs -ădos. *Talkative,* lŏquax, garrŭla. *Resounding,* rĕsŏnābĭlis. *Faithful,* fīda, rīdēlis. *Sportive,* jŏcōsa.

ĕdictum. *An order, an edict.*—EP. *Just,* justum, æquum. *Unjust,* injustum, īnīquum. *Lasting,* firmum, stăbĭle, perpĕtuum, æternum. *Ratified,* rătum. *Powerful,* pŏtens.

effectus, ūs. *Effect.*—EP. *Real,* vērus. *Desired,* optātus.

effĭgies, ēi. *An image.* See imago.

effŭgium. *An escape, a place to which to escape.*—EP. *Safe,* tūtum, incŏlŭme. *Wished for, desirable,* optātum, optābĭle. *Known, customary,* nōtum, sŏlĭtum, consuetum, assuetum. *Obscure,* obscūrum, sēcrētum. *Distant,* longinquum, rĕmōtum. *Ready,* părātum.

ĕgestas. *Want.*—EP. *Hard,* dūra. *Sad,* tristis, mĭsĕra, mĭsĕrābĭlis. *Cruel,* fĕra, sæva, immītis. *Helpless,* ĭnops. *Foul, shameful,* fœda, turpis. *Hateful,* invīsa, ŏdiōsa, inămābĭlis.

32   EGR—EUR

ēgressus, ûs. *A going out, a passage by which to go out.*—EP. *Easy,* făcĭlis. *Safe,* tūtus, incŏlŭmis. *Well-known,* nōtus. *Open,* pătens, ăpertus.

ĕjŭlātio, onis, fem. ĕjŭlātus, ûs. *A wailing.*—EP. *Feminine,* fœmĭneus, mŭliĕbris. *Effeminate,* mollis. *Sad,* tristis, mĭser —ĕri, mĭsĕrābĭlis, lūgūbris. *Loud,* clārus. *Sudden,* sŭbĭtus. *Querulous,* quĕrŭlus. *Shameful,* turpis.

ēlectrum. *Amber.*—EP. *Liquid,* lĭquĭdum. *Pure,* pūrum. *Yellow,* flāvum, crŏceum, lūteum. *Eastern,* 'Eōum.

ēlectus, ûs. *Choice.* See delectus.

ĕlĕgēia. *Elegy.*—EP. *Mournful,* tristis, mæsta, flēbĭlis, lūgūbris, mĭsĕrābĭlis. *Tuneful,* rhythmĭcal, cănōra, argūta, nŭmĕrōsa. *Querulous,* quĕrŭla.

ĕlēmenta, ōrum, plur. neut. *Elements, beginnings.*—EP. *Original,* prīma. *Hard,* dūra. *Fortunate,* fausta, fēlīcia. *Unfortunate,* infausta, măla, infēlīcia. *Trifling,* parva, exĭgua.

ĕlĕphantus. 1. *An elephant.*—2. *Ivory.*—EP. 1. See below.—2. See ebur.

ĕlĕphas, antis, masc. *An elephant.*—EP. *Huge,* vastus, ingens. *Bearing a castle on his back,* turrītus. *Indian, Eastern,* Indus, Indĭcus, 'Eōus. *Docile,* dŏcĭlis, tractābĭlis. *Gentle,* mītis, mansuetus. *Wise,* săpiens, săgax.

ēlŏquium. *Eloquence.* See facundia.

ēlŭvies, ēi, fem. *A torrent.* See torrens.

Ēlўsium. *Elysium.*—EP. *Extensive,* lātum, spătiōsum, amplum. *Sacred,* săcrum, săcrātum. *Pious* (i. e. *the abode of the pious*), pium. *Quiet,* quiētum, tranquillum, sĕrēnum. *Happy,* fēlix, beātum, lætum.

emptor, ōris, masc. *A buyer.*—EP. *At a high price,* prētiōsus. *Careful, cautious,* cautus.

ensis, is, masc. *A sword.*—EP. *Iron, brazen,* ferreus, ferrātus, æreus, ahēneus ahēnus. *Causing wounds,* vulnĭfĭcus. *Deadly,* fătālis, fătĭfer —ĕri. *Sharp,* ăcūtus. *Glittering,* cŏruscus. *Moving like lightning,* fulmĭneus. *Trusty,* fīdus, fĭdēlis. *Bloody,* cruentus, sanguĭneus, sanguĭnŏlentus. *Drawn,* strictus, rĕclūsus. *Raised to strike,* sŭblātus. *Double-edged,* anceps —ĭpĭtis. *Noric* (*Noricum being famous for steel*), Nōrĭcus. *Cruel,* fĕrus, sævus, crūdēlis. *Horrible,* horrendus, horrĭbĭlis, dīrus.

ĕphippia, orum, plur. neut. *Horse-trappings.* See phaleræ.

ĕpistŏla. *A letter.*—EP. *Written,* scripta. *Sent,* missa. *Long,* longa, verbōsa. *Welcome,* grāta, accepta. *Eloquent,* făcunda, ēlŏquens. *Faithful,* fīda, fĭdēlis. *Silent,* tăcĭta.

ĕpŏs, only nom. and acc. sing. neut. *An epic poem.*—EP. *Noble,* nōbĭle. *Heroic,* hērōum.

ĕpŭlæ, ārum, plur. fem. *A feast.*—EP. *Rich,* luxurious, lautæ, ŏpīnæ. *Of various dishes,* vāriæ. *Festive,* festæ. *Cheerful,* lætæ, hĭlāres. *Late,* sēræ.

ĕquĕs, ĭtis, masc. *A horseman, a knight.*—EP. *Active,* impĭger —gri, ācer —cris. *Brave,* fortis, impăvĭdus. *Swift,* vēlox, cĭtus, răpĭdus, cēler —ĕris. *Skilful,* pērītus. *Armed,* armātus. *Armed with a lance,* hastātus.

ĕquus, ĕqua. *A horse, a mare.*—EP. *Swift,* răpĭdus, vēlox, cēler —ĕris. *Let go at his full pace,* admissus. *Docile,* dŏcĭlis. *With hard hoof,* cornĭpes —ĕdis. *Thracian,* Thrācius, Thrēĭcius. *Elean,* Ēlēus, in fem. Elīās —adæ. *Panting,* ănhēlans, ănhēlus. *Ready,* părātus. *Saddled,* instrātus (c. abl. *of the trappings*). *Harnessed to a carriage,* junctus. See Gradus.

Ērĕbus. *Hell.* See Orcus.

errātum. *An error.*—EP. *Wrong,* mălum, prāvum. *Silly,* stultum. *Base,* turpe, fœdum. See crimen.

errātus, ûs, error, ōris, masc. 1. *A wandering.*—2. *A mistake.*—EP. 1. 2. *Ignorant,* ignārus. *Unfortunate,* infēlix, tristis, mĭser —ĕri. *Doubtful,* incertus, dŭbius. 1. *Long,* longus.—2. *Pathless,* āvius, dēvius. *Intentional,* dēlībĕrātus. *Pleasant,* grātus, dulcis.

esca. 1. *Food.*—2. *Bait.*—EP. 1. See cibus.—2. *Deceitful,* fallax. *Destructive,* exĭtiōsa, exĭtiālis, fătālis.

essĕdum. *A chariot.* See currus.

ēventum, ēventus, ûs. *An event.* See casus.

Eumĕnĭdes, um, fem. *The Furies.* See Furiæ.

Eurus. *The South East Wind.*—EP. *Stormy,* prŏcellosus. *Rainy,* plŭvius, plŭviālis, āvĭdus, ăquōsus, imbrĭfer —ĕri, nimbĭfer. *Violent,* viŏlentus. *Wintry,* hўbernus, hўēmālis. *Fierce,* trux trŭcis, trŭcŭlentus. fĕrus, ănĭmōsus, indŏ

EXC—FAB 33

mītus. *Wanton*, prŏtervus. *Swelling*, tŭmĭdus, tŭmens. *Black*, nĭger –gri, āter –tri.

excĭdium. *Destruction*. See exitium.

excŭbiæ, ārum, plur. fem. *A night-watch, any watch.*—EP. *Vigilant*, vigĭles, pervigĭles. *By night*, nocturnæ. *Active*, ācres, impĭgræ. *Unwearied*, indēfessæ.

excŭbĭtor, ōris, masc. *A watcher*. See above.

excursus, ûs. *A running out, a sally.*—EP. *Brief*, brĕvis. *Sudden*, sŭbĭtus, rĕpentīnus. *Daring*, audax, fortis.

exemplar –āris, neut. exemplum. *An example.*—EP. *To be imitated*, ĭmĭtābĭle, ĭmĭtandum. *Useful*, ūtĭle. *Excellent, noble*, ēgrĕgium, insigne, nōbĭle. *Pious, good*, pium, prŏbum. *Evil, base*, mălum, turpe.

exercĭtus, ûs. *An army.*—EP. *Brave, fearless*, fortis, audax, vălĭdus, impăvĭdus. *Glittering with arms*, flōrens ære, cŏruscus, splendĭdus, splendens. *Armed*, armātus. *Armed with spear, or sword, or shield*, hastātus, ensĭfer –ĕri, clўpeātus. *Victorious*, victor. *Dense*, densus.

exĭtium. *Destruction.*—EP. *The last*, ultĭmum, sŭprēmum. *Sad*, triste, mĭsĕrum, mĭsĕrābĭle, lŭgūbre, flēbĭle, *Dire*, dīrum, horrendum, horrĭbĭle. *Bloody*, cruentum, sanguĭneum. *Sudden*, sŭbĭtum, ĭnŏpīnum, nĕcŏpīnum. *Irremediable*, immĕdĭcābĭle.

exĭtus, ûs. 1. *A going out.*—2. *An event.*—EP. 1. See egressus.—2. See casus.

exordium, exorsum. *A beginning.*—EP. *First, original*, prīmum. *Ancient*, antīquum, priscum, vĕtus –ĕris. *Fortunate*, fēlix, faustum.

exortus, ûs. *A rising*. See ortus.

expĕrientia. *Experience.*—EP. *Long*, longa. *True, trustworthy*, vēra, fīda, certa. *Wise*, săpiens. *Ancient*, prisca, vĕtus –ĕris, antīqua.

explōrātor, ōris, masc. *A spy.*—EP. *Bold*, audax, fortis, impăvĭdus. *Crafty*, callĭdus, versūtus, văfer –fri. *Trusty*, fīdus, fĭdēlis. *Who has been sent*, missus. *Sagacious*, săgax, subtīlis.

exsĕquiæ, ārum, plur. fem. *A funeral, funeral rites.*—EP. *Last*, sŭprēmæ, ultĭmæ. *Sad*, tristes, mĭsĕræ, flēbĭles, lŭgūbres. *Sacred*, sācræ, sanctæ. *Funereal*, fūnĕbres, fūnĕreæ.

exsĭlium. *Exile.*—EP. *Sad*, triste, mĭsĕrum, mĭsĕrābĭle. *Distant*, longinquum, rĕmōtum, distans. *Long*, longum, diŭturnum. *Short*, brĕve. *Deserved*, mĕrĭtum. *Undeserved*, immĕrĭtum, indignum. *Hard, cruel*, durum, crŭdēle, immīte. *Hated*, invīsum, ŏdiōsum, ĭnămābĭle.

exsul, ŭlis, masc. fem. *An exile.*—EP. *Sad*, tristis, mĭsĕrābĭlis, mĭsĕrandus. *Helpless*, ĭnops –ŏpis. *Undeserved*, immĕrens, immĕrĭtus. *Poor*, pauper –ĕris, ĕgēnus. *Complaining*, quĕrūlus. *Hopeless*, exspes (*only found in nom.*). *Solitary*, sōlus, gen. sōlīus, dēsertus.

exta, ōrum, plur. neut. *Entrails (esp. of animals sacrificed).*—EP. *Ominous, prophetic*, præsāga, prænuntia. *Fortunate*, sĕcunda, fausta. *Ill-omened, adverse*, infausta, măla. *Inmost*, intĭma. *Still quivering with life*, spīrantia. *Bloody*, cruenta, sanguĭnea. *Sacred*, sācra.

exŭviæ, ārum, plur. fem. *Spoils.*—EP. *Rich, splendid*, ēgrĕgiæ, amplæ, insignes. *Blood-stained*, cruentæ, sanguĭneæ. *Warlike*, bellĭcæ. *Wished for*, optātæ. *Victorious, tokens of victory*, victrīces.

F.

Făba. *A bean.*—EP. *Productive*, fĕcunda, fĕrax. *Heating*, călĭda.

făber –bri. *A smith, an artificer.*—EP. *Skilful, ingenious*, doctus, pĕrītus, ingĕniōsus. *Celebrated*, inclўtus, insignis, nōtus. *Excellent*, ēgrĕgius. *Hardy*, dūrus.

făbrĭcātor, ōris, masc. *A maker.*—EP. *Ingenious*, ingĕniōsus. *Wise*, prūdens, săpiens.

făbella, făbŭla. *A fable, a story.*—EP. *Well-known*, nōta, vulgāris, cĕlĕbris,

D

34 FAC—FAT

superl. cĕlĕberrĭma. *Ancient,* vĕtus –ĕris, prisca, antīqua. *Ingenious,* ingĕniōsa. *Silly,* stulta, ănīlis. *Suitable,* apta, ĭdōnea.

făcĭes, ēi, fem. *A face.*—EP. *Beautiful,* pulchra, formōsa, dĕcōra. *Fair,* candĭda, nĭvea, ĕburnea, ĕburna. *Dark,* fusca. *Lovely,* ămābĭlis. *Juvenile,* jŭvĕnĭlia. *Of a virgin,* virgĭnea, puellāria.

făcĭnus, ŏris, neut. *A deed (esp. an atrocious deed).*—EP. *Bold, audacious,* audax, ătrox. *Cruel,* sævum, fĕrum, crūdēle, immīte, immāne. *Sad,* triste, mĭsĕrum, mĭsĕrābĭle. *Impious,* impium, scĕlĕrātum. *Irremediable, irrevocable,* irrĕvŏcābĭle. *Unheard of,* ĭnaudītum, insŏlĭtum.

factum. *A deed.*—EP. *Pious,* pium. *Kind,* ămīcum, bŏnum, bĕnignum. *Brave,* forte, impăvĭdum. *Noble,* nōbĭle, ēgrĕgium. *Celebrated,* clārum, insigne.

făcultas. *Power over, power of.*—EP. *At hand,* părāta. *Desired,* optāta, optābĭlis.

făcundia. *Eloquence.*—EP. *Divine,* dĭvīna. *Powerful,* pŏtens, effĭcax. *Various,* vāria. *Rapid,* răpĭda, torrens. *Persuasive,* blanda; *Attic, such as that of Demosthenes,* Cĕcrōpia. *Irresistible, victorious,* victrix –īcis. *Avenging,* vindex –īcis. *Pious, just,* pia, justa. *Cultivated,* culta. *Abundant,* larga.

fæx, cis, fem. *The dregs.*—EP. *Lowest,* īma. *Worthless,* vīlis.

făgus, i, fem. *A beech-tree.*—EP. *Spreading,* pătŭla. *Shady,* umbrōsa, ŏpāca. *High,* alta, ardua. *Leafy,* frondea, frondōsa.

fallācia. *Deceit.* See dolus.

falx, cis, fem. *A sickle, a pruning-knife.*—EP. *Sacred to Ceres,* Cĕreālis. *To Saturn,* Sāturnia. *Curved,* curva, incurva, rĕcurva, unca, ădunca. *Sharp,* ăcūta. *Iron,* ferrea, ferrāta. *Belonging to the farmer,* ăgrestis.

fāma. 1. *Fame.*—2. *Report.*—EP. 1. *Immortal,* ætĕrna, immortālia. *Enduring after the life of man,* sŭperstes –ĭtis. *Illustrious,* clāra, inclyta, cĕlĕbris; superl. cĕlĕberrĭma. *Golden,* aurea. *Desired,* optāta, exoptāta.—2. See rumor.

fāmes, is. *Hunger, famine.*—EP. *Terrible,* dīra, terrĭbĭlis, horrenda. *Long,* longa, diūturna. *Cruel,* fĕra, sæva, crūdēlis, immītis. *Intolerable,* intŏlĕrābĭlis. *Maddening,* vēsāna, fŭriōsa, răbĭda. *Pale,* pallĭda, pallens. *Ill-omened, evil,* obscœna, inīqua. *Helpless,* inops –ōpis. *Destitute of food,* jējūna.

fămŭlus, fămŭla. *A servant.* See servus.

fānum. *A temple.* See templum.

far, farris, neut. *Wheat.*—EP. *Sacred to Ceres,* Cĕreāle. *White,* album, candĭdum. *Genial, nutritious,* almum. *Golden (when ripe),* flāvum, aureum.

fărīna. *Meal, flour.*—EP. *Sacred to Ceres,* Cĕreāles. *White,* alba, candĭda, candens. *Genial,* alma. *Made of wheat,* trĭtīcea. *Ground,* trīta.

fascia. *A bandage.*—EP. *Tight,* arcta, brĕvis. *Narrow,* angusta. *White, purple, gilded, etc.,* alba, purpurea, aurea.

fascĭnum. *Fascination, a magic charm.*—EP. *Magic,* măgĭcum. *Powerful,* pŏtens, effĭcax. *Accustomed,* sŏlĭtum, consuetum, assuetum, nōtum.

fascis, is, masc. 1. *A bundle.*—2. in plur. *the fasces of the Consul.*—EP. 1. *Heavy,* grăvis, magnus. *Small, light,* parvus, exĭguus, lĕvis. *Well arranged,* compŏsĭtus.—2. *Conspicuous, illustrious,* clari, insignes. *Powerful,* pŏtentes. *Severe,* sĕvēri, rĭgĭdi, sævi.

fasti, orum, plur. masc. *Annals.*—EP. *Mindful, recording everything,* mĕmōres. *Truthful,* vēri, vērāces, vērīdĭci. *Ancient,* vĕtĕres, antīqui, prisci. *Hereditary,* pătrii, ăvīti.

fastīdium. *Fastidiousness, disgust.*—EP. *Proud, insolent,* sŭperbum, insŏlens. *Deserved,* mĕrĭtum, justum. *Difficult to deal with,* diffĭcīle. *Morose,* mōrōsum. *Incurable,* immĕdĭcābĭle. *Odious,* invīsum, ŏdiōsum, ingrātum.

fastigium. *A top (esp. of a house).*—EP. *The highest,* summum. See culmen.

fastus, ûs. *Pride.* See fastidium.

fātum. 1. *Fate.*—2. *Death.*—EP. 1. *Inevitable,* inēluctābĭle, inēvĭtābĭle. *Fixed, certain,* certum, stăbĭle. *Divine,* Dīvīnum. *Inexorable,* inexōrābĭle, illăcrȳmābĭle. *Original,* prīmum. *Uncertain, unknown,* incertam, abdĭtum, ignotum, dūbium. *Deserved,* mĕrĭtum, dēbĭtum. *Undeserved,* immĕrĭtum, indēbĭtum. *Ancient,* vĕtus –ĕris, priscum, antīquum. *Sad,* triste, mĭsĕrum, mĭsĕrābĭle, lūgūbre. *Cruel,* crūdēle, sævum. *Happy,* fēlix –īcis, faustum. See Parcæ.—2. See mors.

FAU—FER

fauces, ium, plur. fem., found also in abl. sing., **fauce**. *The jaws.*—EP. *Greedy, voracious,* ăvĭdæ, vŏrāces. *Open,* pătentes, ăpertæ. *Blood-stained (of wild beasts, etc.),* sanguĭnëæ, cruentæ.

făvilla. *Ashes.*—EP. *White,* candens, candĭda. *Smoking,* fumans, fŭmea, fŭmōsa. *Light,* lēvis. *Black,* ātra, nĭgra. *Lamented (when speaking of the ashes of the dead),* flēta, dēflēta. *Sad,* mĭsĕra, tristis, mĭsĕranda, flēbĭlis. *Last,* sŭprēma.

făvor –ōris, masc. *Favour.*—EP. *Eager,* stŭdiōsus. *Friendly,* ămīcus. *General, universal,* commūnis.

faustĭtas. *Good fortune.*—EP. *Genial,* alma. *Desired, desirable,* optāta, exoptāta, optābĭlis. *Propitious,* sĕcunda, dextĕra, *sync.* dextra, auspĭcāta. *Lasting,* longa, diŭturna, stăbĭlis, constans. *Transitory,* brĕvis, frăgĭlis, cădūca, vāna. *Deserved,* mĕrĭta, dēbĭta. *Undeserved,* immĕrĭta.

fautor, ōris, masc.; **fautrix, īcis,** fem. *A favourer.*—EP. *Eager,* stŭdiōsus, ācer, ācris. *Friendly,* ămīcus. *Powerful,* pŏtens, efficax, ūtĭlis. *Constant,* constans, firmus, fīdus, fīdēlis, assĭduus.

făvus. *A honeycomb.*—EP. *Honeyed, sweet,* mellītus, mellĭfer –ĕri, dulcis. *White,* albus, candĭdus, candens, nĭveus. *Sticky,* tēnax. *Dense,* densus. *Full,* plēnus. *Waxy,* cēreus.

fax, făcis, fem. *A torch* (see the Gradus).—EP. *Bright,* splendĭda, clāra. *Fiery,* ignea, flammea, flammĭfĕra, flammans. *Lighted up,* accensa. *Made of pine,* pīnea. *Tipped with sulphur,* sulfūrea. *Tipped with pitch,* pĭcea, cērāta. [*Of the marriage torch*] *Nuptial,* nuptiālis, jŭgālis. *Joyful, festive,* læta, festa. [*Of the funeral torch*], funerea, sĕpulchrālis, fūnĕrea, fūnēbris, fērālis. *Sad,* tristis, mĭsĕra, flēbĭlis. *Last, ultima,* sŭprēma, extrēma. [*As a firebrand*], *mischievous, destructive,* damnōsa, perniciōsa, exĭtiōsa. *Hostile,* hostīlis, hostĭca. *Devouring,* ĕdax. *Furious,* fūriōsa.

fēbris, is, fem. *A fever.*—EP. *Burning,* torrĭda, călĭda. *Dry,* ārĭda, sicca. *Causing panting,* ănhēla. *Deadly,* fatālis, fātĭfĕra.

fel, fellis, neut. *Gall.*—EP. *Bitter,* ăcerbum. *Black,* ātrum, nĭgrum. *Poisoned, poisonous, venomous,* vĕnēnātum.

fēlis, is, fem. *A cat.*—EP. *Soft,* mollis, tĕnĕra. *Tenacious of life,* vīvax. *Spotted,* văria, măcŭlōsa. *Silent, noiseless,* tăcĭta. *Crafty,* callĭda, dŏlōsa.

fēmĭna. *A woman.*—EP. *Beautiful,* pulchra, formōsa, dĕcōra, spĕciōsa, spectābĭlis. *Lovely,* ămābĭlis. *Fair,* candĭda. *Gentle,* blanda, tĕnĕra. *Helpless, unwarlike, timid,* imbellis, tĭmĭda. *Modest, chaste,* pŭdīca, casta. *Faithful,* fīda, fīdēlis. See the Gradus.

fēmur, ŏris, neut. *A thigh.*—EP. *Strong,* vălĭdum, nervōsum, tŏrōsum.

fĕnestra. *A window.*—EP. *Open, admitting light,* pătens, pervĭa, lūcĭda. *Let into the wall,* inserta. *Double,* bĭfōris. *Closed,* juncta, clausa.

fĕra. *A wild beast.*—EP. *African,* Lĭbýca, Gætūla. *Savage,* sæva, crūdēlis, immānis. *Devouring,* ăvĭda, răpax. *Furious,* fūriōsa. *Untamed,* indŏmĭta, immansueta.

fĕrĕtrum. *A bier.*—EP. *The last,* sŭprēmum, ultĭmum. *Laid out,* pŏsĭtum. *Sad,* triste, lăcrўmōsum, lăcrўmābĭle, lūgŭbre.

fĕriæ, ārum, plur. fem. *Holidays.*—EP. *Festive, joyful,* festæ, lætæ, hĭlāres. *Regularly recurring,* sŏlennes. *Customary,* sŏlĭtæ, consuetæ. *Wished for,* optātæ. *Pleasant,* dulces, jūcundæ. *Sacred,* săcræ.

fĕrĭtas. *Savageness.*—EP. *Uncultivated,* inculta, rūdis. *Unamiable,* inămābĭlis, invīsa. *Barbarian,* barbăra. *Cruel,* sæva, immītis, aspĕra.

fĕrōcia. *Cruelty.*—EP. *Unbridled,* indŏmĭta, effrēna. *Savage,* sæva, immānis, immansueta. *Barbarian,* barbăra. *Pitiless, implacable,* immītis, ĭnexōrābĭlis, illăcrўmābĭlis. *Dire,* dīra, horrĭbĭlis, horrenda.

ferrūgo, ĭnis, fem. *Rust.*—EP. *Horrid, foul,* horrĭda, fœda, turpis. *Dark,* obscūra, fusca. *Idle,* segnis, ĭners. *Evil, mischievous,* măla, vĭtiōsa, perniciōsa, damnōsa. *Devouring,* ĕdax.

ferrum. *Iron.*—EP. *Noric,* Nōrĭcum. *Dark,* obscūrum, fuscum. *Hard,* dūrum. *Mischievous, destructive,* nŏcens, noxium, damnōsum, exĭtiāle. *Causing wounds or death,* vulnĭfĭcum, fătāle, fātĭfĕrum. *Sacred to Vulcan or Mars,* Vulcānium, Martium, Māvortium. *Dug out of the earth,* effossum. *Sharpened,* ăcūtum.

fertĭlĭtas. *Fertility.*—EP. *Genial,* alma. *Golden (from the colour of ripe corn),*

D 2

36 **FER—FLA**

aurea, flåva. *Abundant*, plēna, grăvis, grăvĭda, über –ris, esp. in superl. ûberrĭma. *Wished for*, optăta, exoptăta, optăbĭlis. *Such as was in the golden age under Saturn*, Săturnia, aurea. *Heavenly*, coelestis, divīna.

fĕrŭla. *A cane or rod.*—EP. *Severe*, sæva, sĕvēra. *Chastising*, vindex –ĭcis, ultrix –ĭcis.

fervor, oris, masc. 1. *Heat.*—2. *Impetuosity.*—EP. 1. *Burning*, ardens, torrĭdus. *Dry*, siccus, arĭdus.—1, 2. *Violent*, vĭŏlentus, ăcer –cris.—2. *Rash*, præceps –ĭpĭtis, incautus, tĕmĕrărius.

festum. *A festival.*—EP. *Solemn, regularly recurring*, sŏlenne. *Customary*, sŏlĭtum, assuetum, consuetum. *Joyful*, lætum. *Sacred*, săcrum, săcrătum. *Pious*, pium.

fētus, ûs. *Offspring, produce.* See proles, fructus.

fĭbra, æ. *The entrails.* See exta.

fĭbŭla. *A clasp.*—EP. *Tight*, arcta. *Golden*, aurea. *Jewelled*, gemmea. *Joined*, juncta. *Tenacious*, tĕnax.

fictor, ōris, masc. *An inventor.*—EP. *Ingenious*, callĭdus, ingĕniōsus. *Deceitful*, mendax, dŏlōsus. *Faithless*, insĭdus, insĭdēlis, perfĭdus.

ficus, i, and ûs, fem. *A fig-tree, a fig.*—EP. *Sweet*, dulcis. *Syrian*, Sўra, Sўria. *Purple*, purpūrea. *Juicy*, succĭda.

fĭdes, ei. 1. *Faith, fidelity.*—2. *Belief.*—EP. 1. *True, honest*, vēra, prŏba. *Firm*, firma, stăbĭlis, constans. *Sacred*, săcra, sancta. *Lasting*, perpĕtua, mansūra. *Incorruptible, pure*, incorrupta, pūra, lĭquĭda. *White, clad in white garments* [*when personified*], candĭda, căna.—2. *Undoubting*, certa. *Credulous*, crēdŭla. *Rash*, præceps –ĭpĭtis, tĕmĕrăria.

fĭdes, is. *A lyre.* See lyra.

fĭdĭcen. *A harp-player.*—EP. *Skilful*, doctus, pĕrītus. *Tuneful*, argūtus, cănōrus, blandus.

fĭdūcia. *Confidence.*—EP. *Bold*, audax, fortis. *Firm*, firma, certa, stăbĭlis. *Vain*, văna, irrĭta, ĭnānis. *Great*, magna. *Ancient*, prisca, vĕtus –ĕris. *Customary*, sŏlĭta, consueta.

fĭgūra. *A figure.*—EP. *Beautiful*, pulchra, dĕcōra, spĕciōsa. *Large*, grandis, magna. *Curved*, curva, incurva, sĭnuōsa. *To be imitated*, ĭmĭtăbĭlis, ĭmĭtanda. *Novel*, nŏva, insŏlĭta, ĭnaudĭta.

fĭlius, fĭlia. *A son, a daughter.*—EP. *Infant, juvenile*, infans, jŭvĕnĭlis. *Tender, of tender years*, tĕner –ĕri. *Docile*, dŏcĭlis. *Affectionate*, pius, ămans. *Beardless* (*of the son*), imberbis. *Marriageable* (*of the daughter*), nūbĭlis. *Beloved*, cārus, dĭlectus. *Worthy to be loved*, ămăbĭlis.

fĭlix, ĭcis, fem. *Fern.*—EP. *Dry*, sicca, arĭda. *Hard*, dūra. *Waving*, fluĭtans, *Leafy*, cōmans. *Slight*, grăcĭlis.

fĭlum, fem. *A thread* (*often the thread of fate*).—2. *A string of a lyre.*—EP. 1. *Slight*, tĕnue. *Easily drawn out*, ductĭle. *Long*, longum. *Soft*, molle, tĕnĕrum. *Affecting mortal life*, mortăle (see Fate).—2. *Tuneful*, cănōrum, argutum, dulce. *Struck*, ictum. See chorda.

fĭmus. *Dung.*—EP. *Rich, fertilising*, pinguis. *Foul*, fœdus, turpis, immundus.

fĭnis, is, masc., very rarely fem. *An end.*—EP. *Last*, ultĭmus, extrēmus, sūprēmus. *Sad*, tristis, mĭser –ĕri, mĭsĕrandus, mĭsĕrăbĭlis, lūgūbris, flēbĭlis. *Expected, wished*, exspectatus, optătus, spērātus. *Desirable*, optăbĭlis. *Late*, sērus.

fĭrmāmen, ĭnis, neut. *A prop.* See columen.

fiscella, fiscĭna. *A basket.*—EP. *Made of twigs, of osiers*, arbŭtea, vĭmĭnea, rūbea. *Frail*, frăgĭlis. *Light*, lĕvis. *Full*, plēna. *Capacious*, căpax.

fistŭla. *A pipe.*—EP. *Rustic*, rustica, ăgrestis. *Tuneful*, blanda, argūta, cănōra, vōcălis. *Hollow*, căva. *Well put together*, compacta. *Sacred to Apollo*, Ăpollĭnea, Ăpollĭnāria. See tibia.

flăbellum. *A fan.*—EP. *Light*, lĕve. *Of various colours*, pictum, vărium. *Made of feathers*, plūmōsum, plumeum. *Adorned with ivory, or gold, or jewels*, ĕburneum, ĕburnum, aureum, gemmeum. *Causing wind*, ventōsum. *Soft*, molle, tĕnĕrum.

flăbrum, flāmen, ĭnis. *A breeze.*—EP. *Gentle*, lēve, molle. *Summer*, æstīvum. *Pleasant*, grātum, jūcundum, dulce, ămœnum. *Desired, desirable*, optātum, optăbĭle. *Fair, favourable*, sĕcundum, faustum. *Rustling*, sūsurrans, *Cool*, frĭgĭdum.

FLA—FOR 37

flăgellum. *A whip*—EP. *Severe, cruel,* sævum, crūdēle, sĕvērum. *Avenging,* vindex –īcis, ultrix –īcis.

flăgĭtium. *A crime.* See crimen, facinus.

flāmen, Ĭnis, n. *A breeze.* See ventus, aura.

flamma. *Flame.*—EP. *Fiery,* ignea. *Shining,* rŭtĭla. *Shining, flickering,* mĭcans, cŏrusca. *Sudden,* sŭbĭta. *Crackling,* crĕpĭtans. *Smoky,* fūmōsa, fūmea, fūmĭfĕra. *Rising, high,* alta, ardua, sŭblīmis. *Devouring,* ĕdax, răpax, ăvĭda. *Destructive,* exĭtiōsa, exĭtiālis. *Hostile,* hostīlis, hostīca, ĭnĭmīca. *Sulphureous,* sulfūrea. *Of lighted tow (for a firebrand),* stuppea.

flammeum. *A veil.*—EP. *Let down,* dēmissum. See velamen.

flātus, ûs. 1. *Breath.*—2. *A breeze.*—EP. 1. *Warm,* călĭdus, fervens, fervĭdus. *Panting,* ănhēlus. *Divine (i. e. as of inspiration),* dīvīnus, coelestis.—2. See ventus.

flētus, ûs. *Weeping.*—EP. *Abundant,* largus. *Sad,* tristis, mĭser –ĕri, mĭsĕr-abĭlis.

flexus, ûs. *A bending.*—EP. *Crooked, winding,* sĭnuōsus, curvus. *Long,* longus. *Sudden,* sŭbĭtus.

Flōra. *The Goddess of flowers.*—EP. *Beautiful,* pulchra, formōsa, dĕcōra, can-dĭda. *Wearing a garland,* cŏrōnāta. *Bountiful,* bĕnigna.

flos, ōris, masc. *A flower.*—EP. *Purple, rosy, etc.,* purpŭreus, rōseus. *Bloom-ing,* vĭrens. *Flourishing in spring, summer, etc.,* vernus, æstīvus. *Varied,* vărius. *With rich colours,* pictus. *Withered,* marcĭdus, marcens. *Gathered,* lectus.

fluctus, ûs. *A wave.*—EP. *Of the sea,* æquŏreus. *Ebbing and flowing,* rēfluus, rēfluens. *White, foaming,* albus, albens, cānus, spūmeus, spūmōsus. *Swelling, stormy,* tŭmĭdus, prōcellōsus, insānus, fūriōsus, turbĭdus. *Vast,* magnus, ingens, immŏdĭcus. *Roaring, hoarse,* raucus, rēsŏnus, frĕmens.

fluentum, flūmen, Ĭnis, neut. **flūvius.** *A river.*—EP. *Rapid,* răpĭdus. *Violent,* vĭŏlentus. *Descending from the mountains,* montānus. *Swollen,* tŭmĭdus, tŭmens. *Cool,* frĭgĭdus, gĕlĭdus. *Deep,* altus. *Full of fish,* piscōsus. *Pebbly,* lăpĭdōsus. *Clear, pure,* līquĭdus, pūrus. *Blue,* cærŭleus, cærulus. *Gentle, tranquil,* lēnis, quiētus. *Murmuring,* lēne sŏnans. *Brawling,* raucus, strĕpens.

fŏcus. *A hearth.*—EP. *Bright, shining,* splendĭdus, mĭcans. *With lighted fire,* accensus, igneus, flammeus. *Warm,* călĭdus. *Cheerful,* lætus. *Inherited from one's ancestors,* pătrius, ă-ītus. *Simple, humble,* simplex –ĭcis, hŭmĭlis.

fœdus, ĕris, neut. *A treaty, an agreement.*—EP. *Social,* sŏcium. *Faithful,* fīdum, fĭdēle. *Ratified, certain,* rătum, certum. *Lasting,* stăbĭle, mansūrum. *Sacred,* săcrum, sanctum. *Agreed upon,* plăcĭtum, compŏsĭtum, pactum.

fœnum. *Hay.*—EP. *Dry,* siccum, ārĭdum. *Light,* lĕve.

fœnus, ōris, neut. *Usury.*—EP. *Greedy,* ăvĭdum, răpax. *Unjust,* injustum, ĭnīquum. *Costly,* prĕtiōsum.

fŏlium. *A leaf.*—EP. *Green,* vĭrĭde, vĭrens, vĭrĭdans. *Thick,* densum. *Shady,* umbrōsum, ŏpācum. *Light,* lĕve. *Falling, perishable,* cădūcum. *Of a tree,* arbŏreum. *Of oak, of beech, etc.,* quernum, fāgineum, *etc. Soft,* molle. *Trembling, quivering,* trĕmŭlum, mōbĭle. *Grey (of a willow, etc.),* glaucum.

follis, is, masc. *A pair of bellows.*—EP. *Large,* magnus, ingens. *Made of bulls' hide,* taurīnus.

fōmes, Ĭtis, masc. *Fuel.*—EP. *Dry,* siccus, ārĭdus. *Abundant,* largus. *Col-lected,* collectus, congestus.

fons, ontis. *A fountain.*—EP. *Pure, glassy,* pūrus, vĭtreus, lūcĭdus, argenteus, splendĭdus. *Free from mud,* illīmis. *Ever running,* pĕrennis. *Moist,* irrĭ-guus, ūdus, līquĭdus. *Mossgrown,* muscōsus. *Surrounded with grass,* grāmĭ-neus, herbōsus. *Sacred,* săcer –cri, săcrātus. *Brawling,* lŏquax. *Cool,* frĭgĭdus, gĕlĭdus.

fŏrāmen, Ĭnis, neut. *A hole.*—EP. *Hollow,* căvum.

forceps, Ĭpis, masc. *A pair of pincers.*—EP. *Tenacious,* tĕnax. *Hard,* dūrus. *Iron,* ferreus, ferrātus.

fŏri, ōrum, plur. masc. *The seats for rowers.*—EP. *Long,* longi. *Arranged,* pŏsĭti.

fŏris, is, fem. *A door,* usu. in plur.—EP. *External,* externa. *Open, opening, wide,* pătens, pătŭla. See porta.

D 3

38 FOR—FRO

forma. 1. *Form.*—2. *Beauty.*—EP. 1. *Various*, vâria. 1, 2. *Slight*, grăcĭlis. *Elegant*, ĕlĕgans. *Handsome*, pulchra, dĕcŏra, spĕcĭŏsa, spectabĭlis. *Lovely*, ămābĭlis. *Marvellous*, mîra. *Divine*, dîvîna.—2. *Perishable*, *short-lived*. brĕvis, frăgĭlis, cădûca. *Useless*, vâna, ĭnânia, ĭnûtĭlis. *Feminine*, *of a girl*, etc., fœmĭnea, virgĭnea, puellâria.

formîca. *An ant.*—EP. *Little*, parva, parvŭla, exĭgua. *Industrious*, sĕdŭla, ŏpĕrōsa, lăbŏriōsa. *Provident*, prŏvĭda, prŭdens. *Gathering in corn*, frūgĭlĕga.

formīdo, ĭnis, fem. *Fear.* See timor.

fornax, ācis, fem. *A furnace.*—EP. *Fiery, flaming*, ignea, flammans, flammea, flammīfĕra, ardens. *Black*, ātra, nĭgra. *Glowing*, rŭtĭla. *Smoking*, fŭmea, fûmōsa.

fornix, ĭcis, masc. *A vault, or arch.*—EP. *Lofty*, altus, arduus. *Concave*, căvus, concăvus, convexus. *Ceiled*, lăqueātus.

fortūna. *Fortune (often personified as the goddess).*—EP. *Favourable*, făvens, sĕcunda, dextĕra, sync. dextra. *Rich*, dîves –ĭtis, lŏcûples –ētis, ŏpŭlenta. *Happy*, fēlix, beâta, fausta. *Ancient*, prisca, vĕtus –eris, antīqua. *Variable*, *treacherous*, vâria, incerta, mûtābĭlis, mŏbĭlis, perfĭda, infĭda, fallax. *Unfavourable*, adversa, inĭqua. *Unhappy*, infēlix, tristis, mĭsĕra, mĭsĕranda, flēbĭlis. *Cruel*, sæva, immĭtis, aspĕra. *Blind*, cæca.

fŏrum. 1. *The market-place.*—2. *The bar.*—EP. 1, 2. *Full*, plēnum. *Hoarse*, *noisy*, raucum, clāmōsum.— 2. *Eloquent*, dĭsertum, fâcundum, ēlŏquens. *Litigious*, lĭtĭgiōsum.

fossa. *A ditch or trench.*—EP. *Deep*, alta, prŏfunda. *Wide*, lâta. *Wet*, ûda.

fossor, ōris, masc. *A digger.*—EP. *Hardy*, dûrus, rŏbustus. *Industrious*, ŏpĕrōsus. *Rustic*, rustĭcus, ăgrestis.

fŏvea. *A pit.*—EP. *Deep*, alta, prŏfunda. *Deceitful*, fallax. *Hostile*, ĭnimîca.

frænum, acc. plur., fræna and frænos. *A bridle.*—EP. *Which holds back*, tĕnax, mŏrans, rĕmŏrans. *Hard*, *severe*, dûrum, rĭgĭdum, sĕvērum. *Unwelcome*, invîsum, ŏdiōsum. *Covered with foam*, spûmeum, spûmōsum, spûmans. *With a bit affixed to it*, lŭpâtum.

frâga, ōrum, plur. neut. *Strawberries.*—EP. *Growing low*, hŭmĭlia, hŭmi nascentia. *Rosy*, rŏsea, rŭbra, rŭberstia. *Sweet*, dulcia. *Of summer*, æstîva.

fragmen, ĭnis, neut., fragmentum. *A fragment, a piece broken off.*—EP. *Small*, parvum, exĭguum. *Large*, ingens, magnum. *Rough*, aspĕrum. *Thrown down*, dējectum.

frăgor, ōris, masc. *A loud noise (as of anything breaking).*—EP. *Hoarse*, raucus. *Great*, ingens, magnus. *Sudden*, sŭbĭtus. See sonus.

frâter, tris, masc. *A brother.*—EP. *Beloved*, cârus, dîlectus, ămâtus. *Agreeing with one*, ûnănĭmis, concors –dis.

fraus, dis, fem. *Deceit.*—EP. *Dishonest*, *wicked*, măla, imprŏba, inĭqua, scĕlĕrata. *Treacherous*, dŏlōsa, subdŏla, infĭda, fallax, perfĭda. *Base*, turpis, infâmis. *Mischievous*, noxia, nŏcens, pernĭciōsa. *Discovered*, rĕperta.

fraxĭnus, i, fem. *An ash-tree.*—EP. *Tall*, alta, ardua, prŏcēra. *Leafy*, frondens, frondea, frondōsa. *Green*, vĭrĭdis. *Late coming into leaf*, sēra. *Hard*, dûra.

frĕmĭtus, ûs, frĕmor, ōris, masc. *A loud roaring noise.*—EP. *Hoarse*, raucus, *Angry*, irâtus, fûriōsus. *Of shouting*, clāmōsus. See sonus.

frĕquentia. *A crowd.* See turba.

frĕtum. 1. *A strait.*—2. *The sea.*—EP. 1. *Narrow*, angustum, arctum. *Unquiet*, turbĭdum, sollĭcĭtum. *Roaring*, frĕmens, raucum. *Boiling up*, æstuans, exæstuans, æstuosum.—2. See mare.

frîgus, ōris, neut. *Cold.*—EP. *Coming from the north*, Hÿberbŏreum, Bŏreâle. *Icy*, glăciâle. *Wintry*, hÿbernum, hĭĕmâle, brûmâle. *Stormy*, prŏcellōsum. *Causing torpor*, iners, segne, pĭgrum. *Causing trembling*, trĕmŭlum. *Continual*, assĭduum, perpĕtuum. *Pleasant (when meaning modified coolness)*, ămābĭle, ămœnum, dulce, jûcundum.

frondâtor, ōris, masc. *A woodman.*—EP. *Hardy*, dûrus, rŏbustus. *Carrying an axe*, sĕcûrĭger –ĕri. *Strong*, fortis, vălĭdus.

frons, dis, fem. 1. *A leaf.*—2. *A branch.*—EP. 1, 2. *Thick*, densa, plurĭma. *Green*, vĭrĭdis, vĭrĭdans, vĭrens. *Lofty*, alta, ardua. *Shady*, umbrōsa, ŏpâca. *Of oak, of beech, etc.*, querna, rŏbŏrea, fâginea, etc.

FRO—FUR 39

frons, tis, fem. *A forehead, a face.*—EP. *Fair, beautiful,* candĭda, pulchra, dĕcōra. *Noble-looking,* nōbĭlis, ēgrĕgia. See facies.

fructus, ûs. *Fruit, produce.*—EP. *Abundant,* largus, amplus, ûber –ĕris, lætus. *Wished for, hoped for,* optātus, exoptātus, spērātus. *Future,* fūtūrus. *Deserved,* mĕrĭtus. *Yearly,* annuus. *Ripening in summer, or autumn,* æstīvus, autumnālis. *Given,* dătus. *Flourishing,* flōrens.

frūgis, gen. sing. fem.; *more usu. in plur.* **frūges;** see Gradus. *The fruit of the earth, corn.*—EP. *Sacred to Ceres,* Cĕreālia. *Ripening each year,* annua. *Fertile,* fertīlis, fēcunda, fērax. *Yellow (when ripe),* flāva, aurea. *New, gathered this year,* horna. *Wheaten,* trĭtĭcea. *Abundant, large,* læta.

frūmentum. *Corn.* See above.

frustum. *A piece, a slice.*—EP. *Small,* parvum, exĭguum.

frūtex, ĭcis, masc. *A shrub.*—EP. *Lowly,* hŭmĭlis. *Thick,* densus. *Green,* vĭrĭdis, vĭrĭdans, vĭrens. *Rough,* asper –ĕri.

frūtĭcētum. *A shrubbery, a coppice.* See above.

fūcus. *A dye (esp. of purple).* See purpura.

fūcus. *A drone.*—EP. *Lazy,* segnis, ignāvus, ĭners. *Unarmed,* ĭnermis, imbellis. *Useless,* ĭnūtĭlis.

fŭga. *Flight.*—EP. *Rapid,* răpĭda, vēlox. *Timid, frightened,* tĭmĭda, terrĭta, perterrĭta. *Sudden,* sûbĭta. *Safe,* tûta, incŏlŭmis. *Prudent,* prūdens. *Base,* turpis, infāmis, indĕcōra. *Uncowrlike,* imbellis.

fulcĭmen, ĭnis, neut.; **fulcrum.** *A prop.*—EP. *Strong,* firmum, vălĭdum. *Safe,* tūtum, incŏlŭme.

fulgor, ōris, masc. *Brightness.*—EP. *Brilliant,* clārus, splendĭdus. *Brilliant, or quivering,* cōruscus, mĭcans. *Quivering,* trĕmŭlus. *Ethereal,* æthĕrius. *Fiery, glowing,* igneus, ardens, rŭtĭlus. *Golden,* aureus.

fulgur, ŭris, neut. *Lightning.*—EP. *Fiery, glowing, etc.,* igneus, rŭtĭlum, cōruscum, flāgrans. *Forked,* trĭfĭdum, bĭfĭdum, bĭsulcum. *Sacred,* săcrum, dĭvīnum, cœleste. *Angry,* īrācundum, īrātum. *Terrible,* dīrum, mĕtuendum, trĕmendum, horrendum, terrĭbĭle. *Cruel,* sævum, fērum, crūdĕle. *Destructive,* exĭtiāle, exĭtiōsum, fătāle. *Hurled down,* tortum, dēmissum, immissum.

fulmen, ĭnis, neut. *The thunderbolt.*—EP. *Falling,* cădŭcum. *Inevitable,* ĭnēvĭtābĭle. *Invincible,* invictum, indŏmĭtum. *Wrought by Vulcan or the Cyclops,* Vulcānium, Cȳclōpium; see above, fulgur.

fūmus. *Smoke.*—EP. *Black,* āter –tri, nĭger –gri, pĭceus. *Dense,* densus. *Waving,* undans. *Slow,* tardus. *Hot,* călĭdus. *Dark, darkening,* obscūrus, ŏpācus.

fūnāle. *A torch.* See fax.

funda. *A sling.*—EP. *Used in the Balearic isles,* Bălĕāris, Bălĕārĭca. *With sure aim,* certa. *Distant, starting at a distance,* longinqua. *Made of cord,* stuppea. *Revolving,* rĕvŏlūbĭlis. *Whirled round,* intorta.

fundāmen, ĭnis, neut.; **fundāmentum.** *A foundation.*—EP. *Firm, stable,* firmum, stăbĭle. *Solid,* sŏlĭdum. *Of stone,* saxeum. *Adamantine, i. e. strong, lasting, etc.,* ădămantīnum. *Deep,* altum. *The first,* prīmum.

fundus. 1. *The bottom.*—2. *A farm.*—EP. 1. *The lowest,* īmus.—2. *Fertile,* fertīlis, fērax, fēcundus, pinguis, lætus. *Cultivated,* cultus. See ager.

fūnis, is, masc. *A rope.*—EP. *Hempen,* stuppeus. *Strong,* vălĭdus, firmus. *Holding fast,* tĕnax. *Stretched,* contentus.

fūnus, ĕris. 1. *A funeral.*—2. *Death.*—EP. 1. See exsequiæ.—2. See mors.

fur, fūris, masc. *A thief.*—EP. *Wicked,* mălus, imprŏbus, ĭnīquus, injustus. *Base,* turpis, infāmis. *Cruel,* sævus, fērus, immītis, trux trŭcis. *Violent,* vĭŏlentus. *Rapacious,* răpax, ăvĭdus.

furca. *A pitchfork.*—EP. *With two prongs,* bĭcornis. *Iron,* ferrea, ferrāta. *Rustic,* rustĭca, ăgrestis.

Fūriæ, ārum, plur. fem. *The Furies.* (See the Gradus).—EP. *Three,* Tres, ternæ, tergĕmĭnæ. *Infernal,* Infernæ, Stȳgiæ, Tartăreæ. *Causing grief,* luctĭfĭcæ. *Avenging,* ultrīces. *Black,* ātræ, nĭgræ. *Cruel,* sævæ, fēræ, immītes, crūdēles. *With snaky hair,* anguĭcōmæ. *Threatening,* mĭnāces.

furnus. *An oven.*—EP. *Hot,* călĭdus, ardens. *Making a noise,* strĭdens. *Kindled,* accensus.

fŭror, ōris, masc. *Fury, madness.*—EP. *Insane,* insānus, vēsānus, āmens, dēmens, răbĭdus. *Sudden,* sûbĭtus, rĕpentīnus. *Vast,* præceps –ĭpĭtis, tĕmĕ-

D 4

40 FUR—GER

rārius. *Improvident, blind,* cæcus. *Unbridled,* effrænus, infrænis. *Wicked,*
impius, scĕlĕrātus, ĭnīquus. *Horrible,* horrĭdus, horrĭbĭlis. *Pitiless,* immītis.
furtum. *Theft.*—EP. *Wicked,* impius, imprŏbus, ĭnīquum, scĕlĕrātum. *Base,*
turpe. *Concealed,* occultum, sēcrētum. *Crafty,* callīdum, versūtum, dŏlōsum.
fuscīna. *A trident.* See tridens.
fustis, is, masc. *A club.*—EP. *Great,* magnus, ingens. *Heavy,* grăvis. *Made
of oak,* rŏbŏreus, quernus. *Avenging,* vindex –ĭcis.
fūsus. *A spindle.*—EP. *Smooth and round,* tĕres –ĕtis. *Turning round,*
vŏlūbĭlis, rĕvŏlūbĭlis. *Turned round (in use),* i. e. *being used,* versātus. *Full,*
plēnus. *Rapid,* răpĭdus, vēlox. *Moving continually,* assĭduus. *Used by
women, or girls,* fœmĭneus, mŭliĕbris, virgĭneus, puellāris.

G.

Gălea. *A helmet.*—EP. *Brazen,* ærea, ærāta, ahēna, ahĕnea. *Hollow,* căva.
Crested, cristāta, cŏmans. *Waving,* nūtans. *Terrible,* dīra, terrĭbĭlis. *Glitter-
ing,* cŏruscs, mĭcans, fulgens, splendĭda. *Warlike,* bellĭca, Martia, Māvortia.
Wrought by Vulcan (as that of Æneas or Achilles), Vulcānia.
gălĕrus. *A hat.*—EP. *Soft,* mollis.
gallīna. *A hen.*—EP. *Prolific,* fēcunda.
gallus. *A cock.*—EP. *Crested,* cristātus. *Warlike,* pugnax, Martius, Māvortius.
Hoarse, raucus. *Wakeful,* vigil –ĭlis, pervigil. *Early in the morning,* mātū-
tīnus.
garrŭlĭtas. *Talkativeness.*—EP. *Incessant,* assĭdua, perpĕtua. *Hoarse,* rauca.
Unwearied, indēfessa.
gaudium. *Joy.*—EP. *Happy (of good omen),* fēlix, lætum, faustum. *New,*
nŏvum. *Unusual,* insŏlĭtum. *Trembling, causing trepidation,* trĕpĭdum. *Sud-
den, unexpected,* sŭbĭtum, rĕpentīnum, ĭnŏpīnum, nĕcŏpīnum. *Present,*
præsens. *Future,* fŭtūrum, ventūrum.
gĕlu, indecl. *Ice.*—EP. *Hard,* dūrum, rĭgĭdum. *Solidified,* sŏlĭdum, astrictum.
See frigus, glacies.
gĕmĭtus, us. *A groan.*—EP. *Sad,* tristis, mĭser –ĕri, mĭsĕrābĭlis. *Great,*
magnus, ingens. *Deep,* altus, prŏfundus. *Vain,* vānus. ĭnānis. *Heavy,* grăvis.
Continual, frequent, assĭduus, crēber –bri, perpĕtuus.
gemma. 1. *A jewel.*—2. *A bud.*—EP. 1. *Valuable,* prĕtiōsa. *Eastern, Indian,
etc.,* "Eōa, Inda, Indĭca. *Brilliant,* lūcĭda, splendĭda, clāra, līquĭda. *Beau-
tiful, ornamental,* insignis, dĕcŏra. *Hanging down,* pendŭla, dēmissa.— 2.
Swelling, tŭmens, turgĭda. *Green,* virĭdis. *Bursting in spring,* verna.
gĕnæ, arum, plur. fem. *The cheeks.*—EP. *Rosy,* rŏseæ. *Fair, beautiful,* can-
dĭdæ, candentes, nĭveæ, pulchræ, dĕcŏræ. *Youthful, beardless,* imberbes,
intonsæ. *Of a damsel,* virgĭneæ, puellāres.
gĕner, ĕri. *A son-in-law.*—EP. *Wished for, desirable,* optātus, optābĭlis. *Loved,*
cārus, ămātus, dĭlectus. *Faithful,* fīdus, fĭdēlis.
gĕnĕtrix. *A mother.* See mater.
gĕnista. *The broom-plant.*—EP. *Lowly,* hŭmĭlis. *Flexible,* lenta.
gĕnĭtor. *A father.* See pater.
gens, tis. 1. *A family.*—2. *A nation.*—EP. 1, 2. *Noble,* nōbĭlis, gĕnĕrōsa.
Brave, fortis, impăvĭda, vălĭda. *Ancient,* antīqua, vĕtus –ĕris. *Illustrious,*
clāra, insignis, inclўta. *Warlike,* bellĭca, Martia, Māvortia. *Faithful,* fĭda,
fĭdēlis.
gĕnu, in sing. indecl. plur. **genua.** *A knee.*—EP. *Strong,* forte, vălĭdum.
Bending down, bent, falling to the ground (esp. in entreaty), submissum, dēmissum,
prōnum, succĭduum, pŏsĭtum.
gĕnus, ĕris, neut. *Birth, race.*—EP. *Lofty,* altum, gĕnĕrōsum, nōbĭle. *Lowly,*
hŭmĭle, ignōtum.
germen, ĭnis, neut. *A bud, a shoot.*—EP. *Swelling, rising,* tŭmĭdum, tumens,
turgĭdum, nascens. *New,* nŏvum. *Green,* virĭde, vĭrens. *Productive,* fertĭle,
fĕrax, fēcundum. *Seasonable,* tempestīvum. *Seasonable, ripe,* mātūrum. *Ap-
pearing in spring,* vernum. *Of a tree,* arbŏreum.

GES—GRE   41

gestāmen, ĭnis, neut. *Anything worn.*—EP. *Noted*, nōtum, insigne. *Splendid*, splendĭdum, clārum.

gestus, ûs. *Gesture.*—EP. *Becoming*, dĕcens, dĕcōrus. *Well-known, customary*, nōtus, sŏlĭtus. *Silent*, tăcĭtus.

gĭgas, antis, masc. *A giant.*—EP. *Earthborn*, terrĭgĕna, terrēnus. *Vast*, ingens, magnus. *Terrible*, terrĭbĭlis, trĕmendus, dīrus. *Fierce, cruel*, fērus, fĕrox, crūdēlis, sævus, immītis. *Lofty, tall*, altus, prōcērus. See Gradus.

glăcies. *Ice.*—EP. *Slippery*, lūbrĭca. *Rough, sharp*, aspĕra, ăcūta. *Wintry*, byĕmālis, hȳberna, brūmālis. *Brought by the north wind, from the north, northern*, Bŏreālis, Hȳberbŏrea, Arctōa. *Solid*, sŏlĭda. See gelu.

glădius. *A sword.* See ensis.

glans, dis, fem. 1. *An acorn.*—2. *A bullet.*—EP. 1. *From an oak*, querna, rŏbŏrea, iligna. *Abounding in Chaonia, Epirus*, Chăŏnia. *Nutritious*, alma. *Useful*, ūtĭlis. *Unsubstantial*, tĕnuis.—2. *Causing wounds*, vulnĭfĭca. *Deadly*, fătālis, lētĭfĕra. *Terrible*, dīra, terrĭbĭlis, mĕtuenda. *Unerring*, certa.

glārea. *Gravel.*—EP. *Yellow*, flāva, lūtea. *Barren*, stĕrĭlis, jējūna. *Hard*, dūra.

glēba. *A lump of earth, soil.* See terra.

glis, glīris, masc. *A dormouse.*—EP. *Sleepy*, somnĭcŭlōsus. *Lazy*, segnis, iners, ignāvus.

glōria. *Glory.*—EP. *Splendid, celebrated*, splendĭda, clāra, ēgrĕgia, insignis. *Honourable*, hŏnesta. *Immortal*, immortālis, æterna, pĕrennis. *Transitory*, brĕvis, cădūca. *Vain*, vāna, ĭnānis, ventōsa. *Ancient*, prisca, vĕtus –ĕris, antīqua, pristīna. *Late*, sēra. *Surviving its subjects*, sŭperstes –ĭtis.

glūten, ĭnis, neut. *Glue.*—EP. *Sticky*, tĕnax. *Thick*, densum.

Gorgon, ŏnis, fem. *A Gorgon.*—EP. *Terrible*, dīra, terrĭbĭlis, horrĭbĭlis, horrĭda. *Unsightly*, turpis, dēformis, fœda. *Ill-omened*, obscœna. *With snaky hair*, anguĭcŏma. See Gradus.

grācŭlus. *A jackdaw.*—EP. *Black*, nĭger –gri, āter –tri. *Greedy (esp. with ref. to fruit)*, ĕdax, ăvĭdus. *Prophetic (of rain*, etc.), præsāgus, prænuntius.

grădus, ûs. *A step.*—EP. *Rapid*, răpĭdus, cītus. *Long, great*, longus, magnus, ingens. *Slow*, tardus, pĭger –gri.

Græcia. *Greece.*—EP. *Brave*, fortis, impăvĭda. *Warlike*, bellīca, Martia, Māvortia. *Powerful*, pŏtens. *Learned*, docta. *Renowned*, inclȳta, clāra, præclāra, insignis. *Reigned over by Pelops or Agamemnon, or Achilles, or Inachus*, etc., Pĕlŏpēa, Ăgămemnŏnia, Ăchillēa, Ĭnăchia, etc.

grāmen, ĭnis, neut. *Grass.*—EP. *Lowly*, hŭmĭle, ignōbĭle. *Green*, vĭrĭde, vĭrĭdans, virens. *Abundant fertile*, lætum, fĕrax, fertīle. *Soft*, molle, tĕnĕrum. *Mossy*, muscōsum. *Moist, irrigated*, ūdum, irrĭguum. *Shaded*, umbrōsum.

grānārium. *A granary.*—EP. *Full*, plēnum. *Yellow (full of yellow corn)*, flāvum, aureum. *Safe*, tūtum.

grando, ĭnis, fem. *Hail.*—EP. *Terrible*, dīra, terrĭbĭlis. *Cruel*, sæva, fēra. *Heavy*, grăvis. *Poured forth*, effūsa, immissa. *Poured down*, dēmissa. *Destructive*, damnōsa, nŏcens, noxia, pernĭciōsa.

grānum. *A grain.*—EP. *Ripe*, mātūrum. *Yellow*, flāvum, aureum. *Of wheat*, trĭtĭceum. *Sacred to Ceres*, Cĕreāle.

grātes, ium, plur. fem. *Thanks.* See below.

Grātia. 1. *The Grace, one of the Graces.*—2. *Grace, elegance.*—3. *Gratitude, thanks.*—EP. 1. *Triple*, terna, tergĕmĭna, trĭplex –ĭcis. *United*, juncta. *Naked*, nūda.—1, 2. *Beautiful*, dĕcens, dĕcōra, spĕciōsa, ēgrĕgia. *Fair*, can-dĭda. *Modest, chaste*, pŭdīca, casta.—2. *Simple*, simplex –ĭcis.—3. *Just*, justa, æqua, mĕrĭta, dēbĭta, digna. *Willing*, lĭbens. *Pious*, pia. *Lasting*, æterna, pĕrennis, perpĕtua. *Mindful*, mĕmor. *Enduring after the action*, sŭperstes –ĭtis.

grăvĭtas. *Heaviness.*—EP. *Great, excessive*, magna, nĭmia. *Irksome*, tristis, mŏdesta.

grĕmium. *The bosom, the lap.*—EP. *Tender*, tĕnĕrum, molle. *Dear*, cārum, ămātum. *Wished for*, optātum.

gressus, ûs. *A step.* See Gradus.

grex, grĕgis, masc. *A flock.*—EP. *Woolly*, lānĭger –ĕri. *Unwarlike, timid*, imbellis, inermis, tĭmĭdus. See ovis.

42 GRU—HIA

grus, gruis, fem. *A crane.*—EP. *Flying high,* äëria, sŭblīmis, alta. *Haunting the Strymon,* Strȳmŏnia. *Crying loud,* clāmŏsa.
gŭbernātor -ōris, masc. *A steerer.*—EP. *Prudent,* prŭdens, cautus. *Skilful,* doctus, pĕrītus.
gurges, ĭtis, masc. *A whirlpool.*—EP. *Swelling,* tŭmĭdus, tŭmens. *Unquiet,* turbĭdus, æstuŏsus, inquiĕtus. *Roaring,* raucus. *Deep,* altus, prŏfundus. *Devouring,* răpax, ăvĭdus. *Terrible,* dīrus, terrĭbĭlis, mĕtuendus, trĕmendus.
gutta. *A drop.*—EP. *Little,* parva, exĭgua. *Light,* lĕvis. *Falling,* cădūca.
gȳrus. *A circle (esp. one caused by motion).*—EP. *Curved,* curvus, incurvus, rĕcurvus, sĭnuŏsus. *Great,* magnus, ingens. *High,* altus.

H.

Hăbēna. *A rein.*—EP. *Retarding,* lenta, mŏdĕrans. *Loose, hanging,* undans, laxa. *Light,* lĕvis. *Given (to the horse, so that he may go fast),* admissa, concessa, dăta. *Drawn tight,* adducta, pressa, suppressa.
hăbĭtus, ûs. *Condition, state.* See conditio.
hædus, hædŭlus, hædŭlea. *A kid.*—EP. *Wanton, frisking,* lascīvus, prŏtervus. *Butting,* pĕtulans. *Horned,* cornĭger, ĕri. *With horny feet,* cornĭpes –ĕdis. *Playful, playing,* lūdens. *Tender, young,* tĕner –ĕri.
hālĭtus, ûs. *Breath.* See spiritus.
hāmus. *A hook.*—EP. *Hidden,* abdĭtus, occultus, tectus. *Deceitful,* fallax, dŏlōsus. *Hooked,* uncus, ăduncus, curvus, rĕcurvus. *Cruel,* sævus, fĕrus, immītis.
hăra. *A pigstye.*—EP. *Dirty,* immunda, fœda, turpis.
hăruspex, ĭcis. *A soothsayer.* See augur, vates.
hasta. *A spear.*—EP. *Brazen,* ærea, ærāta, abĕnea, ahēna. *Whistling,* stridens, strīdŭla. *Hurled,* missa, immissa, intorta, acta. *Piercing a man,* transfixa. *Quivering,* trĕmĕbunda. *Sharp,* ăcūta. *Mighty, powerful,* magna, ingens, vălĭda. *With ashen shaft,* fraxĭnea. *Warlike,* bellīca, Martia, Māvortia. *Bloody,* sanguĭnea, sanguĭnŏlenta, cruenta. *Hostile,* hostīlis, hostīca, adversa.
haustus, ûs. *A draught.*—EP. *Pure,* pūrus. *Liquid,* lĭquĭdus. *Deep,* altus. *Cool,* frĭgĭdus, gĕlĭdus.
hĕdĕra. *Ivy.*—EP. *Easily twined,* lenta, făcĭlis, nexĭlis, flexĭpes –ĕdis. *Pale,* pallens, pallĭda. *Sacred to Bacchus,* Bacchīca, Bacchĕa, Bacchēia. *Bearing berries,* cŏrymbĭfĕra. *Green,* virĭdis, virĭdans, virens.
Hĕlĭcoon, ōnis, masc. *A mountain in Bœotia sacred to the Muses.*—EP. *Sacred,* săcer –cri. *Theban,* Thēbānus. *Shady,* umbrōsus. *Haunted by the Virgin Muses,* Virgĭneus. *Struck by the hoof of Pegasus, the horse of Bellerophon,* Pĕgăseus.
hĕra. *The mistress of a house.*—EP. *Kind, gentle,* bĕnigna, bŏna, mītis. *Proud, arrogant,* sŭperba, arrŏgans. *New,* nŏva.
herba. 1. *Any herb.*—2. *Grass.*—EP. 1, 2. *Green,* virĭdis, virĭdans, virens. *Cut down, gathered,* dēmessa. 1. *Wholesome,* sălūtāris. *Unwholesome,* nŏcens, pestĭfĕra.
hĕres, ēdis, masc. fem. *An heir, heiress.*—EP. *Kindred,* cognātus. *Unknown,* prŏpinquus. *Last,* ultĭmus, sŭprēmus, extrēmus. *Unworthy,* indignus, immĕrĭtus. *Prodigal,* prŏdĭgus. *Forgetful,* immĕmor –ōris.
hēros –ōis, plur. ōēs, etc. *A hero.*—EP. *Divine,* Dīvīnus. *Celebrated,* inclȳtus, clārus, præclārus, cĕlĕber –bris. *Brave,* fortis, impăvĭdus. *Ancient,* vĕtus –ĕris, priscus, antīquus. *Magnanimous,* magnănĭmus. *Trojan, Greek, Roman,* etc., Dardănius, Ăchīvus, Rōmānus, Ītălus, etc.
hĕrus. *A master of a house, or of servants.* See hera.
Hespĕrus. *The Evening star.*—EP. *Silvery,* argenteus. *Pale,* pallĭdus. *Late,* sĕrus. *Wished for,* optātus, expectātus. *Cool,* frĭgĭdus. See vesper.
hiātus, ûs. *An opening.*—EP. *Vast,* vastus, ingens, immānis. *Open,* pătens. *Black, dark,* ăter –tri, obscūrus. *Dire,* dīrus, horrĭbĭlis.

HIB — HYE   43

hĭbiscum. *Marshmallow.*—EP. *Green,* vĭrĭde. *Moist,* ûdum, mădĭdum. *Lowly,* hŭmĭle.

hinnītus, ûs. *Neighing.*—EP. *Loud, shrill,* clārus, ăcūtus. *Usual,* sŏlĭtus. *Known, familiar,* nōtus.

hinnŭleus. *A fawn.*—EP. *Playful,* prŏtervus, lascīvus. *Young, tender,* tĕner –ĕri. *Timid, induced to flee,* tĭmĭdus, fŭgax. See curvus.

hircus. *A goat.*—EP. *Horned,* cornĭger –ĕri. *With horny feet,* cornĭpes –ĕdis. *Strong-smelling,* ŏlens. *Foul,* fœdus. *Bearded,* barbātus. *Shaggy,* villōsus.

hĭrūdo, ĭnis, fem. *A leech.*—EP. *Greedy,* ăvĭda, vŏrax. *Bloody,* sanguĭnea, sanguĭnŏlenta. *Found in marshes,* pălūdōsa, pălustris.

hĭrundo, ĭnis, fem. *A swallow.*—EP. *Migratory, foreign,* pĕrĕgrīna. *Twittering, tuneful,* argūta, vōcālis, garrŭla. *Swift,* răpĭda, præpes –ĕtis, vēlox. *Daulian,* Daulias. *Herald of spring,* vēris prænuntia. See Progne in the Gradus.

Hispānia. *Spain.*—EP. *Most distant (the ancients looked upon Spain as the extreme end of the world on the western side),* ultīma, extrēma. *Brave,* fortis, impăvĭda, ănĭmosa. *Generous,* gĕnĕrōsa. *Unconquered,* invicta, indŏmĭta. *Producing gold,* aurĭfĕra. *Rich,* dives –ĭtis, ŏpŭlenta.

Histŏria. *History.*—EP. *Faithful,* fĭdēlis, fīda. *Mindful,* mĕmor –ŏris. *Learned,* docta.

histrio, ōnis, masc. *An actor.*—EP. *Skilful,* doctus, pĕrītus, callĭdus.

hŏmo, ĭnis. *A man, a human being.*—EP. *Shortlived,* brĕvis, cădūcus, frăgĭlis. *Mortal,* mortalis. See vir, femina.

hŏnor, ōris, masc. *Honour.*—EP. *Eternal, undying,* æternus, immortālis, pĕrennis. *Illustrious,* clārus, insignis. *Deserved,* mĕrĭtus, dignus. *Surviving the person,* sŭperstes –ĭtis.

hōra. *An hour.*—EP. *Brief,* brĕvis. *Soon passing,* vŏlātĭlis, mōbĭlis. *Irrevocable,* irrĕvŏcābĭlis.

hordeum. *Barley.*—EP. *Rough, bearded,* hirsūtum, barbātum. *Yellow (when ripe),* flāvum, aureum.

horreum. *A barn.*—EP. *Full,* plēnum, ŏnustum. *Safe,* tūtum.

horror, ōris, masc. *Fear, trembling.*—EP. *Making one feel cold,* frĭgĭdus, gĕlĭdus. See timor.

hortāmen, ĭnis, neut., hortātus, ûs. *Exhortation.*—EP. *Brave, spirited,* fortis, ănĭmōsus. *Long,* longus. *Prudent,* prūdens. *Wicked,* impium, scĕlĕrātum, inīquum.

hortator, ōris, masc. *An exhorter.* See above.

hortus. *A garden.*—EP. *Flowery,* flōrĭdus, flōreus, flōrens. *Variegated, full of various coloured flowers,* vărius, pictus. *Fertile,* fertĭlis, fēcundus, fĕrax, pinguis. *Cultivated,* cultus. *Well-watered,* irrĭguus. *Well-fenced,* septus.

hospes, ĭtis, masc. fem., also in fem. hospĭta. *1. A host or hostess.–2. A guest.* 1. *Kind, courteous, friendly,* bĕnignus, făcĭlis, mītis, ămīcus. *Generous,* gĕnĕrōsus. *Rich,* dives –ĭtis, lōcŭples –ĕtis, ŏpŭlentus. *Joined by hereditary ties,* pătrius, ăvītus. 1, 2. *Pleasant,* ămābĭlis, amœnus. *Joyful,* lætus. 2. *Acceptable,* acceptus, grātus. *Strange, foreign,* pĕrĕgrīnus, externus. *Safe,* tūtus, incŏlŭmis. *Wandering,* văgus. *Suppliant,* supplex –ĭcis.

hospĭtium. *Hospitality.* See above.

hostia. *A victim.* See victima.

hostis. *An enemy.*—EP. *Fierce, cruel,* fĕrus, sævus, crūdēlis, immītis. *Foreign, or fierce,* barbārus. *Foreign,* externus. *Distant,* longinquus, rĕmōtus. *Unknown,* ignōtus. *Terrible,* terrĭbĭlis, mĕtuendus, tĭmendus. *Brave, fearless,* fortis, ănĭmōsus, impăvĭdus, interrĭtus, imperterrĭtus. *Invincible,* invictus, indŏmĭtus. *Opposing,* adversus. *Angry, hostile,* īrātus, infensus.

hŭmĕrus. *A shoulder.*—EP. *Broad,* lātus. *Strong,* rōbustus, vălĭdus, nervōsus. tŏrōsus.

hūmor, ōris, masc. *Moisture.*—EP. *Wet,* irrĭguus. *Dropping,* stillans. *Genial (of rain, etc.),* almus.

hŭmus, fem. *The ground.* See terra.

hyăcinthus. *A hyacinth.*—EP. *Purple,* purpŭreus, ferrūgĭneus. *Eloquent,* făcundus. *Mournful,* lūgŭbris. See the Gradus.

hўdrops, ōpis, masc. *Dropsy.*—EP. *Thirsty,* sĭtĭcŭlosus, sĭtiens. *Terrible,* dīrus. *Incurable,* immĕdĭcābĭlis.

hyems, ĕmis, fem. 1. *Winter.–2. A storm.*—EP. *Cold, icy,* frĭgĭda, gĕlĭda,

44 HYS—IMB

glăciālis. *Coming from the North*, Arctŏa, Bŏrealis, Hўperbŏrea. *Causing torpor*, pĭgra, ĭners, segnis. *Unfruitful*, infēcunda, stĕrĭlis, infēlix. *Hated*, ŏdiōsa, invīsa. *Severe*, ācris, aspĕra, rĭgĭda, horrĭda, imprŏba, tristis. *Rainy*, ăquōsa, plŭvia, plŭviālis, nūbĭla. *Unsightly*, informis, squālĭda.—2. See procella.

hystrix, ĭcis, fem. *A porcupine*.—EP. *Prickly*, spĭnōsa.

I. J.

Jactātus, ûs. *A tossing about, a flapping (of wings)*.—EP. *Noisy*, rĕsŏnus, clāmōsus. *Frequent*, crēber, bri. *Rapid*, răpĭdus.

jactūra. *Loss*.—EP. *Sad*, tristis, mĭsĕra, mĭsĕrābĭlis. *Unexpected*, ĭnexspectāta, ĭnōpīna, nĕcōpīna. *Extreme*, extrēma, ultĭma.

jactus, ûs. *A throwing (esp. of darts, etc.)*.—EP. *Hostile*, hostīlis, hostĭcus. *Cruel*, saevus, fĕrus, crūdēlis. *Deadly*, fătālis, lētĭfer -ĕri. *Causing wounds*, vulnĭfĭcus. *Distant*, longinquus, rĕmōtus.

jăcŭlātor, ōris, masc. **jăcŭlātrix** -īcis, fem. *A thrower (esp. of darts), skilful*, doctus, pĕrītus. *Bold*, audax, fortis. *Safe*, tūtus, incŏlŭmis, illaesus. *Hostile*, hostīlis, hostĭcus, ĭnĭmīcus. *Unerring*, certus. *Cruel*, saevus, fĕrus, crūdēlis. *Distant*, longinquus, rĕmōtus.

jăcŭlum. *A dart, a javelin*.—EP. *With ashen shaft*, fraxĭneum. *Sharp*, ăcūtum. *Missile*, missĭle, vŏlātĭle. *Piercing*, pĕnĕtrābĭle. *Cruel*, saevum, fĕrum. *Hurled*, missum. *Quivering*, trĕmŭlum, trĕmĕbundum. *Iron*, ferreum.

jānĭtor, ōris, masc. *A doorkeeper*.—EP. *Severe*, dūrus, rĭgĭdus, sĕvērus. *Hated*, invīsus. *Faithful*, fĭdēlis, fĭdus. *Watchful*, vĭgil -ĭlis.

jānua. *A gate, a door*. See porta.

Ibis, ĭdis, fem. *A stork*.—EP. *Ægyptian*, Ægyptia, Nīlĭaca. *Gentle*, mītis. *Affectionate*, pia. *Sacred*, sācra, sācrāta, sancta.

ictus, ûs. *A blow*.—EP. *Cruel*, saevus, fĕrus. *Bloody*, cruentus. *Frequent*, crēber -bri. *Penetrating*, pĕnĕtrābĭlis. *Iron (i. e. from an iron weapon)*, ferreus. *Fatal*, fătālis, lētĭfer -eri.

jējūnium. *A fast*.—EP. *Long*, longum. *Painful*, triste. *Unwilling*, invītum.

ignāvia. *Idleness*.—EP. *Unproductive*, stĕrĭlis, ĭnūtĭlis. *Lazy*, segnis, pĭgra, ĭners. *Slow*, tarda. *Shameful*, turpis. *Ancient*, prisca.

ignis, is, masc. *Fire*.—EP. *Devouring*, ĕdax, răpax. *Sacred to Vulcan*, Vulcānius. *Rapid*, răpĭdus. *Kindled*, accensus. *Raging*, fŭrens, fŭriōsus. *Glowing*, rŭtĭlus. *Unextinguished*, ĭnexstinctus. *Invincible*, invictus.

ignōmĭnia. *Disgrace*.—EP. *Shameful*, turpis, foeda. *Undeserved*, immĕrĭta, indigna. *Deserved*, mĕrĭta, dēbĭta, digna. *Bringing reproach*, prŏbrōsa. *Lasting*, perpĕtua, aeterna, pĕrennis. *Surviving its cause or object*, sŭperstes, ĭtis.

ignōrantia. *Ignorance*.—EP. *Shameful*, turpis, foeda. *Lazy*, ĭners, pĭgra, segnis. *Incurable*, insānābĭlis. *Excusable*, excūsābĭlis. *Stupid*, stulta.

īlex -ĭcis, fem. *A holm-oak*.—EP. *Green*, vĭrĭdis, vĭrĭdans, vĭrens. *Dark*, ātra, nĭgra. *Shady*, umbrōsa, ŏpāca. *Long-lived*, vīvax. *With shining leaves*, cŏrusca. *Lofty*, ardua, alta, prōcēra, āĕria. *With many branches*, rāmōsa. *Leafy*, frondōsa, frondea.

illĕcĕbrae, arum, plur. fem. *Blandishments, allurements*.—EP. *Caressing*, blandae. *Deceitful*, fallāces, falsae, dŏlōsae. *Pleasant*, dulces, ămoenae, jūcundae. *Customary*, sŏllĭtae. *Victorious*, victrīces.

illŭvies, ĕi, fem. *Dirt*.—EP. *Foul*, foeda, turpis, tētra. *Unsightly*, dēformis, informis. *Squalid*, squālĭda, sordĭda. *Of long standing*, longa, diūturna.

imāgo, ĭnis, fem. *An image*.—EP. *Faithful*, fĭda, fĭdēlis. *Known*, nōta. *False*, deceitful*, falsa, ficta, fallax. *Dear*, cāra, dĭlecta.

imber -bris, masc. *Rain*.—EP. *Poured down*, effūsus, dēmissus. *Wintry*, hўbernus, hyĕmālis. *Dark*, caerūleus. *Violent, stormy*, turbĭdus, viŏlentus. *Fertilising*, fēcundus, fertĭlis, almus. *Vernal*, vernus.

IMB—INF 45

imbrex, ĭcis, masc. *A tile, a coping.*—EP. *Narrow,* ang stus. *Slippery,* lŭbrĭcus.

Imītamen, ĭnis, neut. *An imitation.*—EP. *Crafty,* callĭdum. *False,* fictum, fallax.

Imītātor, ōris, masc., **Imītātrix**, ĭcis, fem. *An imitator.*—EP. *Wise, clever,* săpiens, callĭdus. *Skilful,* doctus, pĕrītus. *Deceitful,* fallax, falsus.

impensa. *Cost.*—EP. *Large,* magna, ingens. *Small,* parva, exĭgua, brĕvis. *Too large,* nĭmia. *Prodigal,* prōdĭga.

impĕrātor, ōris, masc. *A general.* See dux.

impĕrium. *Command, dominion.*—EP. *Extensive,* lātum. *Ancient,* vĕtus –ĕris, antīquum, priscum. *Just,* æquum, justum. *Unjust,* inīquum. *Severe,* dūrum, sĕvērum. *Proud, arrogant,* sŭperbum, arrŏgans. *Powerful,* pŏtens. *Venerable,* vĕrendum, vĕnĕrābĭle.

impĕtus, ûs. 1. *Impetuosity.*—2. *An attack.*—EP. 1, 2. *Sudden,* sŭbĭtus. *Hot, eager,* fervens, fervĭdus, viŏlentus, acer –cris.—2. *Hostile,* hostīlis, hostīlus, adversus. *Fierce,* fĕrus, sævus, crūdēlis. *Bloody,* cruentus, sanguĭneus. *Rapid,* răpĭdus.

impiĕtas. *Impiety.*—EP. *Sad,* tristis. *Odious,* ŏdiōsa, invīsa. *Wicked,* scĕlĕrāta. *Rash,* tĕmĕrāria, præceps –ĭpĭtis. *Bold,* audax. *Fearless,* impăvĭda.

imprūdentia. *Imprudence.*—EP. *Rash,* præceps –ĭpĭtis, tĕmĕrāria, incauta. *Blind,* cæca. *Sad,* tristis, mĭsĕra.

Inauris, is, fem. *An earring.*—EP. *Jewelled,* gemmea, gemmans. *Hanging,* pendŭla, dĕpendens, dĕmissa. *Light,* lĕvis.

incendium. *A conflagration.*—EP. *Destructive,* noxium, pernĭciōsum, exĭtiāle, ĕxĭtiōsum, fātāle. *Rapid,* răpĭdum, vēlox. *Glowing, burning,* ardens, torrĭdum, rŭtĭlum. *Miserable,* mĭsĕrum, mĭsĕrābĭle, triste. *Cruel, terrible,* sævum, horrĭdum. *Devouring,* ĕdax, răpax, ăvĭdum.

inceptum. *An attempt.* See cœptum.

incessus, ûs. *Gait.*—EP. *Lofty, proud,* altus, sŭperbus. *Delicate,* mollis. *Rapid,* răpĭdus. *Slow,* lentus.

inclēmentia. *Inclemency, cruelty.*—EP. *Harsh,* aspĕra, dūra, sæva. *Terrible,* dīra. *Unwonted,* insŏlīta. *Wicked,* imprŏba, inīqua.

incŏla, æ, masc. fem.—EP. *Original,* prīmus. *Ancient,* priscus, vĕtus –ĕris, antīquus. *New,* nŏvus. *Brave,* fortis. *Invincible,* invictus, indŏmĭtus.

inconstantia. *Inconstancy.*—EP. *Fickle,* lĕvis, mōbĭlis, vāria. *Wanton,* lascīva, prŏterva. *Like the wind,* ventōsa.

incrēmentum. *Increase.*—EP. *Great,* magnum. *Sudden,* sŭbĭtum. *Unusual,* insŏlītum, Inassuetum.

incŭnābŭla, ōrum, plur. neut. *A cradle.* See cunabula.

incūria. *Carelessness.*—EP. *Silly,* stulta, ĭnepta. *Rash,* tĕmĕrāria, præceps –ĭpĭtis.

incus, ūdis, fem. *An anvil.*—EP. *Iron,* ferrea, ferrāta. *Hard,* dūra. *Placed below the weapon,* suppŏsĭta.

index, ĭcis, masc. fem. *An informer.*—EP. *Trusty,* certus, fīdus, fĭdēlis, vērax. *Treacherous,* infīdus, perfĭdus. *Known,* nōtus.

indĭcium. *A proof.*—EP. *Certain,* certum. *Doubtful,* dŭbium, incertum. *Old,* vĕtus –ĕris, antīquum. *Open, notorious,* mănĭfestum.

indĭgĕna, æ, masc. fem. *A native.*—EP. *Original,* prīmus. *Ancient,* vĕtus. –ĕris, priscus, antīquus.

indignātio. *Indignation.*—EP. *Unrestrained,* lībĕra. *Deserved,* mĕrĭta, dĕbĭta, digna, justa.

indŏles, is, fem. *Disposition.*—EP. *Happy,* fēlix. *Good,* bŏna. *Friendly, kind,* bĕnigna, ămīca. *Natural,* innate, insĭta. *Noble,* nōbĭlis, gĕnĕrōsa. *Base,* turpis.

indulgentia. *Indulgence.*—EP. *Improper,* prāva. *Foolish,* stulta, dēmens. *Pernicious,* noxia, nŏcens, pernĭciōsa, damnōsa. *Judicious,* dextĕra. *Deserved,* mĕrĭta. *Usual,* sŏlĭta.

industria. *Industry.*—EP. *Persevering,* pertĭnax. *Long-continued,* longa, diŭturna. *Strenuous,* strēnua, impĭgra. *Virtuous,* pia, prŏba. *Marvellous, admirable,* mīra, mīrābĭlis. *Unwearied,* indĕfessa.

Inertia. *Sloth.* See ignavia.

infāmia. *Infamy.* See ignominia.

46 INF—JOC

infans, tis, masc. fem. *An infant.*—EP. *Little*, parvus, parvŭlus. *Helpless*, ĭnops –ŏpis. *Trembling*, trĕmŭlus. *Complaining*, quĕrŭlus. *Tender*, tĕner –ĕri.

infantia. *Infancy.*—EP. *Helpless*, ĭnops –ŏpis. *Tender*, tĕnĕra, mollis. *Complaining*, quĕrŭla. *Weeping*, lăcrўmōsa.

infĕriæ, arum, plur. fem. *Sacrifices to the dead.*—EP. *Last*, extrēmæ, ultĭmæ, sŭprēmæ. *Sad*, tristes. *Pious*, piæ.

infŭla. *A fillet.* See vitta.

ingĕnium. 1. *Disposition.*—2. *Genius.*—EP. 1. See indoles.—2. *Divine*, dĭvīnum. *Eloquent*, dĭsertum, făcundum. *Grand*, grande, sŭblīme, altum. *Tender*, molle, tĕnĕrum.

inglŭvies, ĕi. *The gullet.*—EP. *Greedy*, ăvĭda, vŏrax, ĕdax.

ingressus, ûs. *Entrance.*—EP. *First*, prīmus. *New*, nŏvus.

inĭmĭcĭtia. *Enmity.*— EP. *Fierce*, cruel, trux trŭcis, sæva, fĕra, immītis. *Implacable*, ĭnĕxōrăbĭlis, implăcăbĭlis, illăcrўmăbĭlia. *Long*, lasting, longa, dĭŭturna. *Surviving its object or cause*, sŭperstes –ĭtis. *Eternal*, æterna, pĕrennis. *Hereditary*, pătria, ăvīta. *Ancient*, vĕtus –ĕris, prisca, antīqua.

inĭtium. *A beginning.* See principium.

injŭria. *Injury, injustice.*—EP. *Foul*, fœda, turpis. *Cruel*, fĕra, sæva. *Destructive*, exĭtĭōsa, exĭtĭālia, fătālis. *Of long standing*, longa. *Ancient*, vĕtus, prisca, antīqua. *Indelible*, indēlēbĭlis. *Irremediable*, immĕdĭcăbĭlis. *Undeserved*, immĕrĭta, indigna.

innŏcentia. *Innocence.*—EP. *Pure, chaste*, pūra, candĭda, casta. *Inviolate*, intĕmĕrāta. *Pious*, pia. *Simple*, simplex –ĭcis.

insānia. *Madness.*—EP. *Moody*, ægra, tristis. *Furious*, fŭriōsa, răbĭda. *Rash*, præceps –ĭpĭtis, tĕmĕrāria. *Lasting*, longa.

inscĭtia. *Ignorance.* See ignorantia.

insĭdiæ, ārum, plur. fem. *Snares, ambush.*—EP. *Cunning*, callĭdæ, versŭtæ. *Treacherous*, dŏlōsæ, infĭdæ, perfĭdæ, fallāces. *Dangerous*, pĕrĭcŭlōsæ. *Injurious*, nŏcentes, damnōsæ. *Hostile*, hostīles, hostīcæ, adversæ. *Secret*, tăcĭtæ, cæcæ, lătentes. *Unknown*, ignōtæ.

insŏlentia. *Insolence.*—EP. *Haughty*, sŭperba. *Unbecoming*, indĕcōra. *Undeserved*, immĕrĭta.

insomnium. *A dream.* See somnium.

instĭta. *The border round the lower part of a robe.*—EP. *Lowest*, infĭma, ĭma. *Extreme*, ultĭma, extrēma.

instrūmentum. *An instrument, tool.*—EP. *Useful*, ŭtĭle, aptum, commŏdum. *Ready*, părātum.

insŭla. *An island.*—EP. *In the sea*, æquŏrea. *In the river*, flŭviālis. *Flowed round*, circumflua. *Green*, vĭrĭdis. *White (of an island celebrated for white marble, as Paros, or white cliffs, as England)*, nĭvea, candĭda. *Sacred*, săcra, săcrāta. *Rocky*, scŏpŭlōsa, saxōsa. *Distant*, longinqua, rĕmōta.

interdictum. *An interdict.*—EP. *Severe*, sĕvērum, rĭgĭdum. *New*, nŏvum, insŏlĭtum. *Issued by a king*, rēgium.

intĕrĭtus, ûs. *Death.* See mors.

interpres, ĕtis, masc. fem. *A messenger, an interpreter.*—EP. *Faithful*, fīdus, fĭdēlis. *Sent*, missus. *Sacred*, săcer –cri. *Wise*, săpiens. *Full of foresight*, prōvĭdus, præscius.

intervallum. *A space between.* See spatium.

introĭtus, ûs. *An entrance.*—EP. *Wide*, lātus, amplus, spătĭōsus. *Narrow*, angustus, arctus. *Open*, pătens. *Easy*, făcĭlis.

intŭbum. *Endive.*—EP. *Bitter*, amārum.

inventor, ōris, masc., **inventrix, ĭcis**, fem. *A discoverer.*—EP. *Original*, prīmus. *Ancient*, priscus, vĕtus –ĕris. *Sagacious*, săgax, săpiens, callĭdus, ingĕnĭōsus. *Fortunate*, fēlix. *Useful*, ŭtĭlis. *Celebrated*, clārus, insignis. *New*, nŏvus.

inventum. *An invention.* See above.

invĭdia. *Envy.*—EP. *Malignant*, măla, mălĭgna, ĭnīqua. *Disparaging, biting*, mordax, ĕdax. *Bitter*, ăcerba, aspĕra. *Crooked*, ŏblīqua. *Unjust*, injusta. *Pale*, pallĭda. *Base*, turpis.

jŏcus, plur., jŏci and jŏca. *A jest, joking.*—EP. *Merry, cheerful*, festīvus, lætus. *Light*, lĕvis. *Pleasant*, dulcis, ămœnus, ămăbĭlis.

IRA—JUV 47

Ira. *Anger.*—EP. *Violent*, grăvis, vĭŏlenta, vehěmens. *Short-lived*, brěvis. *Just, deserved*, justa, měrĭta, dēbĭta. *Undeserved*, imměrĭta. *Cruel*, sæva, fěra, trux trŭcis, immītis. *Inexorable*, ĭnexōrābĭlis, ĭllăcrўmābĭlis, implăcābĭlis. *Mindful*, měmor -ŏris. *Rash*, præceps -ĭpĭtis, těměrāria. *Unrestrained*, effrēna, impŏtens. *Vain*, vāna, ĭnānis. *Kindled*, accensa.

Iris, Ĭdis, fem. *The rainbow.*—EP. *Dewy*, roscĭda. *Of various colours*, văria, picta, cŏlōrāta. *High*, alta, sŭblīmis, ardua. *Heavenly*, cœlestis, æthěria. *Sacred*, săcra. *Bringing rain*, imbrĭfěra, ăquōsa, plŭvia, plŭviālis. *Promised*, prŏmissa. *Wished for*, optāta. *Friendly*, ămīca.

irrīsor, ōris, masc. *A laugher.* See risor.

irrītāmen, ĭnis, neut., irrītāmentum. *Anything which excites.*—EP. *Powerful*, pŏtens, effĭcax. *Gentle*, blandum, mīte. *Pleasant*, dulce, ămœnum, ămābĭle, jūcundum.

isthmus, i. *An isthmus.*—EP. *Narrow*, angustus, arctus. *With sea on both sides*, bĭmāris.

Iter, Ĭněris, neut. *A journey or a road.*—EP. *Long, or short*, longum, brěve. *Easy or difficult*, făcĭle, diffĭcĭle. *Out of the way, through out-of-the-way, or pathless, places*, ăvium, dēvium. *Safe*, tūtum. See via.

jŭba. *A mane.*—EP. *Flowing*, dēmissa. *Long*, longa. *Thick*, densa. *Waving*, undans, fluĭtans.

jŭbar, ăris, neut. *A sunbeam.*—EP. *Bright, glowing*, splendĭdum, rŭtĭlum, cŏruscum, clārum. *Shining in the morning*, mătūtīnum. *Rosy*, rŏseum. See Sol.

jŭdex, ĭcis, masc. *A judge.*—EP. *Just*, justus, æquus. *Shrewd*, argūtus, subtīlis. *Rigid*, rĭgĭdus, sěvērus. *Venerable*, věněrābĭlis, věrendus. *Grey-headed*, cānus. *Learned*, doctus. *Incorruptible*, incorruptus.

jŭdĭcium. *Judgment (in any sense).*—EP. *Wise*, săpiens, prūdens. *Honest*, æquum, justum. *Fixed*, stăbĭle, immōbĭle, certum. *Slow*, tardum. *Favourable*, sěcundum. *Unfavourable*, adversum, *unfavourable, or unjust*, ĭnīquum.

jūgěra, um. *Acres.* See ager.

jŭgum. 1. *A yoke.*—2. *The ridge of a mountain.*—EP. 1. *Slavish*, servīle, servum. *Proud*, sŭperbum. *Cruel*, sævum, immīte, crūdēle, aspěrum. *Unaccustomed*, insŏlĭtum, ĭnassuetum. *Unhappy*, infēlix, mĭsěrum, triste. *Undeserved*, imměrĭtum, indignum. *Shameful*, turpe, fœdum. See servitium.—2. See mons.

jūmentum. *A beast of burden.*—EP. *Patient*, pătiens. *Strong*, forte, vălĭdum, *Hardy*, dūrum. *Hard-working*, ŏpěrōsum. *Wretched*, mĭsěrum, mĭsěrābĭle.

junctūra. *A joint.*—EP. *Cunningly made*, callĭda. *Firm*, firma, stăbĭlis. *Tenacious*, těnax.

juncus. *A bulrush.*—EP. *Round and smooth*, těres -ětis. *Long*, longus. *Light*, lěvis. *Growing in mud*, līmōsus. *Growing in marshy places*, pălūdōsus, ūdus.

jurgium. *Strife.*—EP. *Noisy*, clāmōsum, raucum. *Frequent*, crěbrum. *Litigious*, lĭtĭgiōsum. *Serious, great*, magnum, grăve. *Long, lasting*, longum, diūturnum. *Leading to abuse*, prŏbrōsum.

jus, jūris, neut. *Law, right.*—EP. *Eternal*, æternum, perpětuum. *Sacred*, săcrum, sanctum. *Fair, honest*, æquum. *Inviolable*, invĭŏlābĭle, invĭŏlātum. *Ancient*, priscum, větus -ěris, antiquum. *Ratified, established*, rătum. *Stable, unalterable*, stăbĭle, immōbĭle.

jussum, jussus, ūs. *A command.*—EP. *Fair, reasonable*, æquus, justus. *Proud, imperious*, sŭperbus. *Royal*, rēgius. *Cruel*, fěrus, immītis, crūdēlis. *Unjust*, injustus, ĭnīquus, imprŏbus.

justĭtia. *Justice.*—EP. *Golden*, aurea. *Divine*, dīvīna, cælestis. *Fair, clad in white*, candĭda, alba. *Eternal*, æterna. *Sacred*, săcra, săcrāta, sancta.

jŭvenca, jŭvencus. *A heifer, a steer.*—EP. *Wanton, playful*, prŏtervus, lascīvus. *Apt to butt*, pětŭlans. *With horny feet*, cornĭpes -ědis. *Horned*, cornĭger -ěri. *Unbroken*, indŏmĭtus.

jŭvěnis. *A youth.*—EP. *Brave, fearless*, fortis, impăvĭdus. *Strong*, vălĭdus. *Beardless*, imberbia, intonsus. *Cheerful*, hĭlāris, lætus. *Eager, vehement*, fervĭdus, ăcer -cris, vehěmens. *Docile*, dŏcĭlis, făcĭlis, tractābĭlis.

jŭventa. *Youth.*—EP. *Early*, prīma, prīmæva, vĭrĭdis. *Beardless*, imberbis, intonsa, lēvis. *Tender*, těněra, mollis. *Easily influenced*, mōbĭlis, făcĭlis.

48 JUV—LAN

Docile, dŏcĭlis. *Vigorous*, vălĭda, fortis. *Hot*, impătiens, fervĭda, călĭda, impătiens. *Obstinate*, indŏcĭlis. *Wanton*, playful, lascīva, prŏterva.

jŭventus, ūtis, fem. *A body of youth.* See juvenis.

L.

Lăbellum, lăbrum. *A lip.*—EP. *Extreme, the tip of, etc.*, summum, extrēmum. *Rosy*, rŏseum.

lăbes, is, fem. *A stain, a disgrace.*—EP. *Sad*, tristis, mĭsĕra, flēbĭlis. *Base*, foul, fœda, turpis. *Lasting, everlasting*, perpĕtua, pĕrennis. *Indelible*, indēlēbĭlis.

lăbor, ōris, masc. *Labour.*—EP. *Hard*, dūrus, diffĭcĭlis, imprŏbus. *Long*, longus. *Hateful*, invīsus, ŏdiōsus, ingrātus. *Already begun*, inceptus. *Useful*, ūtĭlis. *Vain, fruitless*, vānus, ĭnānis, ĭnūtĭlis. *Strenuous*, strēnuus, impĭger —gra. *Unwearied*, indēfessus. *Of the farmer, etc.*, ăgrestis.

lăbyrinthus. *A labyrinth.*—EP. *Inextricable*, ĭnextrĭcābĭlis. *Like the work of Dædalus*, Dædălĕus. *Difficult*, diffĭcĭlis. *Doubtful* (i. e. *where one is doubtful how to get out*), dŭbius, incertus. *Long*, longus. *Winding*, sīnuōsus. *Dark*, full of hidden ways, cæcus, obscūrus. *Manifold*, multĭplex –ĭcis.

lac, tis, neut. *Milk.*—EP. *White*, nĭveum, candĭdum. *Pure*, pūrum. *Warm*, cālĭdum, fervĭdum. *Foaming*, spūmans, spūmeum.

Lăcĕdæmon, ŏnis, fem. *Lacedæmon.*—EP. *Brave*, fortis. *Patient*, pătiens. *Reigned over by the descendants of Hercules*, Hercūlea. *Unwalled*, immūnīta. *Fearless*, impăvĭda. *Unconquered*, invicta, indŏmĭta.

lăcerna. *A cloak.*—EP. *Thick*, densa. *Shaggy*, villōsa. *Short*, brĕvis. *Embroidered*, picta.

lăcerta. *A lizard.*—EP. *Green*, vĭrĭdis. *Silent*, tăcĭta. *Dwelling in marshes*, pălūdōsa, pălustris, ūda.

lăcertus. *An arm.* See brachium.

lăcryma. *A tear.*—EP. *Numerous*, multa, plūrĭma, crēbra. *Wet*, ūda, mădĭda. *Sad*, tristis, mĭsĕra, infēlix. *Falling*, cădūca. *Poured forth*, fūsa, effūsa. *Just rising to the eye*, ŏbōrta. *Checked*, suspensa. *Dewy*, roscĭda. *Just, due*, justa, mĕrĭta, dēbĭta.

lăcūna.—EP. *Hollow*, căva. *Deep*, alta, prŏfunda. *Wet*, ūda.

lăcūnar, āris, neut. *A ceiling.* See laquear.

lăcus, ūs. *A lake.*—EP. *Large*, magnus. *Wavy, full of waves*, undōsus. *Beautiful*, pulcher, ămœnus, ămābĭlis. *Blue*, cærūleus. *Among mountains*, montānus. *Tranquil*, plăcĭdus, tranquillus, sĕrēnus.

lætĭtia. *Joy.* See gaudium.

lăgēna. *A flagon.*—EP. *Full*, plēna. *Of glass*, vītrea.

lăma. *A slough.*—EP. *Foul*, fœda, turpis, obscœna. *Deep*, alta, prŏfunda. *Muddy*, līmōsa. *Wet*, ūda.

lāmentum. *Lamentation.*—EP. *Loud*, clārum. *Frequent*, crēbrum. *Female*, fœmĭneum, mŭliĕbre. *Sad*, triste, mæstum, mĭsĕrum, mĭsĕrābĭle, lūgūbre. *Long, incessant*, perpĕtuum, assĭduum, longum.

lămia. *A sorceress, perhaps a vampire.*—EP. *Dire*, dīra, terrĭbĭlis. *Wicked*, impia, imprŏba. *Deadly*, fātālis, exĭtiōsa.

lămĭna, sync. lamna. *A plate of metal.*—EP. *Thin*, tĕnuis. *Valuable*, prētiōsa, cāra. *Golden, yellow*, aurea, flāva. *Silvery white*, argentea, candĭda.

lampăs, ădis, fem. *A lamp, a torch.*—EP. *Fiery*, ignea, flammea, flammĭfĕra, flammans, ardens. *Lighted*, accensa. *Ruddy, shining*, rŭtĭla, clāra, cŏrusca. *Full of oil, etc.*, uncta. See tæda.

lāna. *Wool.*—EP. *Soft*, mollis, tĕnĕra. *Thin*, tĕnuis. *Light*, lĕvis. *Dyed*, fūcāta. *Dyed purple*, purpūrea, Tyria. *White*, candĭda. *Easily spun*, tractābĭlis, făcĭlis.

lancea. *A lance.* See hasta.

languor, ōris, masc. *Languor*—EP. *Weak*, dēbĭlis, imbellis. *Indolent*, segnis,

LAN—LEÇ   49

ĭners, ignāvus. *Arising from or like sickness,* æger -gri. *Customary,* sŏlĭtus. *Making useless,* ĭnūtĭlis.

lănista, æ, masc. *A master of gladiators.*—EP. *Fierce,* fĕrus, trux trŭcis. *Hardy,* dūrus. *Skilful,* pĕrītus, callĭdus.

lănius. *A butcher.*—EP. *Cruel,* crudēlis, immītis, sævus. *Blood-stained,* cruentus, sanguĭneus, sanguĭnŏlentus.

lănūgo, ĭnis, fem. *Down, esp. the downy hair upon a young man's face.*—EP. *First appearing, new,* prīma, nŏva. *Soft, tender,* mollis, tĕnĕra. *Doubtful* (i. e. *uncertain whether it might be called beard*), dūbia, incerta.

lanx, cis, fem. 1. *A dish.*—2. *Scales.*—EP. 1. *Luxurious, rich,* lauta, luxŭriōsa, ŏpīma, dīves -ĭtis. *Golden, silver,* aurea, argentea. *Chased, embossed,* cælāta. *Full,* plēna.—2. See libra.

lăpis, -ĭdis, lăpillus. *A stone.*—EP. *Hard,* dūrus. *Valuable,* prĕ̄́iōsus. *Of different colours,* pictus, vărius. *Shining,* splendĭdus, cŏruscus. *Transparent,* pellūcĭdus, pellūcens, vĭtreus.

lappa. *A burr.*—EP. *Tenacious,* tĕnax. *Prickly,* spīnōsus. *Odious,* invīsus, ŏdiōsus. *Useless,* ĭnūtĭlis, stĕrĭlis.

lapsus, ûs. 1. *A fall.*—2. *A gliding motion.*—EP. 1. *Sudden,* sŭbĭtus. *Hurtful,* nŏcens, noxius, damnōsus. *Wounding,* vulnĭfĭcus. *Great,* ingens, magnus.—2. *Gentle,* lēnis. *Silent,* tăcĭtus. *Slow,* tardus.

lăquear, āris, neut. *A ceiling.*—EP. *Lofty,* altum. *Painted,* pictum. *Inlaid with gold, silver, etc.,* aureum, argenteum.

lăqueus. *A noose.*—EP. *Tight,* arctus. *Deceitful,* fallax. *Holding tight,* tĕnax. *Deadly,* fātālis, fātĭfer -ĕri.

Lar, usu. plur. Lāres, masc. *The Household Gods, home.*—EP. *Dear,* cārus. *Hereditary,* pătrius, pāternus, ăvītus. *Well-known, customary,* nōtus, sŏlĭtus. *Ancient,* vĕtus -ĕris, prīscus, antīquus. *Wished for (by an absent man),* optātus. *Safe,* tūtus, incŏlŭmis. *Watchful to protect,* vĭgil -ĭlis. *Humble, simple,* hŭmĭlis, simplex -ĭcis.

lardum. *Bacon.*—EP. *Fat,* pingue.

larva. 1. *A ghost.*—2. *A mask.*—EP. 1. *Seen by night,* nocturna. 1, 2. *Terrible,* dīra, terrĭbĭlis, horrĭbĭlis, horrĭda, horrenda.—2. *Feigned,* ficta, falsa. *Deceitful,* dŏlōsa, fallax. *Painted,* picta.

lărix, ĭcis, fem. *A larch.* See pinus.

lascīvia. *Wantonness.*—EP. *Immodest,* impŭdīca. *Shameful,* turpis, fœda, indĕcōra. *Lascivious,* prŏterva.

lătĕbra, usu. in plur. *A hiding-place.*—EP. *Dark, unseen, secret,* obscūra, cæca, abdīta, sēcrēta. *Safe,* tūta, incŏlŭmis. *Unknown,* ignōta. *Distant,* longinqua, rēmōta. *Hollow (as in a cave, etc.),* căva.

lăter -ĕris, masc. *A brick.*—EP. *Baked,* coctĭlis, coctus.

lătex, ĭcis, masc. *Running water.*—EP. *Perpetual,* perpĕtuus, pĕrennis. *Continually running,* jūgis. *Pure,* pūrus. See aqua.

lātrātor, ōris, masc. *A barker.*—EP. *Watchful,* vĭgil -ĭlis, pervĭgil. *By night,* nocturnus. *Fierce,* fĕrus, sævus. *Hoarse,* raucus.

lātrātus, ûs. *Barking.* See above.

lătro, ōnis, masc. *A thief.* See fur.

lătus, ŏris, neut. *A side.*—EP. *Right,* dextĕrum, sync. dextrum. *Left,* sĭnistrum, lævum. *Both,* ūtrumque.

laudātor, ōris, masc., laudātrix -īcis, fem. *A praiser.* See laus.

laurea, laurus, ûs, fem. *A bay-tree.*—EP. *Sacred to Apollo,* Ăpollĭnea, Ăpollĭnāris, Phœbēa, Phœbēia, Actĭăca, Dēlia, Delphĭca. *Triumphal, emblem of victory,* triumphalis, victrix -īcis. *Learned (forming a crown for poets and learned men),* docta ; *so, Castalian, Parnassian, etc.,* Castălia, Parnassia, Parnassis -ĭdis. *Sacred,* săcra, săcrata. *Green,* vĭrĭdis, vĭrĭdans, vĭrens. *Brittle,* frăgĭlis.

laus, dis, fem. *Praise.*—EP. *Immortal,* æterna, immortālis, pĕrennis. *Surviving its object,* sŭperstes -ĭtis. *Deserved,* mĕrĭta, dēbĭta, digna. *Eminent,* insignis, ēgrĕgia.

lea, læna. *A lioness.* See leo.

lēbes, -ētis, masc. *A cauldron.*—EP. *Brazen,* ahēnus, ahēneus. *Chased,* cælātus.

lectīca. *A litter.*—EP. *Soft,* mollis. *Luxurious,* lectīca. *Carried,* gesta,

E

50 LEC—LIL

lector –ŏris, masc. *A reader.*—EP. *Diligent,* sēdŭlus. *Candid,* candĭdus. *Learned,* doctus. *Patient,* pătiens.

lectŭlus, lectus. *A bed.*—EP. *Strewed, made,* strātus. *Soft,* mollis. *Downy,* cўcnēus, plūmeus, plūmōsus. *Customary, known,* nōtus, sŏlĭtus. *Of marriage,* jŭgālis, nuptiālis.

lēgātus. *An ambassador.*—EP. *Sent,* missus. *Eloquent,* dĭsertus, făcundus. *Faithful,* fĭdus, fĭdēlis. *Wise,* săpiens. *Venerable,* vĕnĕrābĭlis, vĕrendus.

lēgio, ŏnis, fem. *A legion.*—EP. *Long,* longa. *Armed, armed with brass,* armĭfĕra, ærea. *Armed with spear or shield, or crested helmet, etc.,* hastāta, clўpeāta, cristāta, etc. *Invincible,* invicta, indŏmĭta. *Brave, fearless,* fortis, impăvĭda. *Victorious,* victrix –icis. *Martial,* Martia, Mavortia. *Glittering,* splendĭda, fulgens.

lembus. *A boat.* See navis.

lēnīmen, ĭnis, neut. *An alleviation.*—EP. *Sweet,* dulce. *Desired, desirable,* optātum, optābĭle.

leo, ŏnis, masc. *A lion.*—EP. *Tawny,* fulvus. *Fierce,* fĕrus, sævus, asper –ĕri. *Fierce-looking,* torvus. *African,* Gætūlus, Lĭbўcus, Pœnus, Nŭmĭda (æ, masc.). *Shaggy,* hirsūtus. *Devouring,* ăvĭdus, vŏrax, răpax. *Horrid,* horrĭdus, horrĭbĭlis, dīrus. *Swift,* răpĭdus, vēlox.

lĕpor, ōris, masc. *Wit.*—EP. *Pleasant,* festīvus, ămœnus. *Merry,* hĭlāris. *Laughing, jocose,* rīdens, jŏcōsus. *Well-bred,* urbānus, cultus.

lĕpus, ŏris, masc. *A hare.*—EP. *Defenceless, weak,* imbellis. *Timid,* tĭmĭdus, păvĭdus. *Inclined to flee,* fŭgax. *Swift,* cēler –ĕris, vēlox, răpĭdus. *With quick ears,* aurītus. *Crafty,* callĭdus, văfer –fri.

lēthum. *Death.* See mors.

lĕvāmen, ĭnis, neut. *Relief.* See lenimen.

lĕvĭtas. 1. *Lightness.*—2. *Fickleness.*—EP. 1, 2. *Easily moved,* mōbĭlis.—2. *Changeable,* ventōsa, văria, mūtābĭlis.

lex, lēgis, fem. 1. *Law.*—2. *A condition.*—EP. 1, 2. *Fair,* æqua, justa. *Lasting,* stābĭlis. *Ratified,* răta.—1. *Sacred,* săcra. *Ancient,* prisca, vĕtus –ĕris, antiqua.—*Severe,* sĕvēra, rĭgĭda. *Threatening,* mĭnax.—2. *Agreed upon,* pacta, certa.

lībāmen, ĭnis, neut. *A libation.*—EP. *Pious,* pium. *Sacred,* săcrum, să-crātum. *Suppliant,* supplex –icis. *Poured out,* effūsum. *First,* prīmum.

lĭbellus, lĭber –bri. *A book.*—EP. *Written,* scriptus. *Learned,* doctus. *Mindful, preserving facts,* mĕmor –ŏris. *Faithful,* fĭdus, fĭdēlis.

lībertas. *Liberty.*—EP. *Golden,* aurea. *White,* candĭda. *Beautiful,* pulchra. *Sacred,* săcra, săcrāta. *Unrestrained,* effrēna.

lībertīnus, lībertīna, lībertus, lĭberta. *A freed man, a freed woman.*—EP. *Exempt from bondage,* immūnis. *Happy,* fēlix, lætus.

lĭbīdo, ĭnis, fem. *Whim, lust.*—EP. *Wanton,* lascīva, prŏterva. *Self-willed,* pĕtŭlans. *Unchaste,* impŭdĭca. *Unrestrained,* indŏmĭta, effrēna. *Shameful,* turpis, fœda.

lĭbra. *A scale.*—EP. *Fair,* æqua, æquāta, justa.

lĭbum. *A cake.*—EP. *Made of corn, wheaten,* ădōreum, trĭtĭceum. *Sweet,* dulce. *Honey,* mellītum. *Sacred,* săcrum, săcrātum.

Lĭbya, æ, or Lĭbye, es. *Africa.*—EP. *Torrid,* torrĭda, ăvĭda, exusta. *Red,* rŭbens. *Desolate,* dĕserta. *Uncultivated,* inculta. *Barbarous,* barbăra. *Distant,* longinqua, rĕmōta, ultĭma, extrēma. *Inhospitable,* ĭnhospĭta, ĭnhos-pĭtālis.

lĭcentia. *License.* See libertas.

licium. *Thread.* See filum.

lĭgāmen, ĭnis, neut. *A ligature.*—EP. *Tight,* arctum. *Light,* lĕve. *Tenacious, firm,* tĕnax, firmum.

lignum. *Wood.*—EP. *Hard,* dūrum. *Easily cut,* sectĭle. *Foreign,* pĕrĕ-grīnum, externum. *Of ash, oak, etc.,* fraxĭneum, quernum, etc.

lĭgo, ōnis, masc. *A spade.*—EP. *Hard,* dūrus. *Heavy,* gravis. *Iron, ferreus,* ferrātus. *Rustic,* rustĭcus, ăgrestis.

lĭlium. *A lily.*—EP. *White,* candĭdum, candens, album, nĭveum, argenteum. *Open,* hians. *Sweet,* suavĕŏlens, ŏdōrātum. *Variegated,* pictum, vărium. *Beautiful,* pulchrum, dĕcōrum. 2. *Modest,* pŭdĭcum. *Tall,* altum, prŏcērum.

LIM—LUE 51

līma. A file, polish.—EP. Finishing, ultǐma, extrēma, nǒvissǐma. Severe, sěvēra, rǐgǐda.

līmax, ăcis, masc. A snail.—EP. Slow, tardus.

limbus. A fringe.—EP. Forming the extremity, ultǐmus, extremus. At the bottom, īmus. Embroidered, pictus. Set off with gold, aureus, aurātus. Purple, purpūreus, Tўrius.

līmen, ǐnis, neut. A threshold.—EP. Outermost, prīmum, extrēmum. Friendly, ǎmīcum, běnignum. See porta.

līmes, ǐtis, masc. A boundary.—EP. Outermost, extrēmus, ultǐmus. Ancient, větus -ěris, priscus, antīquus. Known, nōtus. Extensive, lātus. Sacred, săcer -cri. Marked out, signātus.

līmus. Mud.—EP. Foul, fœdus, immundus, turpis, sordǐdus. Thick, densus. Deep, altus, prǒfundus.

līnea. A line, a string.—EP. Thin, těnuis. Long, longa.

lingua. 1. A tongue.—2. Language.—EP. 1. Talkative, lǒquax, garrǔla. Eloquent, dīserta, făcunda. Learned, docta. Fluent, făcǐlis.—2. Native, pătria. Foreign, externa, pěrěgrīna.

linter, tris, masc. A bark. See navis.

linteum. 1. A linen cloth (esp. in plur.).—2. Sails.—EP. 1. Thin, těnue.—2. See vēlum.

līnum. Flax.—EP. Dry, siccum, arǐdum. Strong-smelling, grăvěolens.

liquor, ōris, masc. Any liquor.—EP. Flowing, fluǐdus. See aqua, vinum, etc.

līs, lītis, fem. Strife (esp. legal strife).—EP. Long, longa. Vexatious, grăvis, mǒlesta. Hateful, invīsa, ǒdiōsa. Noisy, clāmōsa.

littěra. A letter.—EP. Written, scripta. Sent, missa. Conveying news, nuntia. Frequent, crēbra, multa, plūrǐma. Secret, arcāna, sēcrēta. Trustworthy, fīda, fīdēlis.

littus, ōris, neut. EP. Sandy, ǎrēnōsum. Of the sea, æquǒreum, mǎrīnum. Dry, siccum. Wet, ūdum, mādǐdum. Rocky, saxōsum. Hoarse, resounding, raucum, rěsǒnans. Winding, curvum, sǐnuōsum. Covered with foam, spūmeum, spūmōsum, spūmans. Distant, longinquum. Of one's native land, pătrium. Barren, stěrǐle, infēcundum.

lītūra. A smear, a blot.—EP. Foul, unsightly, fœda, dēformis.

lītuus. 1. A trumpet.—2. An augur's wand.—EP. 1. See tuba.—2. Sacred, săcer -cri, sanctus, sācrātus. Prophetic, fātǐdǐcus. Curved, curvus, rěcurvus, incurvus.

līvor, ōris, masc. Envy. See invidia.

lǒcǔlus. A purse. See crumena.

lǒcus, plur. loci and loca.—EP. Known, used, nōtus, sǒlǐtus. Distant, longinquus, rěmōtus. Near, prǒpinquus.

lǒquēla. Speech, language. See lingua.

lōrīca. A breastplate.—EP. Iron, brazen, ferrea, ærea, ahēna. Scaly, squāmea, squāmōsa. Solid, sǒlǐda. Trusty, fīda, fīdēlis. Impenetrable, impěnětrābǐlis. Handy, well-fitting, hăbǐlis, apta. Light, lěvis. Embossed, cælāta. Inlaid with gold, aurea.

lōrum. A rein. See habena.

lōtus, i, fem. The lotus-tree.—EP. Milky, lactea. Soft, mollis, těněra.

lūcerna. A candle. See lampas.

lǔcrum, lǔcellum. Gain.—EP. Honest, prǒbum, æquum. Desired, quæsǐtum, optātum. Great, magnum. Sudden, sūbǐtum. New, nǒvum.

luctāmen, ǐnis, neut. A wrestling.—EP. Hard, durum. Long, longum.

luctātor, ōris, masc. A wrestler.—EP. Strong, rǒbustus, vălǐdus, lăcertōsus. Fearless, fortis, impăvǐdus. Skilful, pěrītus.

luctus, ûs. Grief. See dolor.

lūcus. A grove.—EP. Of ash, of beech, etc., fraxǐneus, făgǐneus, etc. Green, vǐrǐdis, vǐrǐdans. Shady, umbrōsus, umbrǐfer -ěri, ǒpācus. Old, větus -eris, antīquus. Sacred, săcer -cri, sācrātus, sanctus. Leafy, frondōsus, frondens.

lūdǐbrium. Ridicule.—EP. Deserved, měrǐtum, dēbǐtum. Well-known, nōtum.

lūdus. Sport, play, a game.—EP. Merry, joyful, hǐlāris, lætus. Festive, festus. Solemn, recurring at stated periods, sǒlennis. Short, brěvis. Sacred, săcer -cri, sācrātus.

lues, is. A plague.—EP. Wasting, tābǐda. Destructive, fatal, nǒcens, noxia, damnōsa, fātālis, exǐtiōsa, lētǐfěra. Sent from heaven, cœlestis. Ill-omened,

E 2

52   LUM—MAG

obscœna. *Pale, making pale*, pallĭda. *Sad*, tristis, mĭsĕra, mĭsĕranda, mĭsĕrābĭlis.

lūmen, ĭnis, neut. *Light.* See lux.

lūna. *The moon.*—EP. *Pale*, pallĭda. *Silvery*, argentea. *Golden*, aurea. *Shining by night*, nocturna, noctĭvăga. *Horned, crescent-shaped*, bĭcornis. *Dewy*, roscĭda. *Trembling*, trĕmŭla.—*Bright*, clara, splendĭda, fulgens. *Full*, plēna. *Beautiful*, pulchra, candĭda. *Delian* (*because Diana was born at Delos*), Dēlia. *High in heaven*, alta.

lŭpātum. *A bit.* See frenum.

lŭpa, lŭpus. *A wolf.*—EP. *Greedy*, răpax, ăvĭdus. *Insatiable*, insătiăbĭlis. *Pale*, pallĭdus. *Bloody*, sanguĭneus, sanguĭnŏlentus. *Sacred to Mars*, Martius, Māvortius. *Treacherous*, perfĭdus. *Ill-omened, ill-looking*, obscœnus, informis, turpis. *Cowardly*, tĭmĭdus. *Howling*, ŭlŭlans. *Dwelling on mountains or in woods*, montānus, sylvestris.

luscĭnia. *A nightingale.* See Philomela.

lūsor, ōris, masc. *A player.*—EP. *Cheerful*, hĭlăris, lætus. *Festive*, festus.

lustrum. *A haunt of wild beasts, or of any other living thing.*—EP. *Wild*, fĕrum. *Desert, in a desert place*, dēsertum. *Inhospitable*, inhospĭtum, inhospĭtāle. *Blood-stained*, cruentum, sanguĭneum. *Secret*, sēcrētum, lătens, abdĭtum.

lūsus, ūs. *Play, sport.* See ludus.

lŭtum. *Mud.* See limus.

lux, lūcis, fem. *Light.*—EP. *Golden*, aurea. *Bright*, splendĭda, clara, cŏrusca. *Of day*, diurna. *Of heaven*, cœlestis, æthĕria. *Of the sun*, Phœbēa, Phœbēa. *Wished for, desirable*, optāta, optābĭlis. *Lovely*, ămœna, ămābĭlis. *Warm*, călĭda, fervĭda. *Fiery*, ignea, flammea.

luxŭria and luxŭries, ĕi; luxus, ūs. *Luxury.*—EP. *Rich*, dīves –ĭtis, ŏpŭlentus, ŏpīmus. *Wanton*, lascīvus. *Mischievous*, nŏcens, noxius, damnōsus, pernĭciōsus. *Modern*, nŏvus, rĕcens. *Excessive*, nĭmia. *Unprecedented, unusual*, insŏlĭtus, ĭnaudītus. *Proud*, sŭperbus, fastĭdiōsus.

lychnus. *A lamp.* See lampas.

lympha. *Water.* See aqua.

lynx, cis, masc. fem., usu. fem. *A lynx.*—EP. *Spotted*, măcŭlōsa, vāria. *Sacred to Bacchus*, Bacchĭcus, Bacchēius. *Indian*, Indus, Indĭcus, ˘Eōus. *Fierce, Untameable*, trux trŭcis, fĕrus, indŏmĭtus.

lȳra. *A lyre.*—EP. *Tuneful*, cănōra, argūta. *Sacred*, sācra. *Sacred to Apollo*, Ăpollĭnea, Ăpollĭnāris, Phœbēa, Phœbēia. *Sacred to the Muses*, Ăŏnia, ˘Ausŏnia. *Golden*, aurea, aurāta, ĭnaurāta. *Effeminate*, imbellis, mollis. *Cheerful*, jŏcōsa, festīva. *Curved*, curva, incurva, rĕcurva. *Made of the shell of a tortoise*, testūdĭnea.

M.

Măcellum. *Shambles.*—EP. *Dirty*, turpe, fœdum, squālĭdum. *Bloody*, cruentum, sanguĭneum.

māchĭna. *A machine, an engine.*—EP. *Ingenious*, ingĕniosa, callĭda. *Warlike*, bellica. *Destructive*, fătālis, exĭtiōsa. *Hostile*, ĭnĭmīca, infensa. *Employed against*, oppŏsĭta.

măcies, ĕi, fem. *Leanness, wasting.*—EP. *Consuming*, tābĭda. *Sick, arising from sickness, making sick*, ægra. *Ill-looking*, turpis, horrĭda, dēformis. *Excessive*, sŭprēma, summa, ultĭma.

măcŭla. *A spot, a stain.*—EP. *Foul, unsightly*, turpis, dēformis, fœda, tētra. *Disgraceful*, turpis, fœda, prŏbrōsa. *Lasting*, perpĕtua, pĕrennis. *Surviving its cause or object*, sŭperstes, ĭtis.

măga. *A sorceress, a witch.*—EP. *Thessalian* (*the Thessalians were notorious for such practices*), Thessăla, Thessălis –ĭdis, Thessălĭca. *Wicked*, impia, imprŏba, scĕlĕrāta. *Mischievous*, noxia, nŏcens, pernĭciōsa. *Poisoning*, vĕnēfĭca. *Powerful*, pŏtens, effĭcax. *Skilful*, docta, pĕrīta.

măgister, tri. *A director, a teacher.*—EP. 1. *Learned*, doctus. *Skilful, wise*,

MAG—MAT 53

pērītus, prūdens. *Kind*, bŏnus, bĕnignus. *To be respected*, vĕnĕrābĭlis, vĕrendus. *Aged, hoary*, sĕnex, vĕtŭlus, cānus.

măgistrātus, ūs. *A magistrate.*—EP. *Sacred*, sǎcer -crī, sanctus. *Just*, justus, prŏbus, æquus. *August*, augustus, vĕnĕrābĭlis, vĕrendus. *Severe*, sĕvērus, rĭgĭdus.

măgus. *A magician.* See maga.

majestas. *Majesty.*—EP. *Sacred*, sǎcra, sancta, sǎcrāta. *Divine*, dīvīna, cœlestis. *August*, augusta, vĕnĕrābĭlis, vĕrenda. *Ancient*, antīqua, prisca, vĕtus -ĕris.

māla. *The cheek.*—EP. *Tender*, mollis, tĕnĕra. *Beardless*, imberbis, intonsa. *Rosy*, rŏsea. *Fair*, candĭda, nĭvea.

mălĕdictum. *Reproach.* See convicium.

malleus. *A hammer.*—EP. *Iron*, ferreus, ferrātus. *Heavy*, grăvis. *Loud*, clārus. *Lifted up* (*to give a blow*), sŭblātus.

mālum. *An apple.*—EP. *Golden*, aureum, flāvum. *Rosy*, rŏseum. *Sweet*, dulce. *Ripe*, mātūrum. *Hanging*, pendens.

mălum. *Evil.*—EP. *Sad*, triste, mĭsĕrum, mĭsĕrābĭle, flebĭle. *Inevitable*, Inēvĭtābĭle. *Impending*, fŭtūrum, ventūrum.

mālus. *A mast.*—EP. *Tall*, altus, arduus, prōcērus. *Bending* (*in a storm*), trĕmens, nūtans. *Round, smooth, taper*, tĕres -ĕtis. *Covered with sails*, vēlĭvŏlus.

mancĭpium. *A slave.* See servus.

mandātum. *A command.* See jussum.

māne, indecl. neut., used as nom. acc. and abl. *Morning.*—EP. *New, early*, nŏvum, primum. *Rising, just risen*, ortum, exortum. *Dewy*, roscĭdum, pruīnōsum. *Cool*, frĭgĭdum, gĕlĭdum. *Shining*, clārum, rădians. *Ruddy*, rŏseum, purpŭreum.

mānes, ĭum, plur. masc. *The spirits of the dead, the shades below.*—EP. 1, 2. *Dwelling below*, inferni, prŏfundi, ĭmi. *Sad*, tristes, mĭsĕri. *To be worshipped by night*, nocturni. *Unsubstantial*, tĕnues, lĕves, exĭles. *Pale*, pallĭdi, pallentes. *Silent*, tăcĭti, sĭlentes.—1. *Dear*, cāri, dilecti, ǎmāti. *Lamented*, flēti. *Lifeless*, exănĭmis.—2. *Dark*, obscūri, opaci.

mănīca. *A fetter.* See vinculum.

mannus. *A horse.* See equus.

mantĭca. *A wallet.*—EP. *Full*, plēna. *Heavy*, grăvis.

mănus, ūs, fem. 1. *A hand.*—2. *A band.*—EP. 1. *Right*, dextĕra, sync. dextra. *Left*, læva, sĭnistra. *Able to grasp*, căpax. *Strong*, vălĭda, pŏtens. *Fair*, candĭda, nĭvea. *Armed*, armāta. *Bearing a sword or shield*, ensĭfĕra, clўpeāta. *Unarmed*, inermis. *Ingenious*, ingĕnĭŏsa.—2. See caterva.

măre, is, neut. *The sea.*—EP. *Deep*, prŏfundum, altum. *Passed over by ships or sails*, vēlĭvŏlum. *Treacherous*, infĭdum, perfĭdum. *Stormy*, prŏcellōsum, inquiētum, turbĭdum. *Full of waves*, undōsum. *Tranquil*, tranquillum, sĕrēnum, strātum. *Salt*, salsum. *Long, vast*, longum, vastum. *Blue*, cærūleum, cærŭlum. *The realm of Neptune, of Nereus*, Neptūnium, Nĕrēium. *Ebbing and flowing*, rĕfluum, rĕfluens. *Untractable*, indōcĭle. *Dashed against the shore*, illīsum scŏpŭlis.

margo, ĭnis, masc. fem. *An edge.*—EP. *Outermost*, extrēmus, ultĭmus. *Long*, longus. *Surrounding*, circumfūsus.

mărītus. *A husband.*—EP. *Dear*, cārus, dīlectus, ǎmātus. *Faithful*, fīdus, fĭdēlis.

marmor, ŏris, neut. *Marble.*—EP. *White*, nĭveum, candĭdum. *Variegated*, vărium. *Easily carved*, sculptĭle. *Carved*, sculptum. *Parian, Carystian, Tænarian, etc.*, Părium, Cărystium, Tænărium.

massa. *A mass, a lump.*—EP. *Great*, ingens, magna. *Heavy*, grăvis. *Ductile* (*of metal*), ductĭlis, tractābĭlis.

māter, tris, fem. *A mother.*—EP. *Tender*, tĕnĕra. *Loving, affectionate*, ǎmans, pia. *Loved*, cāra, ǎmāta, dilecta. *Anxious*, anxia, sollĭcĭta, stŭdĭōsa. *Watchful*, vĭgĭl -ĭlis, vĭgĭlans.

mātĕria and mātĕries, eī, fem. *Matter, materials.*—EP. *Sufficient*, ampla. *Valuable*, prĕtĭōsa. *Worthless*, vīlis.

mātrōna. *A matron.*—EP. *Chaste*, casta, pŭdīca, vĕrēcunda. *Respectable*, vĕnĕrābĭlis, vĕnĕranda, vĕrenda. *Aged*, vĕtŭla, annōsa, grandæva.

E 3

54 MED—MET

mĕdĭcāmen, ĭnis, neut. **mĕdĭcīna**. *Medicine.*—EP. *Wholesome*, sălūbris, sălūtāris, sălūtĭfĕra. *Useful*, ūtĭlis, pŏtens. *Sacred to Apollo*, Āpollīnea, Āpollīnāria, Phœbēa, Phœbēia. *Or to Machaon*, Māchāŏnia. *Giving life*, vītālis. *Giving aid*, auxĭliāris. *Fitting*, apta, ĭdōnea. *Wished for*, *desirable*, optāta, optābĭlia.

mĕdĭcus. *A physician.*—EP. *Skilful*, doctus, pĕrītus. *Friendly*, ămīcus. *Giving present aid*, præsens. *Bringing aid*, ŏpĭfer -ĕri. See above.

mĕdulla. *The marrow.*—EP. *Inmost*, intĭma, ĭma.

mel, **mellis**, neut. *Honey.*—EP. *Sweet*, dulce. *Made of flowers*, flōreum. *Fragrant*, frāgrans, ŏdōrum, ŏdōrātum. *Yellow*, flāvum, aureum. *Pur*, pūrum, lĭquĭdum. *Attic*, *Hymettian*, *Matine*, *etc.*, Cēcrŏpium, Hȳmiettium, Mātīnum. *Sticky*, tĕnax.

mĕlōs, indecl. neut. *Melody.*—EP. *Tuneful*, cănōrum, argūtum, lĭquĭdum. *Divine*, dīvīnum. *Of the lyre*, lȳrĭcum. *Learned*, *skilfully composed*, doctum. *Ancient*, *well-known*, priscum, vĕtus -ĕris, nōtum.

mĕmōria. *Memory.*—EP. *Faithful*, fīda, fĭdēlis. *Tenacious*, tĕnax.

menda, **mendum.** *A blemish.*—EP. *Unsightly*, dēformis, turpis, fœda. *Old*, prisca, vĕtus -ĕris. *Conspicuous*, conspĭcua, conspĭcienda.

mendācium. *A lie.*—EP. *False*, fictum. *Cunning*, callĭdum, dŏlōsum. *Base*, turpe, fœdum. *Perfidious*, perfĭdum, infĭdum. *Wicked*, impium, imprŏbum.

mendĭcus. *A beggar.*—EP. *Wandering*, văgus. *Lying*, falsus, fallax. *Helpless*, ĭnops -ŏpis. *Poor*, pauper -ĕris, ĕgēnus.

mens, **tis**. *The mind.*—EP. *Wise*, săpiens, săgax. *Prudent*, *full of foresight*, prūdens, prŏvĭda. *Pious*, *good*, pia, casta. *Anxious*, anxia, sollĭcĭta. *Timid*, tĭmĭda. *Prophetic*, præscia, præsāga.

mensa. *A table.*—EP. *Made of oak*, *beech*, *etc.*, querna, fāgĭnea. *Simple*, *simplex* -ĭcis. *Clean*, munda. *Inlaid with gold*, aurea. *Rich*, *luxurious*, dīves -ĭtis, lauta, luxūriōsa, ŏpīma. *Loaded*, grăvis, plēna, ŏnusta.

mensis, **is**, masc. *A month.*—EP. *Swiftly passing*, fūgiens, răpĭdus, brĕvis. *Revolving*, rĕvŏlūbĭlis. See Gradus.

mensūra. *A measure.*—EP. *Just*, *fair*, æqua, justa.

mentum. *A chin.*—EP. *Bearded*, barbātum, hirsūtum. *Beardless*, intonsum, imberbe. *With grey beard*, cānum, incānum.

mēphītis, **is.** *A stench.*—EP. *Bad*, măla, sæva. *Sulphureous*, sulfūrea.

mercātor, **ōris**, masc. *A merchant.*—EP. *Rich*, dīves -ĭtis, ŏpūlentus, lŏcūples -ētis. *Anxious*, anxius, sollĭcĭtus. *Wandering*, văgus. *Eager for gain*, ăvĭdus.

merces, **ēdis.** *Hire*, *reward.*—EP. *Just*, justa, æqua. *Deserved*, mĕrĭta, dēbĭta, digna. *Ample*, ampla, magna.

merges, **ĭtis**, masc. *A sheaf of corn.*—EP. *Of wheat*, trītĭceus. *Sacred to Ceres*, Cĕrĕālis. *Collected*, collecta, coacta. *Abundant*, amplus, largus.

mergus. *A cormorant.*—EP. *Marine*, æquŏreus, mărīnus. *Basking in the sun*, ăprīcus. *Greedy*, ăvĭdus, răpax.

mĕrīdies, **ei**, fem. *Midday.*—EP. *Hot*, fervĭda, torrĭda. *Bright*, clāra, rŭtĭla.

mĕrĭtum. *Desert.*—EP. *Great*, magnum. *Useful*, ūtĭle. *Ancient*, priscum, vĕtus -ĕris.

mĕrum. *Wine.* See vinum.

mĕrŭla. *A blackbird.*—EP. *Tuneful*, cănōra. *Innocent*, innŏcens, innoxia, innŏcua. *Dark*, fusca, nĭgra.

merx -cis, fem. *Merchandise.*—EP. *Foreign*, pĕrĕgrīna, externa. *Distant*, longinqua. *Bought*, empta. *Brought* (*to a place*), advecta.

messis, **is**, fem. *Harvest.*—EP. *Sacred to Ceres*, Cĕrĕālis. *Golden*, aurea, flāva. *Abundant*, immensa, ampla, larga, dīves -ĭtis, ŏpīma. *Ripe*, mātūra. *Of corn*, *of wheat*, spīcea, trītĭcea. *Wished for*, optāta. *Autumnal*, autumnalis. *Productive*, fēcunda, fertĭlis, fĕrax. *Genial*, *nutritious*, alma.

messor, **ōris**, masc. *A reaper.*—EP. *Hardy*, *strong*, dūrus, rŏbustus, vălĭdus. *Sunburnt*, ustus, pĕrustus. *Bearing a sickle*, falcĭfer -ĕri. *Rustic*, rustĭcus, āgrestis. *Unwearied*, indēfessus. *Active*, impĭger -gri, acer -cris.

mēta. *A limit*, *a boundary.*—EP. *Extreme*, extrēma, ultĭma, nŏvissĭma. *Wished for*, optāta.

mĕtallum. 1. *Metal.*—2. *A mine.*—EP. 1. *Hard*, dūrum. *Yellow*, *golden*, *white*, *silver*, *etc.*, flāvum, aureum; album, candĭdum, argenteum.—2. *Inexhaust*-

MET—MON 55

ible, ĭnexhaustum. *Deep*, prŏfundum, altum. *Lowest, the bottom of, etc.*, ĭmum.
—1, 2. *Dug out*, effossum.

mĕtus, ûs. *Fear.* See tremor.

mīca. *A crumb, a grain.*—EP. *Little*, parva, parvŭla, exĭgua.

mīles, ĭtis. *A soldier.*—EP. *Brave, fearless*, fortis, audax, impăvĭdus. *Devoted to Mars*, Martius, Mavortius. *Invincible*, invictus, indŏmĭtus. *Victorious*, victor. *Fierce, cruel*, sævus, fĕrus, immītis. *Armed with spear, shield, crested helmet, etc.*, hastātus, clÿpeātus, cristātus, ensĭfer –ĕri, etc. *Bloodthirsty, bloodstained*, cruentus, sanguĭneus, sanguĭnŏlentus.

mĭlĭtia. *Military service.*—EP. *Cruel*, sæva, fĕra, immītis. See above.

milvius, milgua. *A hawk.*—EP. *Greedy*, ĕdax, ăvĭdus, răpax. *Fierce*, fĕrus, sævus. *Swift*, cĕler –ĕris, răpĭdus, præpes, ĕtis. *Flying high*, sŭblīmis, altus, arduus. *With crooked talons*, uncus, ăduncus.

mīmus, mīma. *An actor, actress.*—EP. *Skilful*, pĕrītus, callĭdus. *Known*, nōtus. *Excellent*, insignis, ēgrĕgius. *Wanton*, lascīvus, prŏtervus.

mĭnæ, plur. fem. *Threats.*—EP. *Terrible*, dīræ, terrĭbĭles. *Cruel, severe*, sævæ, rĭgĭdæ, sĕvēræ. *Angry*, īrātæ, īrācundæ. *Swelling, proud*, tŭmĭdæ, superbæ.

Mĭnerva. *The daughter of Jupiter, etc.* (see the Gradus).—EP. *Mighty in arms*, armĭpŏtens. *Warlike*, bellĭca, armĭsŏna. *Learned*, docta. *Attic*, Cĕcrŏpia. *Born of the head of Jove*, Trĭtōnia. *Virgin*, innupta, casta, pŭdĭca. *Bringing peace*, pācĭfĕra.

mĭnister, trī, mĭnistra. *A servant.* See servus.

mīrācŭlum. *A wonder.*—EP. *Portentous*, prŏdĭgĭōsum. *Strange, unheard of*, nŏvum, ĭnaudītum, insŏlĭtum. *Divine*, dīvīnum, cœleste.

mīrātor, ōris, masc. *A wonderer.*—EP. *Astonished*, attŏnĭtus. *Silent*, tăcĭtus. *Unaccustomed to the thing*, ĭnassuetus, insŏlĭtus.

missus, ûs. *A sending forth.*—EP. *Prudent*, prūdens, prōvĭdus. *Distant*, longinquus, rĕmōtus. *Original*, prīmus.

mītra. *A turban.*—EP. *Eastern, Indian, Persian*, Ēōa, Inda, Indĭca, Persĭca. *Effeminate*, mollis, fœmĭnea, mŭlĭĕbris.

mōbĭlĭtas. *Easiness of motion.*—EP. *Light*, lĕvis. *Easy, handy*, făcĭlis. *Swift*, cĕlĕris, cĭta.

mŏdĕrāmen, ĭnis, neut. *Rule over.*—EP. *Powerful*, pŏtens. *Just*, justum, æquum. *Kind*, bĕnignum, mīte.

mŏdĕrātor, ōris, masc. *A ruler.* See rector.

mŏdestia. *Modesty.*—EP. *Chaste*, casta, vĕrēcunda, pŭdĭbunda, pŭdĭca. *Becoming*, dĕcens, dĕcōra. *Feminine*, fœmĭnea. *Virgin*, virgĭnea, puellāris. *Juvenile*, jŭvĕnīlia.

mŏdŭlātor, ōris, masc. *A musician.*—EP. *Tuneful*, argūtus, dulcis, cănōrus, vōcālis. *Skilful*, callĭdus, pĕrītus.

mŏdus. 1. *A manner.*—2. *Moderation.*—3. *A song, a tune* (*usu. in plur. in this sense*).—EP. 1. *Various*, vărius. *Customary*, sŏlĭtus, assuetus. *Novel*, nŏvus, ĭnaudītus, insŏlĭtus.—2. *Golden*, aureus. *Fair*, æquus, justus.—3. See cantus.

mœnia, um, plur. neut. *Walls, esp. fortified walls.*—EP. *Strong*, fortia. *Safe*, tūta. *Lofty*, alta, celsa, ardua. *Impregnable*, invicta, ĭnexpugnābĭlia. *Inaccessible*, ĭnaccessa.

mœror, ōris, masc. *Grief.* See dolor.

mōla. 1. *A millstone.*—2. *A sacrificial cake.*—EP. 1. *Hard*, dūra. *Heavy*, grăvis. *Of pumice stone*, pūmĭcea.—2. *Sacred*, săcra, săcrāta. *Salt*, salsa.

mōles, is. 1. *A mass.*—2. *Labour.*—EP. 1, 2. *Vast*, ingens, vasta. *Collected*, congesta, coacta.—2. See labor.

mōlīmen, ĭnis, neut. *An effort.* See conamen.

mollĭties, ēi. *Softness.*—EP. *Tender*, tĕnĕra. *Feminine, effeminate*, fœmĭnea, mŭlĭĕbris.

mōmentum. 1. *A moving power, a motive.*—2. *A moment.*—EP. 1. *Serious*, grăve. *Powerful*, pŏtens, effĭcax.—2. *Brief*, brĕve. *Fleeting*, fugax.

mŏnēdŭla. *A jackdaw.*—EP. *Black*, nĭgra, ătra. *Talkative*, lŏquax, garrŭla. *Greedy*, ăvĭda, ĕdax, răpax.

mŏnēta. *Coin.*—EP. *Yellow*, fulva. See pecunia.

mŏnīle, is, neut. *A necklace.*—EP. *Golden*, aureum, aurātum, ĭnaurātum.

56 MON—MUN

Jewelled, gemmeum, gemmans, gemmātum. *Valuable,* prĕtiōsum. *Hanging down,* dēmissum, pendens.

mŏnĭtor, ōris, masc. *An adviser.*—EP. *Wise,* săpiens, prūdens, săgax. *Friendly, kind,* ămīcus, bĕnignus. *Present,* præsens. See below.

mŏnĭtum, mŏnĭtus, ûs. *Advice, warning.*—EP. *Wise,* săpiens, prūdens, săgax. *Friendly,* ămīcus, bĕnignus. *Pious,* pius. *Seasonable,* tempestīvus. *Serious, important,* grăvis. *Useful,* ūtĭlis, aptus, idōneus. *Prophetic,* præscius, præsāgus. *Fortunate,* fēlix –īcis, faustus, sĕcundus. *To be recollected, obeyed,* rĕtĭnendum, servandum.

mons, tis, masc. *A mountain.*—EP. *Lofty,* altus, arduus, aĕrius. *Abrupt,* præruptus. *Snow-capt,* nĭvălis, nĭveus, nĭvōsus. *Cloud-capt,* nūbĭfer. *Precipitous,* præceps –ĭpĭtis. *Lying to the sun,* ăprīcus. *Shady,* umbrōsus, ŏpācus. *Wooded,* nĕmōrōsus, sylvester –tris. *Sacred,* săcer –cri, săcrātus.

monstrător, ōris, masc. *A shower, an inventor.*—EP. *Ingenious,* ingĕniōsus, callĭdus. *Useful,* ūtĭlis. *Celebrated,* clārus, insignis, ēgrĕgius.

monstrum. *A prodigy.*—EP. *Marvellous,* mīrum, mīrābĭle. *Novel,* nŏvum. *insŏlĭtum,* ĭnaudītum. *Heaven-sent,* cœleste, dīvīnum.

mŏnŭmentum. *A monument.*—EP. *Marble,* marmŏreum. *Sculptured,* sculptum. *Lasting,* æternum, pĕrenne. *Surviving its object,* sŭperstes –ĭtis. *Large,* magnum, ingens. *Proud,* sŭperbum. *Mindful,* mĕmor –ŏris.

mŏra. *Delay.*—EP. *Slow,* lenta, tarda. *Lazy,* iners, segnis. *Vexatious,* grăvis, mŏlesta. *Long,* longa. *Hateful,* invīsa, ŏdiōsa.

morbus. *Disease.*—EP. *Long,* longus. *Wasting,* tābĭdus. *Fatal,* fătālis, lētĭfer ēri. *Pale, making pale,* pallĭdus, pallens. *Causing languor,* iners, languĭdus. *Sad,* tristis. *Hated,* invīsus.

mors, tis, fem. *Death.*—EP. *Last,* ultĭma. *Pale,* pallĭda. *Cruel, bitter,* fēra, sæva, crūdēlis, immītis, ăcerba. *Untimely,* immātūra, intempestīva. *Inexorable,* ĭnexōrābĭlis, ĭllācrymābĭlis. *Causing tears,* lăcrўmōsum, flēbĭle. *Stygian, conducting to the Styx,* Stўgia. *Bloody,* crŭenta, sanguīnea, sanguĭnŏlenta. *Cold,* frīgĭda, gĕlĭda. *Sudden,* sŭbĭta. *Violent,* viŏlenta. *Sickening,* ægra. *Glorious,* pulchra, dĕcōra.

morsus, ûs. *A bite.*—EP. *Cruel,* sævus, fērus. *Rapacious,* răpax.

mōrum. *A mulberry.*—EP. *Purple, ruddy,* purpŭreum, sanguĭneum. *Ripe,* mātūrum. *Soft,* molle.

mōrus, i, fem. *A mulberry-tree.*—EP. *Tall,* alta, ardua. *Productive,* fērax, fĕcunda, fertĭlis.

mos, mōris, masc. *A custom.*—EP. *Ancient, old-fashioned,* priscus, vĕtus –ĕris, antīquus. *Hereditary,* pătrius, păternus, ăvītus. *National,* pătrius. *Fixed, lasting,* stăbĭlis, perpĕtuus. *Sacred,* săcer –cri, săcrātus, sanctus. *Pious,* pius. *Good,* prŏbus. *To be imitated,* ĭmĭtābĭlis.

mōtus, ûs. 1. *Motion.*—2. *Tumult.*—EP. 1. *Rapid,* răpĭdus, cĕler –ĕris, cĭtus. *Easy,* făcĭlis. *Graceful,* ēlĕgans, vĕnustus, dĕcōrus, dĕcens. *Joyful,* lætus, hĭlāris. *Tremulous,* trĕmŭlus, trĕmēbundus, trĕmens. *Violent,* viŏlentus. *Slow,* tardus, lentus.

mūcro, ōnis, masc. *A sword.* See ensis.

mūgītus, ûs. *A lowing.*—EP. *Loud,* clārus. *Hoarse,* raucus. *Defenceless,* imbellis.

mūla, mūlus. *A mule.*—EP. *Slow,* lentus, pĭger –gri. *Obstinate,* pertīnax. *Stupid,* bēbes –ĕtis.

mulcta. *A fine.*—EP. *Heavy,* grăvis. *Deserved,* mĕrīta, dēbīta. *Just,* justa, æqua. *Undeserved, unjust,* immĕrīta, ĭnīqua.

mulctra, mulctrāle, is, neut. *A milkpail.*—EP. *Full,* plēna. *Foaming,* spūmea, spūmosa, spūmans. *Full of white liquor,* nĭvea, alba, candĭda, candens.

mŭlier –ĕris. *A woman.* See fēmina.

mundĭtia. *Cleanliness, neatness.*—EP. *Pure,* pūra. *Simple,* simplex –ĭcis. *Becoming,* dĕcens, dĕcōra. *Rustic,* rustĭca, ăgrestis. *Chaste, modest,* casta, pŭdīca.

mundus. *The world.*—EP. *Vast,* vastus, ingens. *Revolving,* rĕvŏlūbĭlis. *Eternal,* æternus. *Perishable,* frăgĭlis, cădūcus. See the Gradus.

mūnia, ōrum, plur. neut. *Offices, duties.*—EP. *Important,* magna, grăvia. *To be performed,* pĕrăgenda.

mūnīmen, ĭnis, neut. *A fortification.*—EP. *Strong,* vălĭdum, forte. *Iron,* terreum. *Threatening*, minax. *Inaccessible*, inaccessum. *Invincible, impregnable*, inexpugnabile, invictum.

munitor, oris, masc. *A fortifier.*—EP. *Skilful*, doctus, peritus, callidus, *Warlike*, bellicus. *Brave, fearless*, fortis, impavidus. *Invincible*, invictus.

munus, eris, neut. *A gift.* See donum.

murex, icis, masc. 1. *A shellfish from which purple was obtained.*—2. *Purple.* —EP. 1, 2. *Purple*, purpureus. *Marine*, aequoreus, marinus. *Tyrian*, Tyrius, Sidonius. *Eastern*, Eous.

murmur, uris, neut. *A murmur.*—EP. *Great, loud*, magnum, clarum. *Hoarse*. raucum. *Indistinct*, caecum. *Slight, gentle*, tenue, leve, lene. *Threatening*, minax. *Unmeaning*, inane.

murus. *A wall.*—EP. *High*, altus, arduus, celsus. *Built up*, congestus. *Strong*, validus. *Unshaken*, immobilis, inconcussus. *Tottering*, labans, caducus.

mus, muris, masc. *A mouse.*—EP. *Little*, parvus, exiguus. *Greedy*, edax, avidus.

musa. *The muse.*—EP. *Aonian, Castalian, etc.*, Aonia, Castalia, Pieria, etc. *Tuneful*, canora, arguta, vocalis. *Sacred*, sacra. *Pious*, pia. *Mindful*, memor –oris. *Learned*, docta. *Divine, eternal*, divina, aeterna. *Virgin*, virginea, casta. See the Gradus.

muscus. *Moss.*—EP. *Green*, viridis, viridans, virens. *Soft*, mollis, tener –eri. *Damp, moist*, udus, humidus, madidus.

myrtus, i, fem. *A myrtle.*—EP. *Sacred to Venus*, Cytherea. *Green*, viridis, viridans, virens. *Sweet-smelling*, fragrans, odora, odorata, suaveolens. *Simple*, simplex –icis. *Growing on the shore*, littorea. *Dark-coloured*, nigra, atra. *Loved by shepherds*, pastoralia. *Tender*, tenera.

mysterium. *A mystery.*—EP. *Sacred*, sacrum, sacratum, sanctum. *Obscure*, obscurum, abditum, ignotum, incognitum. *Ancient*, vetus –eris, priscum, antiquum.

N.

Naenia. *A dirge.*—EP. *Sad*, tristis, maesta, flebilis, lacrymosa. *Tuneful*, canora, numerosa. *Funereal*, funebris, funerea.

nanus. *A dwarf.*—EP. *Little*, parvus, exiguus. *Unsightly*, deformis.

nardus. *Spikenard.*—EP. *Assyrian*, Assyrius. *Sweet, fragrant*, dulcis, fragrans, odoratus.

naris, is, fem. *A nostril.*—EP. *Acute*, acuta. *Open (to snuff the breeze)*, patula, patens. *Hooked*, unca, adunca.

narratus, us. *A relation, the telling of a story.*—EP. *Long*, longus. *True*, verus, verax. *Well-known*, notus.

nasus. *The nose.* See naris.

nata, natus. *A daughter, a son.* See filius.

natator, oris, masc. *A swimmer.*—EP. *Strong*, fortis. *Skilful*, peritus. *Fearless*, impavidus.

natio, onis, fem. *A nation.* See gens.

natura. *Nature.*—EP. *Original*, prima. *Genial*, alma. *Implanted*, insita.

navale, is, neut. *A dock.*—EP. *Capacious*, magnum, capax. *Built*, structum. *Hollow*, cavum. *Safe*, tutum, incolume.

naufragium. *Shipwreck.*—EP. *Sad*, triste, miserum, miserabile, flebile, lugubre. *Fatal*, funestum, fatale. *Ruinous*, exitiosum, exitiale.

navigium. 1. *A ship.*—2. *Navigation, a voyage.*—EP. 1. See navis.—2. *Rapid*, rapidum. *Safe*, tutum. *Stormy*, procellosum. *Dangerous*, periculosum. *Of doubtful result*, dubium, incertum.

navis, is, fem. *A ship.*—EP. *Made of pine*, pinea. *Of oak*, roborea, querna. *Smeared with pitch*, uncta, cerata. *Using sails*, velivola. *Swift*, rapida, velox, cita. *Safe*, tuta, incolumis. *Travelling over the sea*, aequorea, caerulea, caerula. *Hollow*, cava, cavata. *With brazen prow*, aerea, aerata. *Curved*, curva, incurva, curvata, inflexa, adunca. *Tossed about*, jactata. *Wrecked*, fracta, naufraga

58 NAV—NOV

(never used with navis *itself, but with its synonymes,* puppis, *etc.).* See the
Gradus.

nāvīta, nauta, æ, masc. *A sailor.*—EP. *Skilful,* pērītus. *Bold, fearless,*
audax, fortis, impăvīdus. *Active,* impĭger –gri, ācer –cris.

nēbŭla. *A mist, a cloud.*—EP. *Dense,* densa. *Dark,* obscūra, ŏpāca, cæca.
Damp, ūda, hūmīda, hūmens. *Thin,* tĕnuis. *Light,* lĕvis.

nĕcessĭtas. *Necessity.*—EP. *Cruel,* sæva, aspĕra, crūdēlis. *Fixed,* certa. *Im-
moveable,* immōta, immōbĭlis. *Last, extreme,* ultĭma, sŭprēma, extrēma.
Victorious, victrix.

nectar, ăris, neut. *Nectar.*—EP. *Divine,* dīvīnum, cæleste. *Sweet,* dulce.
Etherial, æthĕrium.

nĕfas, indecl. neut. *Wickedness.*—EP. *Sad,* triste, mĭsĕrum. *Disgraceful,* turpe,
fœdum, măcŭlōsum. *Impious,* impium, imprŏbum.

nĕgōtium. *Business.*—EP. *Long,* longum. *Hateful,* invīsum, ŏdiōsum. *Sad,
disagreeable,* triste, mŏlestum, grăve. *Usual,* sŏllĭtum.

nĕmus, ŏris, neut. *A grove.* See lucus.

nĕpos, ōtis, masc. 1. *A grandson.*—2. *A spendthrift.*—EP. 1. *Dear,* cārus,
dīlectus, ămīcus. *Youthful, beardless,* jŭvĕnis, tĕner –ĕri, imberbis, intonsus.
—2. *Prodigal,* prōdĭgus. *Foolish,* dēmens, imprŭvīdus. *Luxurious,* lux-
ūriōsus.

nĕquĭtia. *Wickedness.* See nefas.

nervus. 1. *A sinew.*—2. *A string of a bow, or of a musical instrument.*—EP.
1. *Strong,* vălīdus, vĭgens.—2. (*Of a lyra, etc.*) *Tuneful,* cānōrus, vōcālis,
argūtus. *Struck,* ictus, percussus. *Resounding,* rĕsŏnābĭlis [see chorda, lyra].
(*Of a bowstring*) *Drawn towards one,* adductus. *Made of horsehair,* ĕquīnus.

nex, nĕcis. *Death by being slain.*—EP. *Bloody,* cruenta, sanguĭnea, sanguĭnŏ-
lenta. See mors.

nexus, ūs. *A twining together, a fold.*—EP. *Entwined,* implĭcĭtus. *Winding,*
sĭnuōsus.

nīdor, ōris, masc. *A strong smell.* See odor.

nīdus. *A nest.*—EP. *High,* altus, sŭblīmis. *In a tree,* arbŏreus. *Made of
grass, of moss, etc.,* grāmĭneus, muscōsus. *Concealed, secret,* sēcrētus, abdĭtus. *Safe,*
tūtus, incŏlŭmis. *Inaccessible,* ĭnaccessus. *Rocky, placed on a rock,* saxōsus,
saxeus.

nimbus. 1. *A cloud.*—2. *Rain.*—EP. 1. See nubes.—2. See nuber.

nīsus, ūs. *An effort.*—EP. *Strong,* vălīdus. *Repeated,* crēber –bri, gĕmĭnātus,
ingĕmĭnātus. *Successful,* lætus, fēlix –īcis. *The first,* prīmus.

nītor, ōris, masc. *Brightness.*—EP. *Shining,* clārus, splendĭdus.

nix, nĭvis, fem. *Snow.*—EP. *Deep,* alta, prŏfunda. *Wintry,* hyĕmālis, hўberna,
brūmālis. *Cold,* frĭgĭda, gĕlĭda. *White,* alba, candĭda, candens. *Soft,* mollia.
Slippery, lūbrĭca. *Horrid,* horrĭda, horrĭbĭlis.

nōbĭlĭtas. *Nobility.*—EP. *Highborn,* gĕnĕrōsa, ingĕnua. *Ancient,* vĕtus –ĕris,
prisca, antīqua. *Hereditary,* pătria, păterna, ăvīta. *Illustrious,* clāra, insignis.

noctua. *An owl.*—EP. *Wise,* săpiens. *Sacred to Minerva,* Pallădia. *Athenian,*
Attĭca, Cēcrŏpia. *Hoarse,* rauca. *Late,* sēra.

nōdus. *A knot.*—EP. *Tight,* arctus. *Entangled,* implĭcĭtus. *Joined,* junctus,
conjunctus. *Difficult to untie,* diffĭcĭlis.

nōmen, ĭnis, neut. *A name.*—EP. *Ancient,* vĕtus –ĕris, priscum, antīquum.
Hereditary, pătrium, păternum, ăvītum. *Known,* nōtum. *Illustrious,* clārum,
præclarum, insigne, ēgrĕgium. *Venerable,* vĕnĕrābĭle, vĕrendum. *Sacred,*
săcrum, sanctum. *Powerful,* pŏtens. *Useless, empty,* ĭnāne, ĭnūtĭle.

norma. *A rule.* See lex.

nōta. *A mark of any kind.*—EP. *Conspicuous,* conspĭcua. *Indelible,* indēlēbĭlis.
Discreditable, fœda, turpia.

Nŏtus. *The South-west Wind.*—EP. *Stormy,* prŏcellōsus, vĭŏlentus, turbĭdus,
inquiētus. *Rainy,* ăquōsus, plŭvius, plŭviālis, nimbōsus, nimbĭfer –ĕri. *Warm,*
tĕpĭdus.

Nŏvember –bris, masc. *November.*—EP. *Wintry,* hyĕmālis, hўbernus, brūmālis.
Cold, frĭgĭdus, gĕlĭdus. *Stormy,* prŏcellōsus, ventōsus. *Rainy,* ăquōsus, plŭ-
vius, plŭviālia, nimbĭfer –ĕri.

nŏverca. *A stepmother.*—EP. *Harsh,* aspĕra, dūra, rĭgĭda. *Unjust, unkind,*
injusta, ĭnīqua. *Aged,* annōsa, vĕtŭla.

NOV—OBS 59

nŏvĭtas. *Newness, novelty.*—EP. *Unaccustomed,* insŏlīta, ĭnassueta. *Marvellous,* mīra, mīrābĭlis. *Pleasant,* grāta, āmœna.

nox, noctis, fem. *Night.*—EP. *Black, dusky,* nīgra, ātra, fusca. *Obscure, dark,* obscūra, ŏpāca, tĕnĕbrōsa. *Revolving,* rĕvŏlūbĭlis. *Unseasonable for doing anything, intempesta.* *Quiet,* tranquilla, sĕrēna. *Starry,* sĭdĕrea. *Damp, dewy,* hūmĭda, mădĭda, roscĭda. *Cold,* frīgĭda, gĕlĭda. *Bringing sleep,* sŏpōra sŏpōrĭfĕra. *Silent, noiseless,* tăcĭta, sĭlens.

nūbes, is, fem. *A cloud.*—EP. *Black,* ātra, nīgra, pĭcea. *Dark, causing darkness,* obscūra, ŏpāca. *Bringing rain,* ăquōsa, plŭvĭa, plŭvĭalis, imbrĭfĕra. *Low,* hūmĭlis. *Wintry,* hyĕmālis, hўberna, brūmālis. *Dense,* densa. *Light,* lĕvis. *Collected together,* coacta, collecta (these in plur.).

nūgæ, arum, plur. fem. *Trifles.*—EP. *Light,* lĕves. *Empty, vain,* ĭnānes vānæ.

Nūmen, ĭnis, neut. *Deity.* See Deus.

nŭmĕrus. 1. *A number.*—2. (In plur.) *Harmony, song.*—EP. 1. *Great,* magnus. *Collected,* coactus.—2. See cantus.

nummus. *Money.* See pecunia.

nuntius, nuntia. *A messenger.*—EP. *True,* vērus, vērax. *Sent,* missus. *Faithful,* fīdus, fĭdēlis. *Well-known,* nōtus.

nupta. *A bride.*—EP. *New,* nŏva. *Youthful,* jŭvĕnis. *Modest, blushing,* pŭdĭca, pŭdībunda. *Chaste, virgin,* casta, virgĭnea, intacta, intĕmĕrāta. See uxor.

nuptiæ, arum, plur. fem. *A marriage.*—EP. *Festive,* festæ. *Joyful,* lætæ, hĭlāres. See conjugium.

nŭrus, ûs. *A daughter-in-law.*—EP. *Beloved,* cāra, dilecta. See filia.

nŭtrīmen, ĭnis, neut. *nŭtrīmentum.* *Nourishment.*—EP. *Genial,* almum. *Useful,* ūtĭle. *Wholesome,* sălūbre, sălūtāre. *Customary,* sŏlĭtum, assuetum.

nŭtrix, īcis, fem. *A nurse.*—EP. *Faithful,* fīda, fĭdēlis. *Tender,* tĕnĕra. *Prudent, provident,* prūdens, prŏvĭda. *Genial,* alma. *Kind,* bŏna, bĕnigna.

nūtus, ûs. *A nod.*—EP. *Powerful,* pŏtens. *Favourable,* fēlix –īcis, dexter –ĕri, *sync.* –tri. *To be respected,* vĕrendus, vĕnĕrandus.

nux, nŭcis, fem. 1. *A nut-tree.*—2. *A nut.*—EP. 1. *Fruitful,* fertĭlis, fēcunda, fērax. *Brittle,* frăgĭlis. *Leafy,* frondea, frondōsa (see arbor).—2. *Hard,* dūra.

nympha. *A nymph.*—EP. *Of the woods,* sylvestris. *Of the mountains,* montāna. *Wandering,* văga, errābunda. *Divine,* dīvīna. *Chaste,* casta, pŭdīca. See puella.

O.

Ŏbex, ŏbjĭcis, masc. fem. 1. *A bolt.*—2. *A barrier.*—EP. 1, 2. *Hard, difficult to pass,* dūrus, diffĭcĭlis. *Firm,* firmus. *Iron,* ferreus, ferrātus, ădămantīnus. *Perpetual,* perpĕtuus.

objectus, ûs. *A projection.*—EP. *Jutting out,* exstans. *Conspicuous,* conspĭcuus. *Long,* longus.

ŏbĭtus, ûs. *Death.* See mors.

oblectāmen, ĭnis, neut. *A delight.*—EP. *Pleasing,* grātum, jūcundum, āmœnum, dulce, ămābĭle. *Lasting,* longum, perpĕtuum. *Surviving its cause,* sŭperstes –ĭtis. *Wished for,* optātum. *Customary, known,* sŏlĭtum, nōtum.

ŏblīvio, ōnis, ŏblīvium. *Forgetfulness.*—EP. *Envious.* invĭda, lĭvĭda. *Devouring,* ĕdax, mordax. *Ungrateful,* ingrāta. *Lethœan,* Lēthæa. *Careless,* sēcūra. *Injurious,* damnōsa, nŏcens, noxia, pernĭcĭōsa.

obsĕquium. *Compliance.*—EP. *Friendly,* ămīcum. *Gentle,* mīte. *Willing,* lĭbens. *Pleasing,* ămœnum, ămābĭle, grātum, jūcundum. *Wished for,* optātum, spērātum. *Wise,* săpiens, prūdens. *Winning,* blandum. *Unwilling, forced,* invītum, coactum. *Foolish,* stultum, dēmens.

obses, ĭdis, masc. fem. *A hostage.*—EP. *Given up,* dēdĭtus. *Faithful,* fĭdus, fĭdēlis. *To remain,* mansūrus. *To return,* rĕdĭtūrus.

obsessor, ōris, masc. *A besieger.*—EP. *Hostile,* hostĭlis, ĭnĭmīcus, infensus.

OBS—OPE

Surrounding, circumfūsus, circumstans. *Sounding round,* circumsŏnus. *Fierce,* cruel, fĕrus, saevus. *Unwearied,* indēfessus. *Patient,* pătiens. *Tenacious,* tĕnax. *Brave, strong,* fortis, vălĭdus.

obsĭdĭo, ōnis, fem. *A siege.*—EP. *Long,* longa, diŭturna. *Grievous,* tristis, grăvis. *Bloody,* crŭenta, sanguīnea, sanguīnŏlenta. *Severe,* aspĕra, ăcerba. See above.

obtūtus, ûs. *A looking at.*—EP. *Careful,* attentus. *Long,* longus.

occāsus, ûs. 1. *The setting (of sun, stars, etc.).*—2. *The west.*—EP. 1. *Slow,* lentus. *Late,* sērus. *Dark,* obscūrus, tĕnĕbrōsus, ŏpācus.—2. *Distant,* rēmōtus, longinquus. *Most distant,* extrēmus, ultĭmus. See the Gradus.

occursus, ûs. *A meeting.*—EP. *Expected,* spērātus, exspectātus. *Wished for,* desirable, optātus, optābĭlis. *Pleasant,* grātus, jūcundus, ămābĭlis. *Friendly,* ămīcus. *Sudden,* sŭbĭtus.

oceanus. *The ocean.* See mare.

ŏcellus, ŏcŭlus. *An eye.*—EP. *Bright,* nĭtĭdus, nĭtens. *Eager, quick,* ardens. *Quickly moving,* făcĭlis, cĕler -ĕris. *Beautiful,* pulcher, dĕcōrus. *Black,* nĭger -gri. *Blue,* caerŭleus, caerŭlus. *Modest,* pŭdīcus, pŭdībundus, vĕrēcundus. *Cast down,* dējectus, dēmissus.

ŏdĭum. *Hatred.*—EP. *Bitter,* ăcerbum, aspĕrum, vĭŏlentum. *Implacable,* implăcābĭle, ĭnexōrābĭle. *Long, lasting,* longum, diŭturnum. *Ancient,* vĕtus -ĕris, priscum, antīquum. *Everlasting,* perpĕtuum, aeternum, pĕrenne. *Surviving the provocation,* sŭperstes -ĭtis. *Cruel,* saevum, fĕrum. *Mindful,* mĕmor -ŏris. *Brief,* brĕve. *Wicked,* nēfandum, impium, scĕlĕrātum. *Costly, damaging to him who cherishes it,* prĕtiōsum.

ŏdor, ōris, masc. *A smell.*—EP. *Pleasing, sweet,* dulcis, suavis, jūcundus, ămoenus, ămābĭlis. *Fragrant,* frāgrans. *Known,* nōtus. *Penetrating,* pĕnĕtrābĭlis. *Liquid, pure,* lĭquĭdus, pūrus.

oestrus. *A gadfly.*—EP. *Fierce,* saevus, fĕrox. *Flying,* vŏlātĭlis. *Sent against any one,* immissus.

offensa. *An offence.*—EP. *Serious,* magna, grăvis. *Long, lasting,* longa, diŭturna. See culpa.

offĭcīna. *A workshop.*—EP. *Noisy,* clāmōsa, ranca. *Smoky,* fūmea, fūmōsa, fūmans. *Laborious,* ŏpĕrōsa. *Heavy, full of heavy work,* grăvis.

offĭcĭum. 1. *A duty.*—2. *A kindness.*—EP. 1. *Important,* grăve, magnum. *To be done,* pērăgendum. *Solemn, recurring,* sŏlenne.—2. *Useful,* ūtĭle. *Friendly,* ămīcum. *Deserved,* mĕrĭtum, dēbĭtum. *Wished for,* optātum. *Desirable, pleasing,* optābĭle, grātum, jūcundum, ămoenum.

ŏlea, ŏlīva. *The olive.*—EP. *Sacred to Minerva,* Pallădia. *Athenian,* Attĭca, Cĕcrŏpia. *Sicyonian,* Sīcyōnia. *Of Venafrum,* Vĕnăfrāna. *Fruitful,* fertĭlis, fĕrax, fēcunda. *Pacific, the emblem of peace,* păcĭfĕra. *Green,* vĭrĭdis, vĭrĭdans. *Dark,* caerŭlea. *White, silvery,* albens, candĭda.

ŏleum, ŏlīvum. *Oil.*—EP. *Fat,* pingue. *Shining,* nĭtĭdum. *Making supple,* făcĭle.

ŏlĭtor, ōris, masc. *A market-gardener.*—EP. *Hardy,* dūrus, rŏbustus. *Skilful,* pĕrītus. *Rustic,* ăgrestis, rustĭcus. *Contented,* contentus. *Simple,* simplex -ĭcis.

ŏlor, ōris. *A swan.* See cycnus.

ōmen, ĭnis, neut.—EP. *Sent,* missum. *Sent from heaven,* coeleste, dīvīnum. *Favourable,* bŏnum, sĕcundum, faustum, fēlix, dextĕrum, *syno.* dextrum, laevum. *Betokening advantage,* ūtĭle. *Unfavourable,* infaustum, adversum, infēlix, sĭnistrum, mălum. *Pro, hetic,* praesāgum, praenuntium. *To be venerated,* vĕuĕrābĭle. See the Gradus.

ŏnăger -gri, or ŏnăgrus, i. *A wild ass.*—EP. *Timid,* tĭmĭdus. *Wandering,* văgus.

ŏnus, ĕris, neut. *A burden.*—EP. *Heavy,* grăve, magnum. *Light,* lĕve. *Endurable,* tŏlĕrābĭle. *Unendurable,* intŏlĕrābĭle. *Sad, grievous,* triste. *Hated,* invīsum, ŏdiōsum. *Inevitabel,* ĭnēluctābĭle.

ŏnyx, ўcis, masc. *An onyx, a box of onyx.*—EP. *Costly,* prĕtiōsus. *Striped,* vărius. *Carved,* sculptus.

ŏpĕra. *Work, toil.*—EP. *Diligent, constant,* assĭdua, constans, sēdŭla. *Heavy* grăvis, magna. *Long,* longa, diŭturna. *Faithful,* fĭdēlis, fīda.

ŏpes, um, plur. fem. *Riches.* See divitiae.

OPI—OST   61

ŏpĭfex, ĭcis, masc. *A workman.*—EP. *Hardy,* dūrus, rōbustus. *Skilful,* pĕrītus, doctus, ĭngĕnĭōsus. *Diligent, hard-working,* sēdŭlus, impĭger -gri, ŏpĕrōsus. *Known, famous,* nōtus, insignis. *Working early,* mātūtīnus.

oppĭdum. *A town.* See urbs.

opprŏbrium. *A reproach.*—EP. *Sad, triste,* mĭsĕrum, mĭsĕrābĭle. *Deserved,* mĕrĭtum. *Lasting,* longum, diūturnum. *Everlasting,* perpĕtuum, æternum, pĕrenne. *Foul,* fœdum, turpe. *Surviving its cause,* sŭperstes -ĭtis.

ŏpŭlentia. *Wealth.* See divitiæ.

ŏpus, ĕris, neut. 1. *Work, toil.*—2. *A work*—EP. 1. See opera.—2. *Beautiful, excellent,* pulchrum, ĕgrĕgium, nōbĭle. *Lasting,* mansūrum. *Conspicuous,* conspĭcuum, spectābĭle. *Great,* magnum, ingens.

ōra. 1. *An edge.*—2. *A shore.*—3. *A country.*—EP. 1. See margo.—2. See littus. 3. See regio.

ōrācŭlum, *sync.* ōrāclŭm. *An oracle.*—EP. *Prophetic,* præscium, fātĭdĭcum, prænuntium. *Truthful,* vērum, vērax. *Inexplicit, ambiguous,* ambĭguum, incertum. *Deceitful,* fallax. *Divine,* dīvīnum. *Pythian, Dodonean,* etc., Pgthium, Dōdōnæum, etc. *Ancient,* vĕtus -ĕris, priscum, antīquum. *Venerable,* vĕnĕrābĭle. *Sacred,* sācrum, sācrātum. *Favourable,* faustum, fēlix -īcis, sēcundum.

ōrātor, ōris, masc. *An orator, an ambassador.*—EP. *Eloquent,* făcundus, dīsertus. *Sent,* missus. *Faithful,* fīdus, fĭdēlis.

orbis, is, masc. 1. *Anything circular.*—2. *The world.*—EP. 1, 2. *Round,* rŏtundus.—2. *Great,* magnus, ingens. See mundus.

Orcus. *Hell.*—EP. *Infernal,* infernus. *Reigned over by Pluto,* Plŭtōnius. *Stygian,* etc., Stȳgius, Tartārous. *Dark,* obscūrus, tĕnĕbrōsus, tĕnĕbrĭcōsus. *Dark, lurid,* lūrĭdus, nĭger -gri, āter -tri. *Hated, unlovely,* invīsus, ĭnāmābĭlis. *The lowest, the last,* īmus, intĭmus, ultĭmus, extrēmus. *Pale,* pallĭdus, pallens. *Sad, tristis,* mĭser -ĕri, mĭsĕrābĭlis, flēbĭlis, lācrȳmōsus. *Envious,* invĭdus. *Silent,* tăcĭtus, sĭlens. *Unpitying, implacable,* immītis, implācābĭlis, ĭnexōrābĭlis. See the Gradus.

ordo, ĭnis, masc. 1. *Order.*—2. *A row.*—EP. 1. *Regular,* justus, æquus. *Usual,* sōlĭtus, assuetus. 1, 2. *Well-arranged,* compŏsĭtus, *sync.* compostus. *Long,* longus.

orgia, ōrum, plur. neut. *Orgies.*—EP. *Sacred to Bacchus,* Bacchĭca, Bacchēa, Bacchēia. *Furious, mad,* fŭrĭōsa, insāna. *Impious,* impia, scĕlĕrāta. *Celebrated at night,* nocturna. *Ill-omened,* obscœna.

Ŏriens, tis, masc. *The East.*—EP. *Distant,* longinqua, rĕmōtus. *Most distant,* ultĭmus, extrēmus. *Ruddy,* rŭtĭlus, rŭtĭlans, purpŭreus. *First* (i. e. *the first district to see the day*), prīmus. *Rich,* dīves -ĭtis, ŏpŭlentus, lōcŭples -ētis.

ŏrīgo, ĭnis, fem. *Origin, beginning.*—EP. *First, earliest,* prīma. *Ancient,* vĕtus -ĕris, prisca, antīqua. *Well-known,* nōta. *Obscure, lying hid,* obscūra, cæca, lătens.

ornāmentum, ornātus, ûs. *Ornament.*—EP. *Beautiful, becoming,* pulcher -chri, dĕcōrus, dĕcens, spectābĭlia. *Conspicuous,* conspĭcuua. *Excellent,* exĭmius, præstans, ĕgrĕgius. *Feminine,* fēmĭneus, mŭlĭĕbria. *Girlish,* puellāria, virgĭneus. *Polite, elegant,* cultus. *Various,* vărius. *Eastern,* "Eōus.

ornus, i, fem. *A mountain ash.*—EP. *Growing on the hills,* montāna. *Barren, useless,* stĕrĭlis. *Hard,* dura. *Leafy,* frondea, frondōsa, cōmans. *Green,* vĭrĭdis, vĭrĭdana.

orsum, orsus, ûs. *A beginning.* See principium.

ortus, ûs. 1. *Birth.*—2. *Rising of the sun.*—3. *The East.*—EP. 1. *Noble,* nōbĭlis, gĕnĕrōsus. *Illustrious,* clārus, insignis, inclȳtus.—1, 2. *Earliest,* prīmus. —2. *Ruddy,* rŭtĭlus, rŭtĭlans, purpŭreus.—3. See Oriens.

ōs, ōris, neut. 1. *A mouth, a face.*—EP. 1. *Open,* hians, pătens. *Greedy,* ăvĭdum, vōrax, ĕdax. *Eloquent,* făcundum, dīsertum.—2. See facies.

ŏs, ossis, neut. *A bone.*—EP. *Hard,* dūrum, rĭgĭdum.

oscŭlum. *A kiss.*—EP. *Affectionate,* pium, ămans. *Dear,* cārum, dīlectum. *Pleasant,* dulce, grātum, jūcundum, ămābĭle. *Repeated,* crēbrum, rĕpĕtītum.

ostentum. *A prodigy.* See monstrum.

ostium. 1. *A door, a gate.*—2. *The mouth of a river.*—EP. 1. See porta.—2. *Wide,* lātum. *Subject to the ebb and flow of the tide,* rēfluum, rēfluens. *Hospitable, friendly,* ămīcum. *Roaring,* raucum.

ostrum. *Purple.* See purpura.

62   OTI—PAM

ōtĭum. *Ease, leisure.*—EP. *Tranquil,* tranquillum, sĕrēnum. *Inactive,* ĭners, segne, ignāvum. *Long,* longum, dĭŭturnum. *Of old age,* sĕnīle. *Wished for,* optātum, exoptātum. *Pleasant, desirable,* āmābīle, optābīle, āmœnum, grātum, jūcundum. *Ignoble,* ignōbīle, inglōrium. *Shameful,* turpe. *Free from care,* sēcūrum. *Safe,* tūtum.

ŏvīle, is, neut. *A sheepfold.*—EP. *Fenced,* septum. *Safe,* tūtum. See below.

ŏvis, is, fem. *A sheep.*—EP. *Woolly,* lānīgĕra. *Fleecy,* pellīta. *Bleating,* balans. *Unwarlike, helpless,* imbellis, īnops –ōpis. *Timid, frightened,* tīmīda, păvīda, terrīta. *Apt to flee,* fūgax. *Quiet, placid,* plācīda, tranquilla. *With horny feet,* cornīpes –ĕdis.

ŏvum. *An egg.*—EP. *White,* album, candīdum, nīveum. *Round and smooth,* tĕres –ĕtis. *Full,* plēnum. *Fruitful,* fēcundum.

P.

Pābŭlum. *Fodder, food.*—EP. *Abundant,* amplum, largum. *Genial, nourishing,* almum. *Green,* vīrĭde, vīrĭdans, vīrens.

pactum. *A bargain.*—EP. *Fair,* æquum, justum. *Ratified,* rătum. *Stable,* stăbīle, mansūrum.

pænŭla. *A thick cloak.*—EP. *Warm,* cālĭda. *Heavy,* grăvis. *Of fur,* pellīta. *Fit for winter,* hŷberna, hyĕmālis, brūmālis.

păgīna. *A page.*—EP. *White,* alba, candīda. *Written,* scripta.

păgus. *A village.*—EP. *Small,* parvus, exĭguus. *Rustic,* ăgrestis, rustĭcus.

pălæstra. 1. *A wrestling ground.*—2. *Wrestling.*—EP. 2. *Vigorous,* rŏbusta. *Naked,* nūda. *Anointed,* uncta. *Manly,* vĭrīlis.

pălātĭum. *A palace.*—EP. *Lofty,* altum, arduum. *Proud,* sŭperbum. *Marble,* marmŏreum. *With fine ceilings,* lăqueātum. *Royal,* rēgium, rēgāle. *Magnificent,* magnīfĭcum, splendīdum. *Hereditary,* pātrium, pāternum, ăvītum. *Ivory,* ĕburnum, ĕburneum. *Sculptured,* sculptum.

pălātum. *A palate.*—EP. *Delicate,* acute, subtīle, argūtum.

pălea. *Chaff.*—EP. *Worthless, useless,* stĕrīlis, īnānis, īnūtīlis. *Light,* lĕvis. *Tossed about,* jactăta.

pălear, āris, neut. *A dewlap.*—EP. *Long,* longum. *Hanging down,* dēmissum, pendens.

păliūrus. *A bramble.*—EP. *Thorny,* ăcūtus, spīnōsus.

palla, pallium. *A cloak.*—EP. *Long,* longa. *Embroidered,* picta. *Purple,* purpūrea, Tŷria. *Proud-looking,* sŭperba. *Becoming,* dĕcōra, dĕcens.

pallor, ōris, masc. *Paleness.*—EP. *Bloodless,* exsanguis. *Sickly,* æger –gri. *Sudden,* sŭbĭtus. *Trembling,* trĕmŭlus, trĕmēbundus. *Sallow-looking,* lūrĭdus. *Discoloured,* dĕcōlor –ōris.

palma. 1. *The hand.*—2. *The palm-tree.*—3. *The palm of Victory.*—EP. 1. See manus.—2. *Syrian,* Īdūmæa, Sŷria, Sŷra. *Lofty,* ardua, alta, prŏcēra. *Leafy,* frondea, frondōsa, frondens, cōmans. *Fruitful,* fertīlis, fēcunda. *Quivering,* trĕmŭla, trĕmens.—3. *Deserved,* mĕrĭta, dēbĭta. *Proud,* sŭperba, nōbīlis. *Immortal,* immortālia, æterna, pĕrennis. *Surviving the gainer,* sŭperstes –ĭtis. See Victoria.

palmes, ĭtis, masc. *The shoot of a vine.*—EP. *Loaded with fruit,* ŏnustus, grā –vĭdus, grăvis. See vitis.

palmŭla. *The blade of an oar.* See remus.

palpēbræ, ārum, plur. fem. *Eyelids.*—EP. *Cast down,* dēmissæ. *Modest,* pŭ –dīcæ, pŭdībundæ. See oculus.

pălumbes, is, fem. *A dove.* See columba.

pălus. *A stake.*—EP. *Firm,* firmus. *Upright,* rectus. *Made of oak,* rŏbŏreus, quernus.

pălus, ūdis, fem. *A marsh.*—EP. *Wet,* ūda, hūmĭda, mădĭda. *Deep,* alta, prŏfunda. *Producing bulrushes,* juncōsa, juncea. *Unstable, affording no footing,* instăbīlis. *Muddy,* līmōsa.

pampīnus, fem. *The shoot of a vine.* See vitis.

PAN—PAU 63

pānis, is, masc. *Bread.*—EP. *The gift of Ceres,* Cĕreālis. *Made of wheat,* trītīceus. *White,* albus, candīdus. *Nutritious,* almus.

pannus. *A piece of cloth.* See vestis.

panthēra. *A panther.*—EP. *Indian, Eastern,* Inda, Indīca, ˜Eōa. *Spotted,* picta, mācŭlōsa, vāria. *Fierce,* fĕra, fĕrox, sæva.

păpāver, ĕris, neut. *A poppy.*—EP. *Causing sleep,* sōpōrīfĕrum. *Lethean, causing forgetfulness,* Lēthæum, oblīvīōsum. *Freeing from care,* sēcūrum. *Of various colour,* vārium.

păpīlio, ōnis, masc. *A butterfly.*—EP. *Eastern, Persian,* ˜Eōus, Persīcus. *Of varied colour,* vārius. *Purple,* purpūreus. *Splendid, shining,* splendīdus, rŭtĭlus. *Appearing in summer,* æstīvus. *Feeding on flowers,* flōrĭlĕgus. *Flying,* ālātus, vōlātĭlis, vōlŭcer –cris.

păpilla. *A breast.* See pectus.

păpȳrus. fem. *Paper.*—EP. *Egyptian,* Ægyptia, Nīlīāca. See charta.

Parca. *The Fate.*—EP. *Powerful,* pŏtens. *Inexoruble,* ĭnexōrābĭlis. *Threefold,* trīplex –īcis, tergĕmīna. *Favourable,* bŏna, bĕnigna. *Unfavourable,* aspĕra, mĕla, măligna. See Gradus.

părens, entis, masc. fem. *A parent.* See pater, mater.

păries, părĭĕtis, masc. *The wall of a house.*—EP. *Strong,* vălīdus, firmus. *Made of stone,* saxeus. *Of brick,* coctĭlis.

parma, parmŭla. *A shield.* See clypeus.

parra. *A jay.*—EP. *Talkative,* garrŭla, lŏquax. *Variegated,* văria. *Ill-omened,* sīnīstra, obscœna.

pars, tis, fem. *A part.*—EP. *Each,* ūtrăque. *Different,* vāria, dīversa. *Equal,* æqua.

partus, ûs. *A bringing forth.*—EP. *Long,* longus. *Painful, difficult,* tristis, æger –gri, diffīcĭlis. *Fatal,* fātālis. *Expected,* exspectātus.

pascuum. *Pasture land.*—EP. *Green,* vĭrĭde, vĭrĭdans, vĭrens. *Moist,* irrĭguum, ūdum, mădĭdum, hūmĭdum. *Grassy,* grāmineum, herbōsum, herbīfĕrum, herbĭdum. *Fertile,* fertĭle, fēcundum, fĕrax. *Uncropped,* intonsum.

passer –ĕris, masc. *A sparrow.*—EP. *Little,* parvus, exĭguus. *Brown,* fuscus. *Fighting,* pugnax.

passus, ûs. *A step.* See gradus.

pastor, ōris. *A shepherd.*—EP. *Careful,* sēdŭlus, cautus. *Tender,* tĕner –ĕri. *Vigilant,* vĭgil –īlis. *Hardy,* dūrus. *Fond of music,* vōcālis, cănōrus. *Contented,* contentus. *Simple,* simplex –īcis. *Humble,* hŭmĭlis. *Innocent,* innŏcuus, innoxius. *Pious,* pius. *Anxious,* sollĭcĭtus, anxius.

pătella, pătīna. *A dish.* See lanx.

păter –tris. *A father.*—EP. *Affectionate,* pius, āmans. *Beloved,* ămātus, cārus, dīlectus. *Aged,* sĕnex, annōsus, longævus, vĕtŭlus. *Grey-headed,* cānus. *Venerable,* vĕnĕrābĭlis, vĕrendus, vĕnĕrandus. *Wise,* săpiens, prūdens.

pătĕra. *A goblet.* See poculum.

pătientia. *Patience.*—EP. *Long,* longa. *Unwearied,* indēfessa. *Equal,* æqua.

pătria. *One's native country.*—EP. *Dear,* cāra, dīlecta, ămāta. *Sweet,* dulcis, jūcunda, ămābĭlis. *Native,* nātālis. *Genial,* alma.

pătrōnus, pătrōna. *A patron, a patroness.*—EP. *Powerful,* pŏtens, effĭcax, īdōneus. *Useful,* ūtĭlis. *Kind, friendly,* bŏnus, mītis, bĕnignus, ămīcus. *Ancient,* antīquus, priscus, vĕtus –ĕris. *Eloquent,* fācundus, dīsertus. *Customary,* sŏlĭtus, assuetus, consuetus.

pătruus. *An uncle.*—EP. *Severe,* sĕvĕrus, rĭgĭdus, asper –ĕri. *Aged,* sĕnex, vĕtŭlus, longævus. *Rich,* dīves –ĭtis, ŏpŭlentus, lŏcŭples –ētis.

păvīmentum. *Pavement.*—EP. *Marble,* marmŏreum. *Splendid,* sŭperbum, splendĭdum, magnĭfĭcum. *Inlaid,* vărium.

pāvo, ōnis, masc. *A peacock.*—EP. *Sacred to Juno,* Jūnōnius. *With starry tail,* stellātus, st-llans. *Beautiful,* pulcher –chri, spectābĭlis, vĕnustus, formōsus. *Of various colours,* vārius.

păvor, ōris, masc. *Fear.* See timor.

paupĕries, ēi, paupertas. *Poverty.*—EP. *Sad, unhappy,* tristis, infēlix, mĭsĕra, mĭsĕrābĭlis, ærumnōsa. *Cruel,* aspĕra, ăcerba, sæva, fĕra, immītis. *Anxious,* anxia, sollĭcĭta. *Ancient,* antīqua, prisca, pristīna, vĕtus –ĕris. *Simple,* simplex –īcis. *Contented,* contenta. *Harassing, unseasonable,* importūna. *Ignoble,* ignōbĭlis, inglōria, turpis.

64 PAX—PER

pax, pācis, fem. *Peace.*—EP. *White (clad in white),* alba, albens, candĭda, nĭvea. *Genial,* alma. *Tranquil,* plăcĭda, tranquilla, sĕrēna. *Desired,* optāta, exoptāta. *Desirable,* optābĭlis, ămābĭlis. *Sweet,* dulcis, jūcunda, grāta. *Long, lasting,* longa, diŭturna, mansūra. *Perpetual,* perpĕtua, æterna, pĕrennis. See Gradus.

peccātum. *A sin.*—EP. *Impious,* impium, scĕlĕrātum, scĕlestum. *Forbidden,* vĕtitum. *Disgraceful,* turpe, fœdum, prŏbrōsum, infāme. *Known,* nōtum. *Concealed,* sēcrētum, abdĭtum. *Excusable,* excūsābĭle, lĕve.

pecten, ĭnis, masc. *A comb.*—EP. *Ivory,* ĕburnus, ĕburneus. *Tortoiseshell,* testūdĭneus. *Neat, making neat,* nĭtĭdus. *Golden,* aureus, aurātus. *Jewelled,* gemmeus. *With teeth,* dentōsus.

pectus, ōris, neut. *The breast.*—EP. *Soft,* tĕnĕrum, molle. *Of a woman,* fēmĭneum, mŭlĭĕbre. *Of a girl,* virgĭneum, puellāre. *Of a man,* virīle. *Brave,* forte, ănĭmōsum. *Deep,* īmum. *Beautiful,* pulchrum, dĕcōrum. *Fair,* nĭveum, candĭdum, candens, ĕburneum. *Muscular,* tōrōsum. See cor.

pĕcūlium, pĕcūnia. *Property, money.*—EP. *Abundant,* ampla, larga. *Accumulated,* congesta. *Brazen, silver, etc.,* ærea, argentea, etc. See dīvĭtiæ.

pĕcus, ōris, neut. **pĕcus, ŭdis,** fem. *Cattle, sheep, etc.* See armentum, bos, ovis.

pĕdes –ĭtis, masc. *A pedestrian, a foot-soldier.*—EP. *Strong, brave,* fortis, vălĭdus. *Armed,* armātus. *Bearing spear, etc.,* hastātus. See miles.

pĕdĭsa. *A sponge.*—EP. *Deceitful,* fallax, dŏlōsa. *Destructive,* fătālis, exĭtiōsa, exĭtiālis.

pĕdum. *A shepherd's crook.*—EP. *Rustic.* rustĭcum, ăgreste. *Of a shepherd,* pastōrāle. *Curved,* curvum, rĕcurvum, incurvum, ăduncum.

pĕlăgus, i, neut. *The sea.* See mare.

pellăcia. *Cunning.* See dŏlus.

pellis, is, fem. *A skin.*—EP. *Stripped off,* exūta. *Shaggy,* villōsa, hirsūta. *Tawny,* fulvus. *White,* nĭvea, candĭda. *Thin,* tĕnuis.

pelta. *A small shield.*—EP. *Crescent-shaped,* lūnāta. *Made of wicker-work,* arbūtea, vimĭnea. *Light,* lĕvis. See clypeus.

Pĕnātes –ĭum, or **um,** plur. masc. *Household Gods.*—EP. *Ancestral,* pătrii, păterni, ăvīti. *Safe,* tūti. *Honoured, to be honoured,* culti, vĕnĕrandi. *Holy,* săcri, sancti, săcrāti. *Ancient,* vĕtĕres, prisci, antīqui. *Faithful,* fīdi. *Present, powerful to help,* præsentes, pŏtentes. See Lar.

pĕnetrāle, is, neut. *An inner recess of a house.*—EP. *Inmost,* intĭmum. *Secret,* sēcrētum.

penna. *A feather, a wing.*—EP. *Light,* lĕvis. *Rapid,* răpĭda, præpes –ĭtis, cĭta, vēlox, vŏlūcris. *High, bearing the bird on high,* alta, sūblīmis. *Quivering,* mĭcans. *Trembling (esp. with haste),* trĕpĭdans. *Variegated,* văria. *White,* purple, etc., nĭvea, candĭda, purpūrea, etc.

pensum. *A task.*—EP. *Fair,* æquum. *Allotted,* dătum. *Long,* longum. diŭturnum. *Hard,* dūrum, difficĭle, grăve. *Sad,* triste, mĭsĕrābĭle, mĭsĕrum. *Welcome, pleasing,* grātum, jūcundum, ămœnum, ămābĭle. *Suited to man, or to woman,* virīle, fēmĭneum.

pĕnūria. *Want.* See egestas.

pĕnus, ūs. *Food.* See cibus.

pĕplum. *An embroidered robe for the statues of Goddesses (esp. of Minerva).*—EP. *Sacred,* săcrum, sanctum, săcrātum. *Embroidered,* pictum. *Embroidered with gold,* aureum, aurātum.

pĕra. *A wallet.*—EP. *Full,* plēna. *Heavy,* grăvis. *Empty,* văcua. *Made of leather,* pellīta.

perdix, īcis, fem. *A partridge.*—EP. *Brown,* fusca. *Noisy,* garrŭla. See avis.

perfĭdia. *Perfidy.*—EP. *Impious,* impia, scĕlĕrāta, imprŏba, măla. *Injurious,* damnōsa, noxia, nŏcens, pernĭciōsa, exĭtiālis, exĭtiōsa. *Secret,* sēcrēta, tăcĭta, arcāna, lătens. *Unexpected,* inexpectāta, inŏpīna, nĕcŏpīna. *Deceitful,* fallax, falsa, fraudŭlenta. *Wily,* dŏlōsa, versūta. *Carthaginian,* Pūnĭca, Pœna. *Hateful,* invīsa, ōdiosa. *Perjured,* perjūra. *Ungrateful,* ingrāta. *Unmindful,* immĕmor –ōris. *Unpunished,* inulta.

perfŭgium. *A refuge.* See confugium.

PER—PIG 65

pergŭla. *A balcony.*—EP. *Sunny*, ăprīca. *Shady*, umbrōsa. *Cool*, gĕlĭda, frīgĭda. *Covered in*, tecta.

pĕrīcŭlum, *sync.* **pĕrīclŭm.** *Danger.*—EP. *Great*, grande, magnum, ingens. *So great*, tantum. *Fearful*, dīrum, terrĭbĭle, mĕtuendum, tĭmendum. *Fatal*, fātāle. *Extreme*, ultĭmum, extrēmum, summum. *Sudden*, sŭbĭtum, nĕcŏpīnum, īnŏpīnum. *Varied*, vărium. *Of war*, bellĭcum. *Adverse, opposing*, adversum, oppŏsĭtum. *Numerous*, densum, multum. *Bitter*, ăcerbum, aspĕrum. *Surrounding*, circumfūsum, cingens. *Threatening*, mĭnax. *Future*, ventūrum, rŭtūrum. *Of uncertain result*, incertum, dŭbium.

perjūrium. *Perjury.*—EP. *Profane*, impium, scĕlĕrātum, prŏfānum. *Shameful*, turpe, fœdum. *False*, falsum. See perfĭdia.

pernĭcies, **ēi.** *Injury.*—EP. *Fatal*, fātālis. *Extreme*, ultĭma, extrēma, summa. *Incurable*, immĕdĭcābĭlis. *Slow*, tarda. *Unavoidable*, ĭnēvītābĭlis.

Persia. *Persia.*—EP. *Eastern*, ˘Ēōa. *Distant*, longinqua, rĕmōta, ultĭma. *Conquered*, victa, dŏmĭta. *Unwarlike*, imbellis, mollia. *Wearing quivers*, phărĕtrāta.

persōna. 1. *A mask.*—2. *A character (as in a play).*—EP. 1. *Ingenious*, callĭda, ingĕnĭōsa. 1, 2. *Made to represent something*, ficta. *Suitable*, apta.

pes, pĕdis, *masc.* *A foot.*—EP. *Active, quick*, ăgĭlis, cĕler -ĕris, cĭtus, răpĭdus. *Silent*, tăcĭtus. *Steady, moving steadily*, certus.

pestis, is, *fem.* *Pestilence.*—EP. *Destructive, deadly*, fātālis, exĭtiālis, exĭtiōsa, lĕtĭfĕra. *Incurable*, immĕdĭcābĭlis. *Making sick*, ægra. *Sad, pitiable*, tristis, infēlix, mĭsĕra, mĭsĕrābĭlis. *Burning*, ignea. *Making thirsty*, ărĭda. *Wasting away*, tābĭda. See morbus.

pĕtītor, ōris, *masc.* *A candidate.*—EP. *Ambitious*, ambĭtiōsus. *Prodigal*, prōdĭgus. *Anxious*, sollĭcĭtus, anxius. *Suppliant*, supplex -ĭcis.

pĕtŭlantia. *Petulance.*—EP. *Wanton*, prōterva, lascīva. *Obstinate*, tĕnax. *Unrestrained*, indŏmĭta, effrēna. *Talkative*, lŏquax.

phălanx, gis, *fem.* *A phalanx.* See exercĭtus.

phălērae, ārum, *plur. fem.* *Horse-trappings.*—EP. *Embroidered*, pictæ. *Adorned with gold*, aureæ, aurātæ. ĭnaurātæ.

phărētra. *A quiver.*—EP. *Cretan (because the Cretans were great archers).* Gnossia, Cȳdōnia, Cressa. *Full of arrows*, plēna, grăvĭda. *Golden, silver, ivory*, aurea, aurāta, argentea, ĕburna, ĕburnea. *Inlaid*, picta. *Hollow*, căva. *Light*, lĕvis. *Holding arrows*, săgittĭfĕra.

phăsēlus, *masc. fem.* *A small vessel.* See navis.

philtrum. *A love-spell.*—EP. *Of magic power*, măgĭcum. *Powerful*, pŏtens, effĭcax. *Administered*, dătum. *Successful*, fēlix -īcis, victrix -īcis (*esp. in plur.*).

phĭlўra. *The linden-tree.*—EP. *Easily woven*, făcĭlis, lenta. *Slight*, grăcĭlis. *Pale*, pallĭda, pallens.

phōca *and* **phōce, es**, *fem.* *A seal.*—EP. *Vast*, ingens, magna. *Marine*, æquŏrea, mărīna.

phœnix, īcis, *masc.* *A phœnix.*—EP. *Arabian*, Ărăbus, Ărăbius, Săbæus. *Undying*, immortālis, vīvax. *Rising again*, rĕsurgens.

piācŭlum, piāmen, ĭnis, *neut.* *Expiation, atonement.*—EP. *Suppliant*, supplex -ĭcis. *Powerful, useful*, pŏtens, effĭcax, ūtĭle. *Humble*, hŭmĭle. *Sacred*, săcrum, sanctum.

pīca. *A magpie.*—EP. *Chattering*, garrŭla, lŏquax. *Thievish, wicked*, răpax, imprŏba. *Variegated*, vāria.

pictor, ōris, *masc.* *A painter.*—EP. *Celebrated*, inclўtus, clārus, insignis. *Skilful*, doctus, pĕrītus, sŏlers. *Faithful*, fīdus, fīdēlis.

pictūra. *A picture.*—EP. *Drawn*, expressa. *Unsubstantial*, vāna, ĭnānis. *Faithful*, fīda, fīdēlis. *Surviving the original*, sŭperstes, ĭtis. *Undying*, immortālis, æterna. *Coloured*, cŏlōrāta.

pīcus. *A woodpecker.*—EP. *Sacred to Mars*, Martius, Māvortius. *Variegated*, vărius. *Green*, vĭrĭdis.

pĭĕtas. *Piety (esp. when developed in mercy, affection, etc).*—EP. *Gentle*, mītis. *Lovely*, ămābĭlis. *Just*, justa, æqua. *Watchful*, vĭgil -ĭlis. *Tender*, tĕnĕra. *Pure, holy*, casta, sancta, săcra.

pignus, ōris, *neut.* *A pledge.*—EP. *Deposited*, dĕpŏsĭtum, dătum. *Faithful*, fīdum, fīdēle. *To remain, to last*, mansūrum. *Dear*, cārum. *Valuable*, prĕtiōsum. *Which may be relied on*, certum.

F

66 PIG—POC

pĭgrītia. *Laziness.* See ignavia.

pīla. *A pier.*—EP. *Made of stone,* saxea. *In a river,* flŭviālis. *In the sea,* æquōrea, mărīna. *Strong,* firma. *Built out,* exstructa.

pĭla. *A ball.*—EP. *Round,* rŏtunda, tĕres –ĕtis.

pĭleŏlus, pĭleum.—EP. *A hat.*—EP. *Light,* lĕve. *Fitting,* aptum.

pĭlum. *A javelin.* See jaculum.

pĭlus. *Hair on the body.*—EP. *Shaggy,* hirsūtus, hirtus. *Thick,* densus. *Black,* nĭger –gri, āter –tri.

pīnētum. *A grove of pines.* See pinus.

pinna. *A battlement, a pinnacle.*—EP. *Lofty,* alta, ardua. *On the top,* summa. *Threatening,* mĭnax. *Sculptured,* sculpta. *Worlike,* bellĭca.

pīnus, ûs, fem. *A pine.*—EP. *Tall,* alta, ardua, prōcēra. *Green,* vĭrĭdis, vĭrĭdans, vĭrens. *With prickly leaves,* ăcūta, hirsūta. *Flourishing on Ida or in Pontus.* Īdæa, Pontĭca. *Light,* lĕvis. *Soft,* mollis.

pīrāta. *A pirate.* See prædo.

pīrum. *A pear.*—EP. *Sweet,* dulce. *Soft,* molle.

pīrus, fem. *A pear-tree.*—EP. *Fruitful,* fērax, fĕcunda. *Tall,* prōcēra, alta.

piscātor, ōris, masc. *A fisherman.*—EP. *In the morning,* mātūtīnus. *In the evening,* vespertīnus. *Diligent,* sēdūlus, impĭger –gri. *Skilful,* pĕrītus, callĭdus, *Crafty, deceiving,* văfer –fri, dŏlōsus, fallax. *Careful,* cautus. *Watchful,* vĭgil –ilis.

piscis, is, masc. *A fish.*—EP. *Living in a river,* flŭviālis. *Living in the sea,* æquōreus, mărīnus.

pix, pĭcis, fem. *Pitch.*—EP. *Black,* nĭgra, ātra. *Sticky,* tĕnax. *Produced by trees growing on Mount Ida,* Īdæa. *Produced from pines,* pīnea.

plăcenta. *A cheesecake.*—EP. *Sweet,* dulcis. *Honeyed,* mellīta.

plāga. *A blow.* See ictus.

plāga. *A district.* See regio.

plăgæ. *Nets.* See rete.

planctus, ûs, plangor, ōris, masc. *Beating the breast, wailing.*—EP. *Sad,* tristis, mǐser –ĕri, mĭsĕrābĭlis, lūgūbris. *Feminine,* fēmĭneus, mŭlĭēbris. See dolor.

plānĭties, ēi. *Level ground.*—EP. *Plain, even,* æqua. *Easy to travel over,* făcĭlis. *Wide,* lāta.

planta. *A foot.* See pes.

plătănus, fem. *A plane-tree.*—EP. *Tall,* alta, prōcēra. *Green,* vĭrĭdis, vĭrĭdans, vĭrens. *Bearing no fruit,* stĕrĭlis.

plătea. *A street.*—EP. *Broad,* lāta. *Well known,* nōta.

plausor, ōris, masc. *An applauder.* See below, plausus.

plaustrum. *A waggon.*—EP. *Heavy,* grăve. *Creaking,* strīdens, strīdŭlum. *Slow,* tardum.

plausus, ûs. *Applause.*—EP. *Loud,* clārus. *Willing,* lĭbens. *Genuine,* vērus, vērax. *Cheerful,* lætus. *Favouring,* făvens, sĕcundus. *Wondering,* mīrans.

plēbes, is and plēbs, ēbis, fem. *The common people.*—EP. *Rude, uncivilised,* rūdis, inculta. *Simple,* simplex –ĭcis. *Honest,* prŏba. *Virtuous,* casta. *Ancient, old-fashioned,* antīqua, prisca. *Contented,* contenta. *Uncorrupt,* incorrupta.

plectrum. *The quill with which harp-players struck the harp.*—EP. *Skilful,* doctum, pĕrītum. *Tuneful,* cănōrum. *Ivory,* ĕburnum, ĕburneum.

Plēias, ădis, more usu. in plur. *The Pleiades.*—EP. *Daughters of Atlas,* ˉAtlantēa. *Rainy,* ăquōsa, plŭvia, imbrĭfĕra, plūviālis. *Stormy,* prŏcellōsa. *Wintry,* hÿberna, hÿĕmālis, brūmālis.

plūma. *A feather.* See penna.

plumbum. *Lead.*—EP. *Pale,* pallĭdum, pallens. *Heavy,* grăve. *Dug out of the earth,* effossum.

plŭteus. *A penthouse for troops to work under.*—EP. *Covering,* tĕgens.

Plūto, ōnis. *The King of Hell.*—EP. *Dwelling below,* Infernus. *Ruling over Tartarus, Styx, etc.,* Tartāreus Stÿgius. *Cruel,* sævus, fērus, crūdēlis. *Pitiless, implacable,* immītis, implăcābĭlis, illăcrÿmābĭlis. See Orcus.

plŭvia. *Rain.*—EP. *Wet,* ăquōsa, ūda, mădĭda, hūmĭda. *Continual,* assĭdua, longa. *Wintry,* hÿberna, hÿĕmālis, brūmālis. *Cold,* frĭgĭda, gĕlĭda. *Light,* lĕvis. *Fertilising,* fertĭlis. *Sent from heaven,* cœlestis, æthĕria.

pōcŭlum. *A cup, a goblet.*—EP. *Gold, silver,* aureum, auratum, inauratum,

POD—POR

argenteum. *Embossed,* cælatum. *Simple,* simplex –ĭcis. *Made of beech, of maple, etc.,* Făgĭneum, ăcernum. *Full,* plēnum. *Rosy, full of rosy wine,* rōseum, purpūreum. *Crowned,* cŏrōnātum. *Festive,* festum. *Foaming,* spūmeum, spūmans, spūmōsum.

pŏdagra. *Gout.*—EP. *Causing lumps,* nōdōsa. *Slow, making slow,* tarda. *Attacking old men,* sĕnīlis.

poēma, ătis, neut. *A poem.*—EP. *Divine,* dīvīnum. *Immortal,* æternum, immortāle. *Learned,* doctum. *Known,* nōtum. *Admirable,* ēgrĕgium, insigne.

pœna. *Punishment.*—EP. *Heavy,* grăvis. *Deserved, just,* mĕrĭta, dēbĭta, æqua, justa. *Undeserved, unjust,* immĕrĭta, inīqua, injusta. *Avenging,* ultrix –ĭcis, vindex –ĭcis. *Cruel, bitter,* sæva, immītis, ăcerba, aspĕra. *Late,* sēra. *Instant, speedy,* præsens, cĕlĕris. *Bloody,* sanguĭnea, sanguĭnōlenta, cruenta. *Threatening,* mĭnax. *Terrible,* dīra, mĕtuenda, terrĭbĭlis.

pœnĭtentĭa. *Repentance.*—EP. *Real,* vēra. *Pretended,* ficta. *Deserved,* mĕrĭta, dēbĭta. *Late,* sēra. *Sad,* tristis, ægra.

pŏēsis. *Poetry.* See poeta.

poēta, æ, masc. *A poet.*—EP. *Favoured by the Muses,* Pĭĕrius, Hĕlĭcōnius. *Protected by Apollo,* Ăpollĭneus. *Sacred,* săcer, sanctus. *Pious,* pius. *Mindful,* mĕmor –ŏris. *Tuneful,* cănōrus, vōcālis. *Learned,* doctus. *Immortal,* immortālis, æternus. *Illustrious,* clārus, inclўtus, illustris. *Admirable,* ēgrĕgius. See the Gradus.

poētria. *A poetess.* See above.

pollex –ĭcis, masc. *The thumb.* See manus.

pollĭcĭtum. *A promise.* See promissum.

pŏlus. 1. *The pole of the world.*—2. *Heaven.*—EP. 1. *Revolving,* rĕvŏlūbĭlis, rŏtātus. (*Of the N. Pole*), *Northern,* Arctōus, Bŏreālis. *Cold,* gĕlĭdus, frĭgĭdus, glăcĭālis.—2. See cœlum.

pōmārĭum. *An orchard.*—EP. *Full,* plēnum. *Fertile,* fertĭle, fērax, fēcundum. *Golden or rosy (with golden or rosy apples),* aureum, rōseum, purpūreum, etc.

pompa. *A procession.*—EP. *Solemn, taking place on stated festivals,* sŏlennis. *Festive,* festa. *Triumphal,* triumphālis. *Long,* longa. *Splendid,* splendĭda, magnĭfĭca. *Of persons in dresses embroidered with gold, etc.,* aurea. *Of persons clad in white,* candĭda.

pōmum. *Fruit.*—EP. *Produced in autumn,* autumnāle. *Ripe,* mātūrum. *Sweet,* dulce. *Golden, rosy, etc.,* aureum, rōseum, purpūreum. *Abundant,* largum, densum. *Hanging,* pendens, dēpendens. *Gathered,* decerptum.

pōmus, fem. *A fruit tree.*—EP. *Productive,* fērax, fēcunda. *Heavy with fruit,* grăvis. *Golden, purple (bearing golden or purple fruit),* aurea, purpūrea.

pondus, ĕris, neut. *Weight.*—EP. *Great,* ingens, magnum. *Heavy,* grăve. *Unaccustomed,* insŏlĭtum, ĭnassuetum. *Excessive,* nĭmĭum. *Hard to bear,* dūrum, diffĭcĭle, intŏlĕrābĭle.

pons, tis, masc. *A bridge.*—EP. *Of stone,* saxeus. *High,* altus, arduus. *Dry,* siccus. *Raised up,* sublātus. *Wide,* latus.

pontĭfex –ĭcis, masc. *A priest.* See sacerdos.

pontus. *The sea.* See mare.

pŏpīna. *A cookshop.*—EP. *Greasy,* uncta, pinguis. *Luxurious,* lauta, luxŭriōsa.

pŏples, ĭtis, masc. *The back of the knee.* See genu.

pŏpŭlātor, ōris, masc., **pŏpŭlātrix** –ĭcis, fem. *One who lays waste.*—EP. *Hostile,* infensus, hostīlis. *Rapacious,* răpax. *Cruel,* sævus, fērus, immītis, crūdēlis.

pŏpŭlus, fem. *A poplar-tree.*—EP. *White,* alba. *Sacred to Hercules,* Hercŭlea. *Tall,* alta, prōcēra. *Varying in colour,* bĭcŏlor. *Growing near rivers,* flūmĭnea, flŭvĭalis.

pŏpŭlus, masc. *The people.*—EP. *The whole,* tōtus. *Brave,* fortis. *Powerful,* pŏtens. See gens.

porcus, porca. *A pig.*—EP. *Dirty,* immundus, fœdus, sordĭdus. *Fat,* pinguis. *Greedy,* ăvĭdus, vŏrax.

porta. *A gate (esp. of a city).*—EP. *Brazen,* ærea, ærāta, ahēna, ăhēnea.

F 2

68 POR—PRÆ

Strong, vălĭda. *Fortified,* mūnīta. *Solid,* sŏlĭda. *Safe,* tūta, incŏlŭmis.
Open, pătens, ăperta. *Creaking,* strīdens. *Shut,* clausa.

portentum. *A prodigy.* See monstrum.

portĭcus, ûs, fem. *A portico.*—EP. *High,* alta, ardua. *Looking to the sun,*
Aprīca. *Shady,* umbrōsa, ŏpāca. *Cool,* frigĭda, gĕlĭda. *Marble,* marmŏrea.

pertĭtor. *A ferryman.*—EP. *Of a river,* flūmĭneus, flūviălis. *Hardy,* rŏbustus,
vălĭdus. See navita.

portus, ûs. *A harbour, port.*—EP. *Safe,* tūtus, incŏlŭmis. *Large,* ingens,
magnus. *Retiring,* rĕcēdens. *Curved,* curvātus, curvus, incurvus, rĕcurvus.
Tranquil, tranquillus, plăcĭdus. *Friendly,* ămīcus. *Wished for, desirable,*
optātus, exoptātus, optābĭlis. *To be trusted,* fīdus, fīdēlis. See the Gradus.

pŏsĭtus, ûs, pŏsĭtūra. *Position.*—EP. *Convenient,* commŏdus, ūtĭlis, aptus.
Ancient, vĕtus –ĕris, priscus, antīquus. *High,* altus.

postĕrĭtas. *Posterity.*—EP. *Future,* fŭtūra, ventūra. *Late,* sēra. *Most
remote,* ultĭma. *Mindful,* mĕmor, ŏris. *Grateful,* grāta. *Ungrateful, un-
mindful,* ingrāta, immĕmor.

postis, is, masc. *A doorpost.*—EP. *Oaken,* rŏbŏreus, quernus. *Iron,* ferreus,
ferrātus. *Strong,* vălĭdus.

pŏtentia, pŏtestas. *Power.*—EP. *Wide,* lāta. *Lasting long,* longa, diŭturna.
Firm, stable, firma, stăbĭlis. *Ancient,* vĕtus –ĕris, prisca, antīqua. *Royal,*
rēgia. *Proud,* sŭperba. *Desired,* optāta, exoptāta. *Hoped for,* spērāta.
Promised, prōmissa, pollĭcĭta. *Put in one's way,* ŏblāta, dăta.

pŏtor, ōris, masc. *A drinker.*—EP. *Thirsty,* sĭtiens. *Unsatiable,* insătiābĭlis,
ĭnexplētus. *In the morning,* mătūtīnus. *Late,* sērus. *Deep,* ācer –cris.

præceptor, ōris, masc. *A teacher.*—EP. *Learned,* doctus. *Useful,* ūtĭlis.
Kind, gentle, bēnignus, bŏnus, mītis. *Diligent,* sēdŭlus. *Public,* publĭcus.
Eloquent, dĭsertus, făcundus.

præceptum. *A precept, a command.*—EP. *Wise,* săpiens, prūdens. *Full of
foresight,* præscius. *Useful, suited to circumstances,* ūtĭle, ĭdōneum, aptum.
To be recollected, obeyed, rĕtĭnendum, servandum.

præco, ōnis, masc. *A crier.*—EP. *Hoarse,* raucus.

præcōnium. 1. *A proclamation.*—2. *Praise.*—EP. 1. *Loud,* clārum.—2. See
laus.

præcordia, ōrum, plur. neut. *The heart.* See cor.

præda. *Prey, booty.*—EP. *Splendid,* splendĭda, ēgrĕgia. *Ample,* ampla, ingens,
magna. *Procured,* parta, părāta. *Wished for,* optāta, quæsīta. *Desirable,*
optābĭlis. *Collected,* coacta, congesta. *Won in war,* bellĭca.

prædātor, ōris, masc., prædo, ōnis, masc. *A plunderer, a robber.*—EP. *Ra-
pacious, greedy,* răpax, ăvĭdus. *Wicked,* imprŏbus, scĕlērātus. *Violent,* vĭo-
lentus. *Cruel,* sævus, fĕrus, immītis. *Foreign,* externus, pĕrĕgrīnus. *Infest-
ing the sea,* æquŏreus. *Wandering,* văgus. *Terrible,* terrĭbĭlis, mĕtuendus,
tĭmendus.

prædictum. *A prediction.*—EP. *Truthful,* vērum, vērax. *Announcing fate,*
fātĭdĭcum. *False,* falsum. *Vain,* vānum, irrĭtum.

præmium. *A reward.*—EP. *Just, worthy, deserved,* mĕrĭtum, dĕbĭtum, justum,
æquum, dignum. *Promised,* prōmissum, pollĭcĭtum. *Ample, great,* amplum,
magnum, ingens. *Future,* fŭtūrum. *Given,* dătum. *Pleasant,* dulce, grātum,
jūcundum, ămœnum. *Twofold, threefold, etc.,* dŭplex –ĭcis, trĭplex. *Certain,
fixed,* certum.

præmŏnĭtus, ûs. *A forewarning.* See prædictum.

prænōmen. *The first name.* See nomen.

præsāgium. *A presage.* See prædictum.

præsentia. *Presence.*—EP. *Ready,* prompta, părāta. *Powerful,* pŏtens.
Wished for, optāta, exoptāta. *Delightful,* ămābĭlis, grāta, jūcunda, dulcis,
ămœna. *Lasting,* longa.

præsēpe, is, neut. *A stable.*—EP. *Built,* structum. *Fenced,* septum. *Safe,*
tūtum, incŏlŭme. *Warm,* călĭdum.

præses, ĭdis, masc. fem. *A protector, a patron.*—EP. *Powerful,* pŏtens. *Kind,
friendly,* ămīcus, bēnignus, bŏnus. *Constant,* constans, fīdus.

præsĭdium. *A guard, protection, garrison.*—EP. *Powerful,* pŏtens, vălĭdum.
Armed, armātum. *Numerous,* magnum. *Safe,* tūtum. *Immoveable,* im-

PRÆ—PRO 69

mōtum, immōbīle. *Eternal*, æternum, pĕrenne, perpĕtuum. *Likely to remain,* mansūrum.

præstantia. *Excellence.*—EP. *Blameless,* inculpāta, irrĕprehensa. *Eminent,* ēgrĕgia, mīra. *To be imitated,* ĭmĭtābĭlia, ĭmĭtanda. *To be praised,* laudābĭlia, cĕlĕbranda, mĕmŏrābĭlia. *Worthy,* digna. *Honourable,* dĕcōra. *Amiable,* ămābĭlia.

prætōrium. *The general's tent.*—EP. *Proud,* sŭperbum. *Honoured,* hŏnōrātum.

prandium. *Dinner.* See cœna.

prātum. *A meadow.*—EP. *Grassy,* grāmĭneum. *Green,* vĭrĭde, vĭrĭdans, vĭrens. *Mossy,* muscōsum. *Soft,* molle. *By a river,* flŭviāle, flūmĭneum. *Moist,* *irrigated,* irrĭguum, ūdum, hūmĭdum, mădĭdum. *Fertile,* fertĭle, fĕcundum, fĕrax. *Flowery,* flōreum.

prĕces, um, plur. fem., *used also in* abl. sing., prĕce. *Prayers.*—EP. *Humble,* hūmĭles. *Suppliant,* supplĭces. *Pious,* piæ. *Grateful,* grātæ. *Mindful,* mĕmŏres. *Diligent,* assĭduæ. *Perpetual,* perpĕtuæ. *Effectual,* pŏtentes, effĭcāces, audītæ. *Vain,* vānæ, ĭnānes. See Gradus in preces and precor.

prālum. *A winepress.*—EP. *Foaming,* spūmans, spūmeum, spūmōsum. *Full,* plēnum. *Used in autumn,* autumnāle.

prĕtium. *Price.*—EP. *Great,* magnum, ingens. *Small,* vīle, exĭguum, parvum. *Asked,* pĕtītum. *Given,* dătum. *Promised,* prōmissum.

prīmĭtiæ, ārum, plur. neut. *First-fruits.*—EP. *Promised,* prōmissæ, pollĭcītæ. *Offered,* oblātæ, dātæ. *Sacred,* sācræ, sācrātæ. *Rich,* dīvītes, *sync.* dītes, ŏpīmæ. *Excellent,* ēgrĕgiæ. *Expected,* exspectātæ, spērātæ. *Grateful* (i. e. *offered out of gratitude*), grātæ. *Acceptable,* acceptæ, grātæ. *Due,* dēbĭtæ.

primordia, ōrum, plur. neut. *The beginning.* See principium.

prīmōres, um, plur. masc. *Chiefs.*—EP. *Noble,* nōbĭles, gĕnĕrōsi. *Picked out,* lecti, dēlecti. *Brave,* fortes, ănĭmōsi. *Honoured,* hŏnōrāti. *Beloved,* cāri, ămāti.

princeps, ĭpis, masc. fem. *A prince, princess.*—EP. *Of royal blood,* rēgius. *Known,* nōtus. See primores.

princĭpium. *A beginning.*—EP. *Original,* prīmum. *Ancient,* vĕtus -ĕris, prĭscum, antīquum. *Sacred,* sācrum. *Honoured,* hŏnōrātum. *Venerable,* vĕnĕrābĭle. *Obscure, unknown,* obscūrum, cæcum, ignōtum.

preāvus. *An ancestor.* See avus.

prŏbātor, ōris, masc. *An approver.*—EP. *Courteous,* cōmis, urbānus. *Friendly,* ămīcus. *Favourable,* æquus. *Kind,* bŏnus, bĕnignus. *Deserved,* mĕrĭtus.

prŏbĭtas. *Honesty.*—EP. *Just,* æqua, justa. *Severe,* sĕvēra, rĭgĭda. *Old-fashioned,* antīqua, vĕtus -ĕris, prĭsca. *To be imitated,* ĭmĭtābĭlis, ĭmĭtanda. *Incorruptible,* pūra, incorrupta. *Faithful,* fīda, fīdēlis. *Blameless,* irrĕprehensa, inculpāta. *Simple,* simplex -ĭcis. *Rustic,* rustĭca.

probrum. 1. *A sin.*—2. *Disgrace.*—3. *Reproach.*—EP. 1. See crimen.—2. See dedecus.—3. *Shameful,* turpe, fœdum. *Loud, hoarse,* clāmōsum, raucum. *Deserved,* mĕrĭtum, justum. *Injurious,* injūriōsum. *Lasting,* æternum. *Malignant,* mălum, mālignum. *Biting,* mordax. *Envious,* invĭdum, līvĭdum. *Ungrateful,* ingrātum.

prŏcella. *A storm.*—EP. *Windy,* ventōsa. *With North Wind,* Bŏreālis. *Unquiet,* implăcīda, turbĭda, inquiēta. *Swelling,* tŭmĭda, tŭmens. *Threatening,* mĭnax. *Roaring, hoarse,* strīdens, frĕmens, obstrĕpens, rauca. *Destructive,* noxia, pernĭciōsa, nŏcens, exītiālis, exītiōsa. *Sent,* missa, dēmissa. *Raging,* fŭrens, fŭriōsa. *Black,* nĭgra, atra, pĭcea. See Gradus.

prŏcĕres, um, plur. masc. *Nobles.* See primores.

prŏcessus, ūs, masc. *Progress.*—EP. *Continual,* pĕrennis. *Fortunate,* faustus, sĕcundus. *Desired,* optātus. *Hoped,* spērātus. *Pleasant,* grātus, dulcis. *Future,* fŭtūrus.

prŏcūrātor, ōris, masc. *An agent.*—EP. *Careful,* cautus. *Watchful,* vĭgil -ĭlis, vĭgĭlans. *Faithful,* fĭdus, fĭdēlis. *Diligent,* sēdŭlus.

prŏcursus, ūs. *A sally.*—EP. *Sudden,* sŭbĭtus, ĭnōpīnus, nĕcōpīnus. *Fortunate,* fēlix -īcis. *Bold, fearless,* fortis, impăvĭdus.

prŏcus. *A suitor.*—EP. *Eager,* ācer -cris. *Loving,* ămans. *Wanton,* lascīvus, prŏtervus, impŭdīcus. *Suppliant,* supplex -ĭcis. *Acceptable,* acceptus. *Gentle,* mītis. *Joyful,* lætus.

prŏdĭgium. *A prodigy.*—EP. *Prophetic, full of fate,* prænuntium, fātĭfĕrur

F 3

70 **PRO—PRU**

fătăle. *Strange*, mīrum, mīrăbĭle. *Novel*, nŏvum, insŏlītum, ĭnaudītum. *Sent from heaven*, cœleste. *Seen in the sky*, æthĕrium. *Sad*, triste, infēlix. *Of good omen*, fēlix −ĭcis, sĕcundum.

prŏdĭtio, ōnis, fem. *A betrayal.*—EP. *False*, dĕceitful, treacherous, falsa, fallax, perfĭda, infĭda, dŏlōsa. *Base*, turpis, fœda. *Wicked*, impia, imprŏba. *Hateful*, invīsa, ŏdiōsa. *Promised, agreed upon*, pacta, prōmissa.

prŏdĭtor, ōris, masc. *A betrayer.* See above.

prœlium. *A battle.*—EP. *Sacred to Mars*, Martium, Māvortium. *Bloody*, sanguĭneum, sanguĭnŏlentum, cruentum. *Deadly*, fūnestum, fătăle. *Joined*, consertum, commissum. *Cruel*, sævum, fĕrum, fĕrox, crūdēle. *Causing wounds*, vulnĭfĭcum. *Of enemies*, ĭnĭmĭcum. *Horrid*, horrĭdum, horrĭbĭle, dīrum. *Noisy*, clāmōsum, raucum.

prŏfectus, ûs. *Advantage.*—EP. *Useful*, ūtĭlis. *Wished for*, optātus, exoptātus. *Future*, fūtūrus. *Certain*, certus. *Great*, magnus. *Deserved*, mĕrĭtus, dēbĭtus.

prŏgĕnies, ĕi, fem. *Offspring.* See proles.

prŏgĕnĭtor, ōris, masc. *An ancestor.* See avus.

prōles, is, fem. *Offspring.*—EP. *Abundant*, multa. *Beautiful*, pulchra, formōsa, dĕcōra, ĕgrĕgia. *Illustrious*, clāra, inclȳta. *Surviving its parents*, sŭperstes −ĭtis. *Orphan*, orba. *Future*, fūtūra, ventūra. *Promised*, promissa, pollĭcita. *Granted*, dāta. *Wished for*, optāta, exoptāta. *Loved*, cāra, āmāta, dīlecta.

prŏlŭvies, ĕi. *A flowing forth.*—EP. *Rapid*, răpĭda. *Slow*, lenta. *Pure*, pūra. *Foul*, fœda, tētra, sordĭda.

prŏmĕrĭtum. *Desert.* See meritum.

prŏmissor, ōris, masc. *A promiser.* See below.

prŏmissum. *A promise.*—EP. *True*, certain, vērum, certum. *Ratified*, rătum. *Deceitful*, fallax, dŏlōsum, perfĭdum, infĭdum. *Rash*, incautum, præceps −ĭpĭtis, tĕmĕrārium, imprŭdens. *Vain, not to be accomplished*, vānum, irrĭtum, ĭnāne.

prŏmontōrium. *A promontory.*—EP. *High*, altum. *Projecting*, exstans. *Rocky*, saxeum, saxosum. *Beaten*, percussum. *Resounding*, rĕsŏnans.

prŏnĕpos, ōtis. *A grandson.* See nepos.

propāgo (*see Gradus for the quantity of the* o), ĭnis, fem. *A branch.* See ramus.

prŏpŏsĭtum. *An intention.*—EP. *Fixed*, certum. *Wise*, săpiens, prūdens. *Rash*, præceps −ĭpĭtis, tĕmĕrārium. *Mad, foolish*, dēmens. *Failing in its accomplishment*, irrĭtum, ĭnāne, vānum.

prŏpugnācŭlum. *A bulwark.*—EP. *Iron*, ferreum, ferrātum, ădămantĭnum. *Rocky, made of stone*, saxeum. *Strong*, vălĭdum, forte. *Calculated to remain*, mansūrum. *Opposed* (*to enemies*), adversum, oppŏsĭtum. *Inaccessible*, inaccessum. *Impregnable*, ĭnexpugnābĭle, invictum.

prōra. *The prow of a ship.*—EP. *Brazen*, ærea, ærāta, ahēnea, ahēna. *Painted*, picta. *Having a beak*, rostrāta. *Opposed to an enemy*, adversa, oppŏsĭta. *Threatening*, mĭnax. *Attacking*, ingrĕdiens.

proscēnium. *The stage.*—EP. *Built*, structam. *Splendid*, splendĭdum.

Prŏserpĭna. *Proserpine.*—EP. *Dwelling below*, Inferna. *Queen of Hell, of Styx, etc.*, Tartārea, Stȳgia. *Dark-complexioned*, furva, nĭgra. *Cruel*, sæva, fĕra, immītis. *Daughter of Ceres*, Cĕreālia. *Born in Sicily*, Sĭcŭla, Trĭnācria. See Orcus.

prospectus, ûs. *Sight, a view.*—EP. *Extensive*, lātus. *Rapid*, răpĭdus. See visus.

prŏtervĭtas. *Wantonness.*—EP. *Playful*, jŏcōsa, festīva. *Pleasant, amiable*, grāta, ămābĭlis. *Petulant*, pĕtŭlans.

prŏventus, ûs. *Produce, income.*—EP. *Annual*, annuus. *Customary*, sŏlĭtus, assuetus. *Abundant*, dīves −ĭtis, largus, amplus.

prŏverbium. *A proverb.*—EP. *Ancient*, vĕtus −ĕris, antiquum, priscum. *Well-known*, nōtum. *Believed*, crēdĭtum.

prŏvincia. *A province.*—EP. *Taken, conquered*, capta, dŏmĭta, victa. *Added*, adjecta, addĭta. *Friendly*, ămīca. *Rich*, dīves −ĭtis, ŏpŭlenta, lŏcŭples −ĕtis. *Wide*, lāta. *Distant*, rĕmōta, longinqua, ultĭma.

prŏxĭmĭtas. *Nearness.*—EP. *Pleasant*, grāta, ămœna. *Ancient*, vĕtus −ĕris, prisca, antiqua. *Close*, arcta.

prūdentia. *Prudence.*—EP. *Cautious*, cauta. *Diligent*, sĕdŭla, assĭdua.

PRU—PUT 71

Timid, tĭmĭda. *Anxious*, anxia, sollĭcĭta. *Doubtful*, dŭbia, incerta. *Sagacious*, săgax. *Full of foresight*, præscia. *Successful*, fēlix -ĭcis, victrix -ĭcis. *Customary*, sŏlĭta, assueta, consueta. *Known*, nōta. *Eminent*, ēgrĕgia, insignis. *Safe*, tūta.

pruīna. *Hoar-frost.*—EP. *Dewy*, roscida, rōrāta. *Seen in the morning*, mātūtīna. *White*, alba, candĭda, candens, cāna. *Shining*, fulgens, fulgĭda, vītrea, cōrusca. *Damp*, ūda, hūmĭda, mădĭda. *Cold*, gĕlĭda, frĭgĭda.

prūna. *A live coal.*—EP. *Fiery*, ignea, flammans. *Burning*, ardens. *Hot*, călĭda. *Glowing*, rŭtĭla, mĭcans.

prūnum. *A plum.*—EP. *Purple*, purpŭreum. *Soft*, molle. *Ripe*, mātūrum.

psittācus. *A parrot.*—EP. *Talkative*, garrŭlus, lŏquax. *Imitative*, ĭmĭtātor. *Noisy*, clāmōsus. *Indian*, Indus, Indĭcus, ͞Eōus.

pūbes. *Youth.* See juventus.

pūdĭcĭtia. *Modesty, chastity.*—EP. *Chaste*, casta. *Pure, inviolate*, pūra, intĕmĕrāta. *Pious*, pia. *Maiden*, virgĭnea, puellāris. *Venerable*, vĕnĕrābĭlis, augusta. *Genial*, alma. *Becoming*, dĕcens, dĕcōra.

pŭdor, ōris, masc. *Shame, modesty.*—EP. *Bashful*, vĕrēcundus. *Blushing*, rŏseus. See above.

puella. *A girl.*—EP. *Fair*, pulchra, formōsa, dĕcōra, spĕcĭōsa. *Chaste*, casta, intĕmĕrāta. *Modest*, pŭdĭca, vĕrēcunda. *Tender*, tĕnĕra, mollis. *Simple*, simplex -ĭcis. *Fair*, candĭda, nĭvea. *With auburn hair*, flāva. *Dark-complexioned*, fusca. *Carefully dressed*, compta, ornāta. *Cheerful, joyful*, hĭlāris, læta. *Rustic*, rustĭca. *Nobly born*, ingĕnua, gĕnĕrōsa, nōbĭlis. See virgo.

puer, ĕri. *A boy.*—EP. *Unshaven, beardless*, intonsus, imberbis. *Not arrived at the age of puberty*, impūbes. *Playful*, lūdens. *Docile*, dŏcĭlis. See above.

puĕrĭtia, *sync.* puertia. *Childhood.*—EP. *Helpless*, ĭnops -ōpis. *Weak*, infirma, imbellis. *Innocent*, innŏcua, innoxia, pūra. *Tender*, tĕnĕra, mollis. *Early*, prīma. *Green*, vĭrĭdis. *Playful*, jŏcōsa. *Docile*, dŏcĭlis.

puerpĕra. *A mother.* See mater.

puerpĕrium. *Childbirth.*—EP. *Painful*, triste. *Happy*, fēlix -ĭcis.

pūgil -ĭlis. *A boxer.*—EP. *Strong*, vălĭdus, rōbustus. *Hardy*, dūrus. *Skilful*, pĕrītus. *Fierce*, fĕrus, fĕrox. *Known, celebrated*, nōtus, insignis. *Excellent*, ēgrĕgius. *Victorious*, victor.

pugna. *A fight.* See proelium.

pugnātor, ōris, masc. *A fighter.* See miles.

pugnus. *A fist.* See manus.

pullus. *The young of any animal, esp. of a bird.*—EP. *Tender*, tĕner -ĕri, mollis. *Unfledged*, implūmis. *Weak, helpless*, infirmus, ĭnops -opis.

palmo, ōnis, masc. *The lungs.*—EP. *Tender*, tĕner -ĕri, mollis. *Essential to life*, vītālis. *Panting*, ănhēlus, ănhēlans.

pulpĭtum. *A scaffold or stage.*—EP. *Erected*, structum, exstructum. *Lofty*, altum. *Wooden*, ligneum.

pulsus, ûs. *A striking.*—EP. *Repeated*, crēber -bri, rĕpĕtītus. *Hard*, dūrus, vĭŏlentus. *Sudden*, sŭbĭtus.

pulvillus, pulvīnar -āris, neut. (See Gradus). *A pillow.*—EP. *Soft*, mollis. *Of feathers*, plūmeus. *Of straw*, strāmĭneus. *Sacred*, săcer -cri, săcrātus.

pulvis -ĕris, masc. *Dust.*—EP. *Black*, nĭger -gri, āter -tri. *Dense*, densus. *Dirty, foul*, turpia, foedus, immundus, sordĭdus. *Light*, lĕvis. *Flying*, vŏlĭtans, tortus.

pūmex -ĭcis, masc., *rarely fem.*—EP. *Light*, lĕvis. *Soft*, mollis. *Full of holes*, căvus, multĭcăvus.

puppis, is, fem. *The stern of a ship.* See navis.

pūpŭla. *The pupil of the eye.* See oculus.

purgāmen, ĭnis, neut. 1. *The offscouring of anything.*—2. *Atonement.*—EP. 1. *Foul*, sordĭdum, foedum, turpe. *Worthless*, vīle. *Castaway*, abjectum.—2. See piamen.

purpŭra. *Purple.*—EP. *Procured from the sea*, æquŏrea, mărīna. *Tyrian, etc.*, Tyria, Sĭdŏnia, Sarrāna. *Royal*, rēgia, rēgālia. *Splendid*, splendĭda, magnĭfĭca. *Rosy*, rŏsea.

pūtātor, ōris, masc. *A pruner.*—EP. *Skilful*, pĕrītus, doctus, callĭdus. *Hardy*, dūrus. *Rash*, præceps -ĭpĭtis, tĕmĕrārius. *Carrying a knife*, falcĭfer -ĕri.

72   PUT—RAP

pŭteus. *A well.*—EP. *Full,* plēnus. *Wet,* ūdus, mădĭdus, hūmĭdus. *Deep,* altus, prŏfundus.

pȳra. *A funeral pile.* See rogus.

pȳrōpus. *A carbuncle.*—EP. *Fiery looking,* igneus, rŭtĭlus, flammeus. *Rosy,* rŏseus.

pyxis, ĭdis, fem. *A box for perfumes.*—EP. *Scented,* ŏdōrātus, frăgrans. *Full,* plēnus. *Sweet,* dulcis. *Ivory,* ēburna, ēburneus. *Silver,* argenteus.

Q.

Quădrŭpes, ĕdis, masc. *A horse.* See equus.

quæsĭtor, ōris, masc. *An Examiner.*—EP. *Severe,* sĕvērus, rĭgĭdus. *Just,* æquus, justus. *Venerable,* vĕnĕrăbĭlis, vĕnĕrandus, augustus, vĕrendus.

quæstus, ūs. *Gain.*—EP. *Great,* magnus, ingens. *Annual,* annuus. *Wished for, desirable,* optātus, optăbĭlis. See lucrum.

quălus, quăsillus. *A basket.* See calathus.

quercētum. *A grove of oaks.* See below.

quercus, ūs, fem. *An oak.*—EP. *Of Epirus, of Dodona,* Chăōnia, Dōdōnæa. *Spreading,* pătŭla. *Lofty,* alta, ardua, prŏcēra, āěria. *Aged,* annōsa. *Strong,* vălĭda. *Shady,* ŏpāca, umbrōsa. *Leafy,* frondea, frondōsa, frondens. *Sacred,* săcra, săcrāta. *Knotted, gnarled,* nōdōsa. *Bearing acorns,* glandĭfĕra.

quĕrēla, quĕrĭmōnia, questus, ūs. *Complaint.*—EP. *Tearful,* lăcrymōsus, flēbĭlis. *Sad,* tristis, mœstus, mĭser –ĕri, mĭsĕrăbĭlis. *Feminine, effeminate,* fēmĭneus, mollis. *Tuneful,* cănōrus, lĭquĭdus. *Long,* longus. *Continual,* assĭduus. *Ancient,* vĕtus –ĕris, antīquus, priscus. *Inconsolable,* inconsōlăbĭlis.

quies, ētis, fem. *Rest.*—EP. *Tranquil,* tranquilla, plăcĭda. *Unbroken,* irrupta. *Gentle, winning, pleasant,* blanda, dulcis, ămœna, grāta, jūcunda. *Happy,* fēlix –īcis, beāta. *Wished for,* optāta, exoptāta. *Customary,* sŏlĭta, assueta, consueta. *Unaccustomed,* dēsueta. *Free from care,* sēcūra.

quinquennium. *A space of five years.*—EP. *Long,* longum. *Quiet,* plăcĭdum.

R.

Răbies, ēi, fem. *Rage.*—EP. *Insane,* insāna, vēsāna, dēmens. *Furious,* fŭriōsa, imprŏba. *Fierce,* fĕra, fĕrox, sæva. *Indomitable,* indŏmĭta.

răcēmus. *A bunch of grapes.*—EP. *Purple,* purpūreus. *Ripe,* mātūrus. *Hanging,* pendens, dēpendens. *Swelling,* tŭmĭdus, tŭmens. *Dark-coloured,* līvĭdus, līvens. *Heavy,* grăvis.

rădius. *A ray, a sunbeam.*—EP. *Ruddy,* rŏseus, rŭtĭlus. *Shining in the morning, early,* mātūtīnus, prīmus. See jubar.

rădix, īcis, fem. *A root.*—EP. *Deep,* alta. *The lowest,* īma. *Hard,* dūra. *Fruitful,* fēcunda, fertĭlis, fĕrax.

rāmāle, is, neut., rāmus. *A branch.*—EP. *Shady,* umbrōsus, umbrĭfer –ĕri, ŏpācus. *Leafy,* frondeus, frondōsus, frondens. *Dense,* densus. *Bearing fruit,* fertĭlis, fēcundus, fēlix –īcis. *Hanging,* pendens, dēpendens. *Spreading,* pătŭlus. *Luxuriant,* fluens, luxŭrians.

rāna. *A frog.*—EP. *Living in marshes,* pălūdōsa, pălustris. *Chattering,* garrŭla, lŏquax. *Living in wet places,* ūda. *Spotted,* măcŭlōsa, văria.

răpīna. *Rapine.*—EP. *Lawless,* injusta, īnĭqua, imprŏba. *Cruel,* immītis, sæva, fĕra. *Greedy,* ăvĭda. See præda.

raptor, ōris, masc. *One who carries off, who plunders.*—EP. *Greedy,* ăvĭdus. *Cruel, fierce,* fĕrus, sævus, crūdēlis. *Impious,* impius. *Unchastised,* īnultus. *Base,* turpis, fœdus. *Hated,* invīsus, ŏdiōsus. *Hostile,* hostĭlis, infensus. *Lying in ambush,* lătens, abdĭtus.

raptum. *Plunder.* See præda.

RAS—REP 73

rastrum, plur. **rastri**. *A rake, a harrow.*—EP. *Iron*, ferreum, ferrātum. *Sharp*, ācūtum. *Heavy*, grăve. *Continually used*, crēbrum, assĭduum. *Crooked, with crooked teeth*, uncum, ādūncum.

rătio, **ŏnis**, fem. 1. *Reason.*—2. *A manner.*—EP. *Given by God*, dīvīna, cœlestis. *Lofty*, alta. 1. *Pure*, pūra.—2. *Simple*, simplex –īcis. See modus.

rĕceptus, **ûs**. 1. *A retreating.* See below.

rĕcessus, **ûs**. 1. *A retreating.*—2. *A place to retreat to, a retired place.*—EP. 1. *Rapid*, răpĭdus. *Slow*, lentus. 1, 2. *Silent*, tăcĭtus.—2. *Secret*, sēcrētus, abdītus. *Distant*, longinquus, rĕmōtus. *Quiet*, tranquillus, plăcĭdus. *Mossy*, muscōsus. *Shady*, umbrōsus, ŏpācus. *Safe*, tūtus.

rĕcĭtātor, **ŏris**, masc. *A reciter.*—EP. *Continual*, assĭduus. *Unwearied*, indēfessus. *Intolerable, bitter*, ăcerbus, intŏlĕrābĭlis.

rector, **ŏris**, masc. 1. *A ruler.*—2. *A driver, a steerer.*—EP. 1. See rex.— 2. *Skilful*, pĕrītus, doctus. *Cautious*, cautus, prūdens. *Anxious*, sollĭcĭtus, anxius. *Watchful*, vĭgil –īlis. *Guiding the ship by night*, nocturnus. *Fearless*, impăvĭdus, imperterrĭtus.

rĕcursus, **ûs**. 1. *A running back, a return.*—2. *The ebb and flow of the tide.*—EP. 1. See redĭtus.—2. *Of the sea*, æquŏreus, mărīnus. *Refluent*, rēfluus. *Recurring at fixed periods*, certus. *Recurring alternately*, alternus.

rĕdemtor, **ŏris**, masc. *A contractor.*—EP. *Prudent*, prūdens. *Rich*, dīves –ĭtis, ŏpŭlentus. lŏcŭples –ĕtis.

rĕdĭmĭcŭlum. *An ornament for the head or neck.*—EP. *Embroidered, variegated*, pictum, vărium. *Ornamented with gold*, aureum. *Jewelled*, gemmeum, gemmātum.

rĕdĭtus, **ûs**. *A return.*—EP. *Safe*, incŏlŭmis, tūtus. *Wished for*, optātus, exoptātus. *Expected*, exspectātus. *Late*, sērus. *Pleasant*, grātus, jūcundus, āmœnus. *Fortunate*, fēlix, faustus. *Triumphal*, triumphālis. *Victorious*, victrix –īcis. *Promised*, promissus.

rĕgia. *A palace.* See palatium.

rĕgīna. *A queen.*—EP. *Fair*, candĭda, pulchra. See rex.

rĕgio, **ŏnis**, fem. *A region, district.*—EP. *Extensive*, lāta, spătiōsa, ampla. *Celebrated*, nōta, inclўta. *Rich*, dīves –ĭtis, ŏpŭlenta, lŏcŭples. *Dry*, ārĭda, sicca. *Wet*, irrĭgua, ūda, hūmĭda. *Mountainous*, montāna. *Fertile*, fertĭlis, fēcunda, fērax. *Cultivated*, culta. *Barren*, stĕrĭlis. *Uncultivated*, inculta. *Deserted*, dēserta.

rĕgnātor, **ŏris**, masc. *A ruler.* See rex.

rĕgnum. *A kingdom.*—EP. *Extensive*, ingens, lātum, spătiōsum. *Ancient*, antiquum, vĕtus –ĕris, priscum. *Hereditary*, pătrium, păternum, ăvītum. *Rich*, dīves –ĭtis, ŏpŭlentum. *Brave, warlike*, forte, bellĭcum. *Invincible, unconquered*, invictum. *Powerful*, pŏtens. *Proud*, sŭperbum.

rĕgŭla. *A rule.*—EP. *Fixed*, certa. *Reasonable*, æqua, justa. *Old*, prisca, vĕtus –ĕris, antīqua. See lex.

rĕlĭgio, **ŏnis**, fem. *Religion.*—EP. *Ancient*, vĕtus –ĕris, antīqua, prisca. *Sacred*, săcra, săcrata, sancta. *Divine*, dīvīna, cœlestis. *Pure*, pūra, incorrupta. *Pious*, pia. *National*, pătria. *Merciful, gentle*, mītis. *Cruel*, fĕra, effera, sæva.

rĕlĭquiæ, **ārum**, plur. fem. *Relics.*—EP. *The last*, ultĭmæ, extrēmæ, sŭprēmæ. *Miserable*, tristes, mĭsĕræ. *Solitary*, sōlæ. *Dear, care*, cāræ, dīlectæ, ămātæ.

rēmex, **ĭgis**, masc. *A rower.*—EP. *Hardy, strong*, dūrus, rŏbustus, vălĭdus. *Skilful*, pĕrītus, callĭdus. *Active*, ācer –cris, impĭger –gri.

rēmĭgium. *The collection of oars, the art of rowing, etc.* See Gradus.

rĕmŏrāmen, **ĭnis**, neut. *A hindrance.*—EP. *Slow*, lentum. *Hateful*, invīsum, ŏdiōsum. *Useless*, ĭnŭtĭle. *Hurtful*, nŏcens, damnōsum. *Unexpected*, inexspectātum, imprōvīsum, ĭnŏpīnum, nĕcŏpīnum.

rēmus. *An oar.*—EP. *Long*, longus. *Continually plied*, assĭduus. *Swift*, cĕler –ĕris, răpĭdus. *Used with activity*, ăgĭlis. *Dripping*, mădĭdus, mădens. *Foaming, causing foam, etc.*, spūmans, spūmōsus, spūmeus. *On alternate sides*, alternus.

rĕnŏvāmen, **ĭnis**, neut. *A renewing.*—EP. *Entire*, intĕgrum. *Marvellous*, mīrum, mīrābĭle. *Sudden*, sŭbĭtum.

rĕpăgŭla, **ŏrum**, plur. neut. *A bolt, a barrier.* See obex.

rĕpertor, **ŏris**, masc. *An inventor, a discoverer.*—EP. *Wise*, sŏlers, săpiens

74 REP—RIV

callĭdus. *Provident*, prŏvĭdus, prūdens. *Divine*, dīvīnus. *Excellent*, ēgrĕgius. *Useful*, ŭtĭlis, aptus. *Celebrated*, insignis, clārus, inclўtus. *Original*, prīmus.

rĕpĕtītor, ōris, masc. *One who demands back.*—EP. *Strenuous*, strēnuus, ācer —cris. *Eager*, anxius, sollĭcĭtus. *Continual*, untiring, sēdŭlus, indēfessus. *Prompt*, promptus.

rĕpostor, ōris, masc. *A rebuilder, restorer.*—EP. *Diligent*, sēdŭlus. *Pious*, pius. *Friendly*, ămīcus. *Anxious*, sollĭcĭtus.

rĕprehensor, ōris. *A blamer.*—EP. *Severe*, sĕvērus, rĭgĭdus. *Impartial*, æquus. *Deserved*, mĕrĭtus. *Unjust*, ĭnīquus. *Undeserved*, immĕrĭtus.

rĕpulsa. *A repulse.*—EP. *Dishonouring*, indĕcōra, sordĭda, turpis. *Unexpected*, ĭnexspectāta, ĭnŏpīna, nĕcŏpīna, imprŏvīsa. *Bloody*, cruenta, sanguĭnea, sanguĭnŏlenta. *Bitter, sad*, ăcerba, tristis, infēlix —icis.

rĕquies, ēi, fem. *Rest.* See quies.

res, rei, fem. *A thing, a circumstance.*—EP. *Happy, fortunate*, fēlix –icis, fausta, læta. *Unfortunate*, tristis, infēlix, mĭsĕra. *Novel*, nŏva. *Easy*, făcĭlis. *Marvellous*, mīra, mīrābĭlis, mīranda. *Difficult*, dūra, diffĭcĭlis.

respectus, ûs. *Regard.* See cura.

respīrāmen, ĭnis, neut. *The passage of the breath.*—EP. *Essential to life*, vītāle. *Easy*, făcĭle. *Open*, ăpertum, pătens.

responsor, ōris, masc. *Answerer.* See below.

responsum. *An answer.*—EP. *Courteous*, cōme, urbānum. *Friendly, kind*, ămīcum, bēnignum. *Desired, hoped for*, optātum, spērātum. *Acceptable*, grātum, dulce, acceptum, jūcundum. *Harsh*, aspĕrum, ăcerbum, grăve. *Sad*, triste.

rēte, is, neut. *A net.*—EP. *Full of holes*, rārum. *Made of rope*, stuppeum. *Let down in the river or sea*, flūmĭneum, flūvĭăle, æquŏreum, mărīnum. *Capacious*, căpax. *Stretched out*, extentum.

rĕtĭnācŭlum. *Anything which holds, a cable, rein, etc.*—EP. *Strong*, vălĭdum, forte. *Holding*, tĕnax. *Making slow*, lentum. *Hateful*, invīsum, ŏdĭōsum, ingrātum.

rĕvĕrentia. *Respect.*—EP. *Due*, dēbĭta, mĕrĭta. *Humble*, hŭmĭlis. *Worthy*, digna. *Ancient, old-fashioned*, prisca, vĕtus –eris, antīqua. *Pious*, pia. *Silent*, tăcĭta.

rĕvŏcāmen, ĭnis, neut. *A recall.*—EP. *Expected, wished for*, exspectātum, spērātum, optātum. *Acceptable*, acceptum, grātum, dulce. *Slow, delayed*, lentum, tardum. *Sudden*, sŭbĭtum.

reus, fem. rea. *A criminal.*—EP. *Base, infamous*, turpis, infāmis. *Convicted*, mănĭfestus. *Wicked*, improbus, impius.

rex, rēgis, masc. *A king.*—EP. *Just*, justus, æquus. *Merciful*, mītis, clēmens. *Powerful*, pŏtens. *Great*, magnus. *Illustrious*, clārus, præclārus, insignis, inclўtus. *Magnificent*, magnĭficus. *Proud*, sŭperbus. *Purple, clad in purple*, purpŭreus. *Warlike*, bellĭcus, pugnax. *Wise*, săpiens.

rictus, ûs. *The open mouth.* See os, ōris.

rĭgor, ōris, masc. *Stiffness, hardness.*—EP. *Unyielding*, immōtus, immŏbĭlis. *Tenacious*, tĕnax. *Brittle*, frăgĭlis.

rīma. *A fissure, a leak.*—EP. *Open*, hians, pătens. *Wide*, lāta. *New*, nŏva. *Mischievous, destructive*, noxia, nŏcens, pernĭcĭōsa, exĭtĭōsa, exĭtĭālis. *Penetrable*, pĕnĕtrābĭlis. *Weak*, dēbĭlis, infirma, invălĭda.

rīpa. *A bank.*—EP. *Of a river*, flūmĭnea, flūvĭālis. *Grassy*, grămĭnea. *Moss-grown*, muscōsa. *Loaded with reeds or bulrushes*, ărundĭfĕra, juncōsa, juncea. *Damp*, ūda, hŭmĭda, mădĭda. *Green*, vĭrĭdis. *Soft*, mollis. *Sunny*, ăprīca. *Muddy*, līmōsa.

rīsor, ōris, masc. *A laugher.*—EP. *Jesting*, jŏcōsus. *Merry*, hĭlăris, lætus. *Friendly*, ămīcus, bēnignus. *Courteous*, cōmis, hūmānus.

rīsus, ûs. *Laughter.*—EP. *Unrestrained*, sŏlūtus, līber –ĕri. *Long*, longus. *Loud*, clārus. See above.

rītus, ûs. *A rite.*—EP. *Sacred*, săcer –cri, săcrātus, sanctus. *Ancient*, antīquus, vĕtus –ĕris, priscus. *Usual*, sŏlĭtus, assuetus, consuetus. *Barbaric*, barbărus, barbărĭcus, ĭnhūmānus. *Cruel*, sævus, immītis, crudēlis, fĕrus.

rīvālis. *A rival.*—EP. *Emulous*, æmŭlus. *Hostile*, adversus. *To be feared, formidable*, formīdābĭlis, mĕtuendus, tĭmendus. *Victorious, successful*, victor,

RIV—RUM 75

fēlix –īcis. *Ancient,* vĕtus –ĕris, prīscus, antīquus. *Secret,* sēcrētus, tăcītus, ignōtus.

rīvus. *A brook*—EP. *Slight, small,* parvus, exĭguus, tĕnuis. *Leaping along,* sāliens. *Babbling,* sŭsurrans, murmŭrans. *Pebbly,* lăpĭdōsus. See fluvius.

rixa. *A quarrel.*—EP. *Noisy,* clāmōsa. *Horrid,* horrĭda, ŏdiōsa. *Shameful,* turpis, fœda, pŭdenda, prŏbrōsa. *Sudden,* sūbĭta. *Fresh,* nŏva. *Unjust,* injusta, ĭnīqua.

rōbur, ŏris, neut. 1. *Oak.* 2. *Strength.*—EP. 1. See quercus. 2. See vir.

rŏgātum. *A question.* — EP. *Hard,* dūrum, diffĭcĭle. *Obscure,* obscūrum. *Anxious,* anxĭum, sollĭcĭtum.

rŏgus. *A funeral pile.*—EP. *Funereal,* fūnĕreus, fūnĕbris, fērālis. *The last,* ultĭmus, sŭprēmus, extrēmus. *Sad,* tristis, infēlix –īcis, mĭser –ĕri, mĭsĕrābĭlis, lūgūbris, dēflendus. *Kindled,* accensus, succensus. *Devouring,* ĕdax, āvĭdus. *Raised,* structus, exstructus.

Rōma. *Rome.* — EP. *Proud,* sŭperba. *Magnificent,* magnĭfĭca. *Ruling the world,* dŏmĭna. *Brave,* fortis. *Invincible,* invicta, indŏmĭta. *Lasting for ever,* æterna. *Founded by Romulus,* Rōmūlea. *Warlike,* bellĭca, bellātrix. *Warlike, or sacred to Mars,* Martia, Māvortia. *Sacred,* sācra, sancta. *Illustrious,* inclўta, clāra. See the Gradus.

ros, rōris, masc. *Dew.*—EP. *Morning,* mātūtīnus. *Descending from heaven,* cœlestis, æthĕrius. *Shining,* vĭtreus, lūcĭdus. *Moist,* ūdus, mădĭdus, hūmĭdus. *Soft,* mollis, tĕner –ĕri. *Fertilising,* fertĭlis, fēcundus. *Pleasant,* grātus, ămœnus. *Liquid,* lĭquĭdus. *Cool,* gĕlĭdus, frĭgĭdus.

rŏsa. *A rose.* — EP. *Red,* purpūrea. *Sacred to Venus,* Cўthĕrēïa, Ĭdălia. *Sweet-smelling,* dulcis, frāgrans, ŏdōra, ŏdōrāta, ŏdōrĭfĕra. *Persian,* Persĭca. *Easily woven into chaplets,* nexĭlis, lenta. *Festive,* festa. *Thorny,* spīnōsa, ăcūta. *Short-lived,* brĕvis, frăgĭlis, cădūca.

rŏsārium, rŏsētum. *A bed of roses.* See above.

rostrum. 1. *A beak.* 2. *The beak of a ship.* — EP. 1. *Hooked,* uncum, rĕduncum, ăduncum. *Hard,* dūrum. 2. *Brazen,* æreum, ærātum, ahēnum, ahēneum. *Opposed,* adversum, oppŏsĭtum. *Rapid,* răpĭdum, vēlox. *Penetrating,* pĕnĕtrābĭle.

rŏta. *A wheel.* — EP. *Revolving,* rĕvŏlūbĭlis. *Rapid,* răpĭda, cĭta, cĕlĕris. *Glowing,* fervĭda, fervens, ardens. *Brazen iron, bound with brass, iron, etc.,* ærea, ærāta, ferrea, ferrāta. *Crooked, circular,* curvus. *Noisy, rattling,* strĕpens.

rŭbētum. *A bed of brambles.* See rubus.

rūbīgo, ĭnis, fem. 1. *Rust.* 2. *Blight.*—EP. *Dirty,* sordĭda, fœda, immunda. 1, 2. *Devouring,* ĕdax, vŏrax. *Thick,* densa. *Destructive,* nŏcens, noxia, damnōsa, pernĭciōsa. 2. *Cruel,* aspĕra, sæva.

rŭbor, ōris, masc. 1. *Redness.* 2. *A blush.*—EP. 1, 2. *Rosy, purple,* rŏseus, purpūreus. 2. *Modest,* pŭdĭcus, pŭdībundus, vĕrēcundus. *Sudden,* sūbĭtus. *Timid,* tĭmĭdus. *Virgin,* virgĭneus. *Warm,* fervĭdus, fervens, călĭdus.

rŭbus. *A bramble.* — EP. *Prickly,* spīnōsus, ăcūtus. *Rough,* asper –ĕri. *Bristling,* horrĭdus, horrens, hirsūtus.

rŭdens, tis, masc. *A cable.*—EP. *Strong,* firmus, vălĭdus. *Holding,* tĕnax. *Stretched,* contentus. *Of hemp,* stuppeus. *Of iron,* ferreus, ferrātus. *Creaking,* strĭdens, strĭdŭlus.

rŭdimentum. *A beginning.* See principium.

rŭdis, is, fem. *A foil.* — EP. *Blunt,* hĕbes –ĕtis. *Innocent,* innŏcua, innoxia. *Inexperienced, untried,* ĭnexperta.

rūga. *A wrinkle.*—EP. *Aged,* sĕnīlis (*when spoken of an old woman*), ănīlis. *Horrid,* horrĭda. *Deep,* alta. *Severe-looking,* sĕvēra, rĭgĭda. *Sad,* tristis, mĭsĕra. *Languid, denoting languor,* languĭda. *Loose,* laxa, sŏlūta.

ruīna. *Downfall, ruin.*—EP. *Entire,* tōta. *Sudden,* sūbĭta, nĕcŏpīna, ĭnŏpīna. *Great,* ingens, vasta. *Sad,* tristis, mĭsĕra, mĭsĕrābĭlis, flēbĭlis. *Incurable, irrevocable,* immĕdĭcābĭlis, irrĕvŏcābĭlis. *The last, extreme,* ultĭma, extrēma, sŭprēma, summa. *Horrid,* horrĭda, dīra. *Unworthy, undeserved,* indigna, immĕrĭta.

rŭmor, ōris. *Report.* — EP. *Talkative,* lŏquax. *True, certain,* vērus, certus. *To be trusted,* fīdus, fīdēlis. *Vain,* vānus, ĭnānis. *Wandering,* văgus. *Doubt-*

76 RUP—SAL

ful, dŭbius. *Of doubtful origin*, incertus. *New*, nŏvus, rĕcens. *Various*, vărius. *Discreditable*, indĕcōrus, dĕcŏlor. *Wicked*, ĭnīquus.

rŭpes, is, fem. *A rock.*—EP. *Precipitous*, praeceps -ĭpĭtis. *Sloping up*, acclīvis, acclīva. *Sloping down*, dēclīvis, dēclīva, sŭpīna. *Sunny*, ăprīca. *Looking on the sea*, aequŏrea, mărīna. *Lofty*, alta, ardua, aĕria, celsa. *Hard*, dūra, rĭgĭda. *Rough*, aspĕra. *Covered with brambles*, dūmōsa. *Looking like a tower*, turrīta. *Eaten out*, exēsa, ĕdēsa. *Threatening*, mĭnax, *Barren*, stĕrĭlis.

rūrĭcŏla, masc. **rustĭcus.** *A rustic.* See agricola.

rus, rūris, neut. 1. *The country.* 2. *A field.*—EP. 1. *Green*, vĭrĭde. *Tranquil*, tranquillum, plăcĭdum, quiētum. *Innocent*, innŏcuum, insons. *Simple*, simplex -īcis. *Unpolished*, incultum. *Fertile*, fertĭle, fēcundum, fĕrax. 2. See ager.

ruscus. *Furze.*—EP. *Bristling*, fuscus. *Worthless*, vīlis. *Dry*, ărĭdus, siccus.

rustĭcĭtas. *Rusticity.*—EP. *Unpolished*, rūdis, inculta, ĭnurbāna. *Contented*, contenta. *Simple*, simplex -īcis. *Innocent*, innŏcua, insons. *Virtuous*, prŏba. *Old-fashioned*, prisca, vĕtusta, vĕtus -ĕris, antīqua. *Modest*, vĕrēcunda, pŭdĭca, pŭdībunda.

rūtrum. *A mattock.*—EP. *Iron*, ferreum, ferrātum. *Heavy*, grăve. *Rustic*, ăgreste. *Hard*, dūrum.

S.

săbarra. *Gravel used as ballast.*—EP. *Yellow*, flāva. *Heavy*, grăvis.

saccus. *A bag, a purse.*—EP. *Full*, plēnus. *Heavy*, grăvis.

săcellum. *A chapel.* See templum.

săcerdos, ōtis, masc. fem. *A priest or priestess.*—EP. *Pious*, pius. *Sacred*, săcer —cri, săcrātus, sanctus. *Venerable*, vĕnĕrābĭlis, vĕrendus, vĕnĕrandus. *Aged*, hoary, sĕnex, vĕtŭlus, cānus. *Prophetic*, praescius, fātĭdĭcus. *Pure*, castus, pūrus. *Clad in white*, candĭdus, albus.

săcrāmentum. *An oath.*—EP. *Pious*, pium. *Lasting*, stăbĭle. *To be believed*, fĭdum, fĭdĕle. *Everlasting*, aeternum, pĕrenne. *Inviolable*, invĭolābĭle. *Inviolate*, invĭolātum.

săcrārium. *A chapel.* See templum.

săcrĭfĭcium. *A sacrifice.* EP. *Pious*, pium. *Sacred*, săcrum, săcrātum, sanctum. *Suppliant*, supplex -īcis. *Continual*, assĭduum, crēbrum. *Rich*, ŏpīmum, dīves -ĭtis. *Of frankincense*, thūreum. See victima.

saecŭlum, sync. **saeclŭm.** *An age.*—EP. *Coming*, ventūrum, fŭtūrum. *Past*, praetĕrĭtum. *Long*, longum. *Ancient*, vĕtus -ĕris, priscum, antīquum. See tempus.

saevĭtia. *Fierceness, cruelty.*—EP. *Pitiless*, immītis. *Savage*, fĕra, fĕrox. *Barbaric*, barbăra, ĭnhūmāna. *Hateful*, invīsa, ŏdiōsa. *Implacable*, implăcābĭlis. *Furious*, fŭriōsa.

săga. *A witch.*—EP. *Wicked*, impia, scĕlĕrāta. *Aged*, vĕtŭla. *Grey-headed*, cāna. *powerful*, pŏtens. *Learned*, docta. *Thessalian (Thessaly was celebrated for magic)*, Thessăla. *Cruel*, crudēlis, effĕra. *Frantic*, fŭriōsa. *Deceitful*, fallax, dŏlōsa, perfĭda.

săgitta. *An arrow.*—EP. *Sent*, missa. *Winged*, vŏlŭcris, vŏlātĭlis, pennāta. *Swift*, cĕlĕris, cĭta, vēlox. *Poisoned*, vĕnēnāta. *Sharp*, ăcūta. *Cretan (the Cretani were celebrated as archers)*, Cressa, Crētĭca, Cȳdōnia, Gŏrtȳnia, Gŏrtȳnĭăca. *Missile*, missĭlis. *Piercing*, pĕnĕtrābĭlis. *Deadly*, lētālis, lētĭfĕra. *Barbed*, hāmāta,

săgum, săgŭlum. *A military cloak.*—EP. *Warlike*, bellĭcum. *Light*, lĕve. *Short*, brĕve. *Scarlet*, pūnĭceum. *Causing woe*, triste, lūgŭbre, infēlix -īcis.

sal, sălis, masc. and neut. *Salt.*—EP. *From the sea*, aequŏreus, mărīnus. *Bitter*, ămārus. *Bright*, lūcĭdus. *Pure*, pūrus.

sălebrae, arum, pl. fem. *Rough places.*—EP. *Rugged*, aspĕrae. *Uncultivated*, incultae. *Barren*, stĕrĭles. *Stony*, lăpĭdōsae, saxeae. *Pathless*, dēviae, ăviae. *Inaccessible*, ĭnaccessae.

sălictum. *A willow-bed.* See salix.

SAL—SCI 77

sālīnum. *A saltcellar.*—EP. *Made of gold or silver,* aureum, aurātum, argenteum. *Of maple,* ācernum.

sālix, ĭcis, fem. *A willow.*—EP. *Growing by a river,* flūmĭnea, flūviālis. *Growing in a marsh,* pālustris, pālūdōsa. *Moist,* ūda. *Flexible,* lenta, fācĭlis, flexĭlis. *Of a silver-grey leaf,* glauca. *Soft,* mollis.

saltus, ûs, masc. *A leap.*—EP. *Active,* ăgĭlis. *Long,* longus. *Repeated,* crēber –bri, rĕpĕtītus. *Rustic,* ăgrestis, rustĭcus. *Strong,* vălĭdus.

saltus, ûs. *A grove, a lawn.* EP. *Green,* vĭrĭdis, vĭrĭdans, vĭrens. *Pleasant,* jūcundus, dulcis, ămœnus. *Woody,* sylvester *or* sylvestris, nĕmŏrōsus. *Grassy,* grāmĭneus. *Mossy,* muscōsus. *Low,* hŭmĭlis. *Sacred,* săcer, săcrātus, sanctus. *Hollow,* căvus. *Deep,* prŏfundus, altus. *Shady,* umbrōsus, ŏpācus.

sălum. *The sea.* See mare.

sălus, ūtis, fem. 1. *Safety.*—2. *Health* (rare in this sense).—EP. 1. *Secure,* tūta, incŏlŭmis. *Wished for,* optāta. *Hoped for,* spērāta. *Promised,* prōmissa. *Granted,* dāta. *Dear,* căra. 2. See valetudo.

sanguis, ĭnis, masc. *Blood.*—EP. *Red,* rŏseus, purpūreus. *Warm,* călĭdus, fervĭdus. *Full of life, cause of life, etc.,* vītālis. *Shed,* effūsus.

sănies, ēi. *Gore.* See above.

săpientia. *Wisdom.*—EP. *Divine,* dīvīna, cœlestis. *Pure,* pūra. *Provident,* prŏvĭda, prūdens, præscia. *Cautious,* cauta. *Crafty,* callĭda. *Celebrated,* clāra, inclyta. *Eminent,* insignis, ēgrĕgia.

săpor, ōris, masc. *A taste.*—EP. *Sweet,* dulcis. *Rich,* lautus, ŏpīmus.

sarcĭna. *A bundle, a burden.* See onus.

sărissa. *A kind of spear.* See hasta.

săta, orum, pl. neut. *Corn-land, crops.*—EP. *Abundant, fertile,* læta, fēcunda, pinguia. See arvum, seges.

sătelles, ĭtis, masc. *A body-guard.*—EP. *Armed, helmeted, etc.,* armātus, cristātus. *Clad in scarlet,* pūnĭceus. *Strong, brave,* vălĭdus, fortis. *Faithful,* fīdus, fĭdēlis. *Royal,* rēgius.

sătio, ōnis, fem. *A sowing.*—EP. *Provident,* prudens, prŏvĭda. *In proper season,* tempestīva. *Abundant,* larga.

sător, ōris, masc. *A sower.* See above.

sătyra. *Satire.*—EP. *Biting,* mordax. *Envious,* invĭda, līvĭda. *Bitter,* aspĕra, ăcerba. *Unrestrained,* lībĕra.

saxum. *A rock, a stone.* See rupes.

scăbies, ēi, fem. *The itch.*—EP. *Sad,* tristis. *Shameful,* turpis, fœda.

scālæ, ārum, pl. fem. *Ladders, stairs.*—EP. *Lofty,* altæ, arduæ, ăĕriæ. *Of oak,* rŏbŏreæ, quernæ. *Moveable,* mōbĭles. *Moved quickly,* cĕlĕres. *Ready,* părātæ. *Put against a wall, etc.,* admōtæ. *Of stone,* saxeæ.

scamnum. *A bench.* See sedile.

scăpha. *A boat.* See navis.

scăpŭlæ, arum, pl. fem. *The shoulder-blades.* See humerus.

scătēbra, oftenest in pl. *The bubbling of water.*—EP. *Murmuring,* murmŭrans, sŭsurrans. *Babbling,* lŏquax, garrŭla. *Light,* lĕvis. *Gentle,* lēnis. *Cool,* frĭgĭda, gĕlĭda.

scĕlus, ĕris, neut. *Wickedness.*—EP. *Impious,* impium. *Audacious,* audax, ătrox. *Base,* turpe. *Unspeakable,* nĕfandum, infandum, nĕfārium. *Unheard of.* Inaudītum. *Cruel,* sævum, immīte.

scēna. *A scene, a theatre.*—EP. *Purple,* purpūrea. *Painted,* picta. *Let down,* dēmissa *or* sŭblāta (*for in ancient theatres the scenes were raised from the floor*). *Ingenious,* ingĕniōsa. *Giving a faithful representation,* fīda, fĭdēlis.

sceptrum. *A sceptre.*—EP. *Royal,* rēgium, rēgāle, rēgĭfĭcum. *Powerful,* pŏtens. *Ivory,* ĕburnum, ĕburneum. *Golden,* aureum, aurātum, ĭnaurātum. *To be respected,* vĕnĕrābĭle, vĕrendum, augustum. *To be feared,* tĭmendum, trĕmendum, mĕtuendum. *Hereditary,* pătrium, păternum, ăvītum.

scientia. *Knowledge.*—EP. *Profound,* alta, prŏfunda. *Varied,* vāria. *Learned,* docta. *Divine,* dīvīna, cœlestis.

scintilla. *A spark.*—EP. *Bright,* lūcĭda, splendĭda. *Fiery, glowing,* ignea, flammans, flammĭfĕra, ardens, flăgrans. *Sudden,* sŭbĭta. *Leaping out,* exsĭliens, ēmĭcans. *Little,* exĭgua, parva. *Destructive,* exĭtiōsa, exĭtiālis, damnōsa.

scirpea *A mat.*—EP. *Of rushes,* juncea. *Of straw,* strāmĭnea. *Worthless,* vīlis. *Dirty,* fœda, turpis, sordĭda.

78 SCO—SEP

scŏpŭlus. *A rock.* See rupea.

scorpĭŏs, i, masc. *A scorpion.*—EP. *Poisonous,* vĕnĕnātus. *Fierce,* fĕrus, sævus.

scrīnium. *A writing desk.*—EP. *Full,* plēnum.

scriptum. *A writing.* See liber.

scrobs, scrōbis, fem. See fossa.

scurra, masc. *A buffoon.*—EP. *Ridiculous,* rĭdĭcŭlus. *Worthless, low,* vīlis.

scŭtĭca. *A whip.* See flagellum.

scŭtum. *A shield.* See clypeus.

scўphus. *A cup.* See poculum.

sĕcessus, ûs. *A place of retirement, retirement.*—EP. *Safe,* tūtus, incŏlŭmis. *Quiet,* plăcĭdus, tranquillus, quiētus. *Pleasant,* āmœnus, grātus, dulcis, jūcundus. *Remote,* rĕmōtus, sēcrētus.

sĕcūris, is, fem. *An axe.*—EP. *Iron,* ferrea, ferrata. *Hard,* dūra. *Heavy,* grăvis. *Sharp,* ăcūta. *Brought against that which it is to cut,* adducta, admōta. *Cruel,* sæva, fĕra. *Fearful,* mĕtuenda, tĭmenda. *Sacrificial,* sācrĭfĭca. *Curved,* falcāta, curva.

sēdes, is, fem. 1. *A seat.* 2. *An abode.*—EP. 1. *Cool,* frĭgĭda, gĕlĭda. *Sunny,* ăprīca. *Grassy, mossy,* grāmĭnea, muscōsa. *Ivory,* ēburna, ēburnea. *Golden,* aurea. *Soft,* mollis.—1, 2. *Shady,* umbrōsa. *Rocky, placed among rocks,* or *made of stone,* saxea. *Lofty, high,* alta, ardua, sŭblīmis. *Humble,* hŭmĭlis. *Simple,* simplex –īcis. *Rustic,* rustica. *Proud,* sŭperba. *Safe,* tūta. *Well-known,* nōta. *Usual,* sŏlĭta, consueta. *Desired, desirable,* optāta, optābĭlis. *Pleasant,* dulcis, grāta, āmœna, jūcunda. 2. *Hereditary or native,* pātria. *Hereditary, ancestral,* ăvīta, păterna. See domus.

sĕdīle, is, neut. *A seat.* See above.

sĕdĭtio, onis, fem. *Sedition.*—EP. *Wicked,* impia, scĕlĕrāta. *Cruel,* sæva, fĕra. *Bloody,* sanguīnea, sanguĭnŏlenta, cruenta. *Ignoble,* ignōbĭlis. *Implacable,* implācābĭlis. *Civil,* cīvīca. *New,* nŏva. *Sudden,* sŭbĭta. *Turbulent,* turbĭda. *Swelling, angry,* tŭmĭda, tŭmens, irāta, fūrĭosa. *Discontented,* ægra.

sĕdŭlĭtas. *Industry.*—EP. *Continued,* assĭdua, longa. *Unwearied,* indēfessa. *Virtuous,* prŏba. *Innocent,* innŏcua, innoxia.

sĕges, ĕtis, fem. 1. *Corn-land.*—2. *The crop.*—EP. 1. *Cultivated,* culta, exercīta. *Fertile,* fēcunda, fĕrax, fertĭlis, pinguis, læta. *Warm,* călĭda.—2. *Abundant,* læta. *Yellow,* flāva. *Sacred to Ceres,* Cĕrealis. *Expected,* expectāta, spērāta. *Wished for,* optāta. *Seasonable,* tempestīva. *Ripe,* mātūra. *High,* alta. *Thick,* densa. *Strong,* vălĭda.

segnĭties, ei. *Laziness.* See ignavia.

sella. *A seat.* See sedes.

sēmen, ĭnis, neut. *Seed.*—EP. *Fruitful,* fēcundum, pingue, lætum. *Chosen,* lectum. *Sown, cast,* jactum, pŏsĭtum. *Buried in the earth,* ōbrŭtum. *Swelling,* tŭmens, tŭmĭdum. *Grateful, likely to make a return,* grātum.

sēmentis. *Sowing.* See satio.

sēmĭta. *A path.* See via.

sĕnātor, ōris, masc. *A senator.*—EP. *Wise,* săpiens. *Aged,* sĕnex, vĕtŭlus. *Hoary,* cānus. *Venerable, august,* vĕnĕrābĭlis, augustus, vĕrendus. *Dignified,* grăvis. *Prudent,* prūdens. *Powerful,* pŏtens. *Nobly born,* nōbĭlis, gĕnĕrōsus. *Chosen.* lectus.

sĕnātus, ûs. *A senate.*—EP. *Of the country,* pătrius. *Numerous,* frēquens. See above.

sĕnecta, sĕnectus, ūtis, fem. *Old age.*—EP. *Hoary,* cāna, alba. *Weak,* imbellis, infirma, dēbĭlis. *Venerable,* vĕnĕrābĭlis, vĕnĕranda, vĕrenda. *Frail,* frăgĭlis. *Slow,* tarda, pĭgra. *Worn out,* effēta. *Wrinkled,* rūgōsa. *Cold,* gĕlĭda, frĭgĭda. *Inactive,* iners. See Gradus.

sensus, ûs. *Sense, feeling, etc.*—EP. *Acute,* ăcūtus. *Dull, blunt,* hĕbes –ĕtis. *New,* nŏvus. *Customary,* sŏlĭtus. *Inmost,* intĭmus, īmus.

sententia. 1. *Opinion.*—2. *Meaning.*—EP. 1. *Wise,* săpiens. *Slowly formed,* tarda. *Late,* sēra. *Cautious,* cauta.—1, 2. *Fixed,* certa. *Variable,* vāria.

sentis, is, masc. *A thorn.*—EP. *Sharp,* ăcūtus. *Rough,* asper –ĕri. *Thick,* numerous, densus.

sēpes, is, fem. *A hedge.*—EP. *Thick,* densa. *High,* alta. *Thorny,* spīnōsa.

septum. *Any place fenced in.*—EP. *Safe,* tūtum. *Narrow,* angustum, arctum. *Inviolable,* invĭŏlābĭle.

sĕpulchrum. *A tomb.*—EP. *Built up,* structum, exstructum. *Last,* ultĭmum

SEP—SIM 79

sŭprēmum, extrēmum. *Sad, to be lamented*, triste, mĭsĕrum, mĭsĕrābĭle, lăcrȳmōsum, flēbĭle, deflendum. *Marble*, marmŏreum. *Magnificent, proud*, magnĭfĭcum, sŭperbum. *Quiet*, tranquillum, plăcĭdum, quiētum. *Ancestral, family*, pătrium, păternum, ăvītum.

sĕpultūra. *Burial.* See above.

sĕra. *A bolt.*—EP. *Iron*, ferrea, ferrāta. *Hard*, dūra. *Unkind*, ĭnīqua, imprŏba, mălīgna. *Shut*, clausa. *Tenacious*, tēnax. *Obstinate*, pertīnax.

sĕries, ēi, fem. *A series.*—EP. *Long*, longa. *Regular*, justa. *Unbroken*, intĕgra.

sermo, ōnis, masc. *Discourse, conversation.*—EP. *Long*, longus. *Friendly*, ămīcus. *Lasting by day, or by night*, diurnus, nocturnus. *Learned*, doctus. *Various*, vărius. *Envious*, invĭdus, līvĭdus. *Malignant*, mălignus. *Satirical*, mordax.

serpens, tis, masc., rarely fem. *A serpent.*—EP. *Venomous*, vĕnēnātus. *Biting*, mordax. *Heavy*, grăvis. *Long*, longus. *Scaly*, squāmōsus, squāmeus. squāmĭger -eri. *Curling*, sĭnuosus. *Curled up*, contractus. *Hissing*, sĭbĭlus, *Dark-coloured*, āter -tri, caerūleus, caerŭlus. *Erect*, arrectus. See the Gradus.

serra. *A saw.*—EP. *Sharp*, ăcūta. *Creaking*, argūta, strīdŭla, strīdens. *With teeth*, dentōsa. *Iron*, ferrea, ferrāta. *Hard*, dūra, rĭgĭda.

sertum. *A garland.*—EP. *Of roses*, rŏseum. *Of flowers*, flōreum. *Easily woven*, nexĭle. *Put on*, impŏsĭtum. See corona.

servātor, ōris, masc. *A preserver.*—EP. *Powerful*, pŏtens, vălĭdus. *Great*, magnus. *Ancient*, vĕtus -ĕris, priscus, antīquus. *Honoured*, hŏnōrātus. *Loved*, ămātus, cārus, dīlectus. *Watchful*, vĭgil -īlis. *Eager, active*, ācer -cris, impĭger -gri, strēnuus.

servĭtium, servĭtus, ūtis, fem. *Slavery.*—EP. *Sad*, tristis, mĭsĕra, mĭsĕrābĭlis. *Hard*, dūra. *Hateful*, invīsa, ŏdĭōsa, ĭnāmābĭlis. *Base*, turpis, foeda. *Heavy*, grăvis. *Long*, longa, diūturna. *Everlasting*, aeterna. *Unwilling*, invīta. *Helpless*, ĭnops -ŏpis.

servus, serva. *A slave.*—EP. *Useful*, ūtĭlis. *Trusty*, fīdus, fĭdēlis. *Aged*, sĕnex, vĕtŭlus. *Honest*, prŏbus. *Known*, nōtus.

sēta. *A bristle.*—EP. *Rough*, aspĕra, horrĭda, horrens. *Thick*, densa. *Terrible*, terrĭbĭlis, dīra. *Shaggy*, hirta, hirsūta.

sĭbĭlus, in pl. sĭbĭla, ōrum. 1. *A hiss.* 2. *The noise of the wind or of a wind instrument.*—EP. 1. *Horrible, fearful*, horrĭbĭlis, dīrus, mĕtuendus. *Threatening*, mĭnax. 2. *Soft*, mollis. *Sweet*, dulcis, ămoenus. *Cool*, frĭgĭdus, gĕlĭdus. *Gentle*, lēnis.

sĭca. *A dagger.* See ensis.

sīdus, ĕris, neut. *A star.*—EP. *Shining*, lūcĭdum, splendens, fulgens, cŏruscum, rădians. *High*, altum, sublīme. *Fixed in heaven*, caeleste, aethĕrium. *Eternal*, aeternum. *Shining by night*, nocturnum. *Wandering*, văgum. *Giving omens of the future*, praenuntium. *Golden*, aureum. *Cold*, frĭgĭdum, gĕlĭdum. See astrum.

sĭgillum. 1. *A little image.* 2. *A seal.*—EP. 1. *Small*, parvum, exĭguum. *Ornamental*, dĕcens, dĕcōrum. 2. *Carved*, sculptum, exsculptum. *Trusty*, fīdum, fĭdēle. *Waxen*, cēreum.

signum. 1. *A sign, a signal.* 2. *A standard.* 3. *A statue.*—EP. 1. *Certain, true*, certum, vērum. *Well known*, nōtum. *Expected, wished for*, optātum, spērātum. 2. *Warlike*, bellĭcum, Māvortium. *Victorious*, victrix -īcis. *Safe*, tūtum, illaesum, servātum. *Dear*, cārum, dēlectum. *National*, pătrium. 3. See statua.

sĭlentium. *Silence.*—EP. *Tranquil*, plăcĭdum, tranquillum, quiētum. *Unbroken*, irruptum. *Pleasant*, grātum, dulce, ămoenum, ămābĭle. *Existing by night*, nocturnum. *Faithful, keeping a secret*, fīdum, fĭdēle. *Mute*, mūtum, tăcĭtum, tăcĭturnum. *Obstinate*, pertīnax.

sĭler, ĕris, neut. *A withy.* See vimen.

sĭlex, ĭcis, masc. fem. *A flint.*—EP. *Hard*, dūra. *Containing fire*, igneus, flammĭfer -ĕri. *Struck*, percussus, ictus.

sĭlĭqua. *A husk.*—EP. *Useless*, ĭnūtĭlis, vīlis. *Light*, lĕvis. *Empty*, ĭnānia.

simplĭcĭtas. *Simplicity, honest*, prŏba. *Rustic*, rustĭca, ăgrestis. *Contented*, contenta. *Old-fashioned*, prisca, antīqua, vĕtus -ĕris. *Unpolished*, inculta, rŭdis.

80   SIM—SOL

sĭmŭlācrum. 1. *A likeness, an image.* 2. *A phantom.*—EP. *Skilfully made,* ĕgrĕgium, insigne. *Faithful,* fĭdēle, fĭdum. *Sacred,* săcrum, săcratum, sanctum. *Marble,* marmŏreum. *Ivory,* ĕburnum, ĕburneum. *Painted,* pictum. 2. *Seen by night,* nocturnum. *Horrid,* horrĭdum, dīrum, horrībĭle, mĕtuendum, tĭmendum. *Of ill omen,* obscœnum, sĭnistrum. *Pale,* pallĭdum, pallens.

sĭmŭlāmen, ĭnis, neut. *A representation.* See above, 1.

sĭmŭlātor, ōris, masc. *A pretender.*—EP. *Deceitful,* fallax, falsus. *Cunning,* callĭdus, dŏlōsus. *Base,* turpis. *Malignant,* mălus, mălignus. *Wicked,* imprŏbus.

sĭmultas. *Enmity.*—EP. *Old,* prisca, vĕtus –ĕris, vĕtusta, antīqua. *Bitter,* ăcerba, aspĕra. *Undeserved,* immĕrīta. *Lasting,* longa, diūturna. *Everlasting,* æterna.

sĭngultus, ûs. *A sob, sobbing.*—EP. *Panting,* ănbēlus. *Heavy,* grăvis. *Repeated,* crēber –bri. *Sad,* tristis, miser –ĕri, mĭsĕrābĭlis. *Broken,* fractus. *Long,* longus. *Shaking the person,* concŭtiens. *Silent,* tăcĭtus, sĭlens.

sĭnum. *A pail.*—EP. *Of maple, of beech, etc.,* ăcernum, făgīneum, făgīnum. *Full,* plenum. *Foaming,* spūmans, spūmōsum.

sĭnus, ûs. 1. *The bosom.*—2. *Any hollow or bend.*—3. *A bay.*—EP. 1. *Tender,* tĕner –ĕri, mollis. *Affectionate,* pius, ămans, cārus. *Wished for,* optātus. *Friendly,* ămīcus. *Swelling* tŭmĭdus, tŭmens —2, 3. *Curved,* curvus, falcātus. 2. *Gentle,* lēnis.—3. *In the sea,* æquŏreus, mărīnus. *Deep,* altus, prŏfundus. *Safe,* tūtus. *Lying back, concealed,* lătens.

Sīren, ēnis. *A Siren* (See Gradus).—EP. *Threefold,* trĭplex –ĭcis. *Tuneful,* vōcālis, cănōra, argūta. *Learned,* docta. *Clever,* ingĕniosa, săpiens. *Victorious,* victrix. *Powerful,* pŏtens.

Sīrius. *The Dog-star.*—EP. *Rapid, vehement,* răpĭdus, vehĕmens, viŏlentus. *Burning,* torrĭdus, torrens, igneus, ardens, æstĭfer –ĕri. *Shining in summer,* æstīvus.

sistrum. *A timbrel.*—EP. *Egyptian,* Ægyptium, Nīliăcum. *Barbaric,* barbărum, barbărīcum. *Rattling,* crĕpĭtans.

sĭtis, is, fem. 1. *Thirst.*—2. *Drought.*—EP. 1, 2. *Dry, parching,* ărĭda, ărens, sicca. *Burning,* ignea, torrĭda, torrens. *Long,* longa, diūturna.—1. *Causing sickness or pain,* ægra, tristis.—2. *Causing barrenness,* stĕrĭlis, tristis.

sĭtus, ûs. *Situation.* See positus.

sĭtus, ûs. *Rust.* See rubigo.

smăragdus. *An emerald.*—EP. *Green,* vĭrĭdis. *Eastern,* Eŏus, Indus, Indĭcus, *Hard,* dūrus. *Brilliant,* splendĭdus, lūcĭdus, splendens.

sŏbŏles. *Offspring.* See proles.

soccus. *A slipper.*—EP. *Low,* hŭmĭlis. *Soft,* mollis. *Comic,* cōmĭcus. *Jocose,* jŏcōsus. See Gradus.

sŏcer, ĕri. *A father-in-law.*—EP. *New,* nŏvus. See pater.

sŏcius. *A companion, an ally.*—EP. *Dear,* cārus, dīlectus, ămātus. *Customary,* sŏlĭtus, consuetus, assuetus. *Old, ancient,* priscus, vĕtus –ĕris, antīquus, vetustus. *Useful,* ūtĭlis, aptus. *Worthy,* dignus, prŏbus. *Trusted, trusty,* fīdus, fĭdēlis. *Powerful,* pŏtens. *Assisting,* ŏpĭfer –ĕri. *Pleasant, wished for,* grātus, ămābĭlis, optātus, optābĭlis. *Tried,* spectātus.

sŏcrus, ûs, fem. *A mother-in-law.* See socer.

sŏdālis. *A companion. Companionship,* sŏdālĭtium. See socius.

sol, sōlis, masc. *The sun.*—EP. *Rising,* ŏriens. *Setting,* occĭdens, occĭduus. *Shining in the morning,* mātūtīnus. *Mid-day,* mĕdius. *Brilliant,* splendĭdus, rŭtĭlus, fulgens. *Shining in heaven,* cœlestis, æthĕrius. *High, supreme,* sŭblīmis, altus, sŭprēmus, summus. *Ripening fruit,* mātūrus. *Fiery, burning,* igneus, torrĭdus. *Warm,* călĭdus. *Delightful,* dulcis, jūcundus. *Golden,* aureus. *Sacred,* săcer –cri. See Gradus.

sōlāmen, ĭnis, neut. sōlātium. *Comfort.*—EP. *Wished for, desirable,* optātum, exoptatum, optābĭle. *Sweet,* dulce, jūcundum, grātum. *Slow, late,* tardum, sērum. *Enduring,* longum, mansūrum. *Gentle,* lēne, blandum. *Sure,* certum. *Deserved,* mĕrĭtum. *Fortunate, happy,* fēlix –īcis.

sōlātor, ōris, masc. *A comforter.*—EP. *Wise,* săpiens. *Skilful, ingenious,* sōlers, ingĕniōsus. *Friendly,* ămīcus. *Kind,* bŏnus, bĕnignus. See above.

sōlertia. *Skill, wisdom in action.*—EP. *Great,* magna. *Prudent, skilful,* prūdens, pĕrīta, docta. *Proved,* spectāta. *Known,* nōta. *Crafty, ingenious,* cal-

SOL—SPE 81

lǐda, ingĕnĭōsa. *Successful*, victrix –ĭcis, fēlix –ĭcis. *Useful*, ūtĭlis. *Varied*, vărĭa.

sŏlium. *A throne.*—EP. *Royal*, rēgium, rēgăle, rēgĭfĭcum. *Powerful*, pŏtens. *Golden*, aureum, aurātum, ĭnaurātum. *Ivory*, ĕburnum, ĕburneum. *National*, pătrium. *Hereditary*, pătrium, păternum, ăvītum. *Ancient*, antĭquum, vĕtustum. *Honoured, honourable, august*, hŏnōrātum, augustum, vĕnĕrăbĭle. *To be feared*, mĕtuendum. *Sacred*, săcrum, săcrātum, sanctum. *High*, altum, sŭblīme.

sollĭcĭtūdo, ĭnis, fem. *Solicitude.*—EP. *Anxious*, anxia. *Doubtful*, dūbia, incerta. *Fearful*, tĭmĭda. *Long*, longa, diŭturna. *Past*, praetĕrĭta. *Abiding*, mansūra. *Sad*, aegra, tristis, lăcrȳmōsa. *Bitter*, ācerba. *Unceasing*, perpĕtua, aeterna.

solstĭtium. *The solstice, esp. the summer solstice.* See aestas.

sŏlum. *The ground, soil.*—EP. *Dirty*, turpe, foedum. *Fertile*, pingue, fertĭle, fēcundum, fērax. *Muddy*, līmōsum. See terra.

somnium. *A dream.*—EP. *Seen*, vīsum. *Seen by night*, nocturnum. *Doubtful*, ambĭguum, incertum. *Of good omen*, faustum, fēlix –ĭcis, dextĕrum, *sync.* –trum. *Of bad omen*, sĭnistrum, infaustum. *True*, vērum. *Prophetic*, praenuntium, praesāgum. *Empty, vain*, vānum, ĭnāne.

somnus. *Sleep.*—EP. *Enjoyed at night*, nocturnus. *Light*, lēvis. *Tranquil*, tranquillus, plăcĭdus, quiētus. *Deep*, altus. *Sweet, wished for*, dulcis, ămoenus, jūcundus, optātus. *Causing forgetfulness*, lēthaeus, oblĭvĭōsus. *Wholesome*, sălūber –bris. *Languid*, languĭdus. *Inactive*, ĭners, segnis. See Gradus.

sŏnĭtus, ûs, sŏnor, ōris, masc. sŏnus. *A noise.*—EP. *Loud*, clārus, grăvis. *Hoarse*, raucus. *Tuneful*, lĭquĭdus, argūtus. *Distant*, longinquus. *Sweet, soft*, blandus, dulcis. *Well known*, nōtus. *Slight*, tĕnuis. *Re-echoed*, rĕpercussus. *Sudden*, sŭbĭtus, rĕpentīnus. *Sounding in the air, coming from heaven*, aethĕrius, coelestis. *Marvellous*, mīrus, mīrăbĭlis.

sŏpor, ōris, masc. See somnus.

sordes. *Dirt.* See situs, ûs.

sŏror, ōris, fem. *A sister.*—EP. *Dear*, cāra, ămāta, dīlecta. *Beautiful*, pulchra, candĭda, dĕcōra, formōsa. *Agreeing with one*, ūnănĭmia, concors –dis. *Affectionate*, pia, ămans. *Faithful*, fīda, fĭdēlis. *Of the same age*, aequaeva, aequālis.

sors, tis, fem. 1. *Fortune, chance.*—2. *A lot.*—EP. 1. See fortuna.—2. *Cast*, jacta. *Unfortunate*, adversa. *Deceitful*, fallax, perfĭda, infīda. *Decision*, arbĭtra.

spătium. 1. *A racecourse.*—2. *Space, room.*—EP. 1. *Dusty*, pulvĕreum, pulvĕrŭlentum. *Measured out, marked out*, ēmensum, signātum.—1, 2. *Known, usual*, nōtum, sŏlĭtum, consuetum.—2. *Ample*, magnum, amplum, ingens. *Short, small*, parvum, exĭguum, brĕve.

spĕcies, ēi, fem. 1. *Appearance, what is seen, likeness.*—2. *Beauty.*—EP. 1. *Real*, vēra. *Seen*, vīsa. *Deceitful*, falsa, fallax.—2. See forma.

spĕcĭmen, ĭnis, neut. *A specimen.*—EP. *Trustworthy*, fīdum, fĭdēle.

spectācŭlum, *sync.* **spectăclum.** *A spectacle.*—EP. *Splendid*, splendĭdum. *Solemn, recurring at fixed times*, sŏlenne. *Sacred*, săcrum, săcrātum, sanctum. *Festive*, festum. *Much frequented*, cĕlĕbre.

spectātor, ōris, masc. spectātrix, īcis, fem. *A spectator.*—EP. *Joyful*, laetus, felix. *Coming together*, coiens, congrĕdiens. *Assembled*, collectus, lectus (*these last 4. usu. in plur.*). *Invited*, vŏcātus. *Clad in white*, candĭdus. *Eager*, cŭpĭdus, ācer –cris. *Attentive*, intentus. *Anxious*, anxius, sollĭcĭtus. *Fearful*, tĭmĭdus. *Present*, praesens, adstans. *Surrounding*, circumstans.

spĕcŭla. *A watchtower.*—EP. *High*, alta, ēdĭta. *Built*, structa, exstructa. *Fortified*, mūnīta. See turris.

spĕcŭlātor, ōris, masc. *A scout.*—EP. *Light*, lēvis. *Active, quick*, ăgĭlis, cĕler –ĕris. *Trusty*, fīdus, fĭdēlis. *Sent out*, missus, ēmissus. *By night*, nocturnus, *Cautious*, cautus. *Crafty*, dŏlōsus, callĭdus. *Returning, having returned*, rĕdux –ŭcis.

spĕcŭlum. *A mirror.*—EP. *Glassy*, vītreum. *Faithful*, fīdum, fĭdēle.

spĕcus, ûs, spēlaeum, spēlunca. *A cave.* See antrum.

spes, ĕi. *Hope.*—EP. *Anxious*, anxia, sollĭcĭta. *Credulous*, crēdŭla. *Eager*, acris, ăvĭda, cŭpĭda. *Certain*, certa. *Ratified*, răta. *Deceitful*, falsa, fallax,

G

82 SPI—STI

mendax, perfĭda. *Doubtful*, dŭbia, incerta. *Foreboding*, præsaga. *Mingled*, mista. *Sanguine*, bŏna. *Passing, shattered*, brĕvis, frăgĭlis, cădūca. *Vain*, vāna, ĭnānis, irrīta.

spīca. *An ear of corn.*—EP. *Ripe*, mātūra. *Yellow*, aurea, flāva. *Full*, plēna, grăvĭda, grăvis.

spĭcŭlum. *A javelin.* See jaculum.

spīna. *A thorn.*—EP. *Rough, sharp*, aspĕra, ăcūta. *Bristling*, horrĭda, horrens. *Projecting*, exstans. *Piercing*, pĕnĕtrābĭlis.

spīnētum. *A thorny brake.* See above.

spīra. *A fold.*—EP. *Winding*, sĭnuosa. *Twisted*, torta, contorta. *Compressed*, pressa, compressa.

spīrācŭlum, spīrāmentum. *A breathing-hole.*—EP. *Hollow*, căvum.

spīrĭtus, ûs. 1. *Breath, breathing.*—2. *Spirit.*—3. *Life.*—EP. *Of life*, vītālis. *Deep*, altus, prŏfundus. *Quick, panting*, ănhēlus, ănhēlans. *Difficult*, æger, diffĭcĭlis. 2. *Vigorous, animated*, ănĭmōsus. *Noble*, nōbĭlis, gĕnĕrōsus. *Divine*, dīvīnus. 3. See vita.

splendor, ōris, masc. *Splendor.*—EP. *Brilliant*, fulgĭdus, rădians. *Royal*, rēgius. *Magnificent*, magnĭfĭcus. *Marvellous*, mirus, mīrābĭlis. *Remarkable*, insignis, ēgrēgius. *Golden*, aureus. *Conspicuous*, conspĭcuus, conspĭciendus.

spŏlium. *Spoil.*—EP. *Great*, magnum, amplum. *Rich*, dīves -ĭtis, ŏpŭlentum, splendĭdum, ēgrēgium. *Wished for*, optātum. *Enjoyed*, pŏtītum. *Token of victory*, victrix -īcis. *Warlike*, bellĭcum. *Stripped off an enemy*, exūtum. *Glorious*, clārum, præclārum, insigne.

sponsa. *A bride.*—EP. *Promised*, pollĭcĭta, prōmissa. See uxor.

sponsus. *A husband.* See maritus.

sprētor, ōris, masc. *A despiser.*—EP. *Proud*, sŭperbus, arrŏgans. *Impious*, impius. *Audacious*, audax. *Cruel*, sævus, fĕrus, immītis. *Old, ancient*, vĕtus -ĕris, antīquus. *Accustomed*, sŏlĭtus, assuetus, consuetus. *Open*, mănĭfestus, ăpertus.

spūma. *Foam, froth.*—EP. *White*, alba, albĭda, albens, nĭvea, candens. *Fresh*, nŏva, rĕcens. *Of the sea*, æquŏrea, mărīna. *Rising up*, exsurgens. *Lying on the top*, summa.

squālor, ōris, masc. *Dirt.*—EP. *Unseemly*, turpis, dēformis. *Wretched*, mĭser -ĕri, mĭsĕrābĭlis. *Poor*, ĭnops -ŏpis, pauper -ĕris.

squāma. *A scale of a fish, serpent, etc.*—EP. *Shining*, lūcĭda, nĭtens, fulgens. *Close*, densa, conserta. *Variegated*, văria, picta. *Crackling*, crĕpĭtans.

stăbŭlum. *A stable.*—EP. *Safe*, tūtum. *Shut up*, clausum. *Full*, plēnum. *Rustic, of a farmer*, rustĭcum, ăgreste.

stădium. *A racecourse.* See spatium.

stagnum. *A pool, a marsh.*—EP. *Low*, hŭmĭle. *Wet*, irrĭguum, ūdum, hŭmĭdum, mădĭdum. *Shaking*, trĕmŭlum. *Muddy*, līmōsum. *Deep*, altum, prŏfundum. *Sticky*, tĕnax.

stāmen, ĭnis, neut. *A thread.* See filum.

stătio, ōnis, fem. *A station.*—EP. *Fixed*, fixa, certa. *Safe*, tūta, incŏlŭmis. *Ancient*, prisca, antīqua, vĕtusta, vĕtus -ĕris. *Original*, prīma. *Proper*, digna.

stătua. *A statue.*—EP. *Brazen*, ærea, ærāta, ahēna, ahēnea. *Marble*, marmŏrea. *Golden*, aurea. *Sculptured*, sculpta. *Faithful (as a likeness)*, fĭda, fĭdēlis. *Likely to last*, mansūra. *Excellent*, ēgrēgia, insignis. *Celebrated*, nōta, inclўta, clara. *Erected*, pŏsĭta, stans.

stătus, ûs. 1. *An attitude.*—2. *A condition, or state.*—EP. 1. *Firm*, firmus. *Threatening*, mĭnax. *Graceful*, dĕcōrus, decens. 2. See conditio.

stella. *A star.* See sidus.

stellio, ōnis, masc. *A sort of lizard.*—RP. *Long*, longus. *Green*, vĭrĭdis. *Loving marshy places*, pălūdōsus, păluster -tris.

stercus, ōris, neut. *Dung.* See fimus.

stĭmŭlus. 1. *A goad.*—2. *A stimulus.*—EP. 1, 2. *Sharp*, acer -cris, ăcūtus. 1. *Sharpened at the point*, præăcūtus. *Iron*, ferreus, serrātus. 2. *Powerful*, pŏtens. *Unseen, secret*, cæcus, tăcĭtus. *Wished for, needed*, optātus.

stĭpendium. *Pay.*—EP. *Large*, magnum, amplum. *Deserved*, mĕrĭtum. *Expected*, spērātum, exspectātum. *Given, received*, dătum, acceptum.

stīpes, ĭtis, masc. *A stake, a trunk of a tree.*—EP. *Of oak, beech, maple, etc.* rōbŏreus, quernus, făgĭneus, făgĭnus, ăcernus, etc. *Hard*, durus. See arbor.

STI—SUC 83

stĭpŭla. *Stubble, straw.*—EP. *Dry,* arĭda, sicca. *Light,* lĕvis. *Poor, humble* (*when used for the thatch of a cottage, or the bed of a poor man*), pauper –ĕris, hŭmĭlis, tĕnuis, simplex –ĭcis. See stramen.

stĭria. *An icicle.*—EP. *Cold,* frĭgĭda, gĕlĭda, glăcĭālis. *Stiff,* horrĭda, horrens, rĭgĭda. *Hanging down,* pendens, dēpendens, pendŭla. *Wintry,* hўberna, hўĕmālis, brūmālis.

stirps –pis, fem. 1. *The root or stem of a tree.*—2. *A family.*—EP. *Deep,* alta, prŏfunda. *The lowest,* ima. *Hard,* dūra.—1, 2. *Ancient,* vĕtus –ĕris, vetusta, antĭqua, prisca. 2. *Noble,* nŏbĭlis, gĕnĕrōsa. *Illustrious,* clāra, præclāra, insignis.

stīva. *A plough-tail.* See aratrum.

stŏla. *A woman's robe.* See toga.

strāges. *Ruin, slaughter.*—EP. *Vast,* vasta, magna, ingens. *Cruel,* sæva, fĕra, immītis. *Bloody,* cruenta, sanguĭnea, sanguĭnōlenta. *Sad,* tristis, mĭsĕra, mĭsĕrābĭlis. See clades.

strāgŭlum. *A counterpane.*—EP. *Soft,* molle. *Placed on anything,* impŏsĭtum.

strāmen, ĭnis, neut.—EP. *Dry,* arĭdum, ārens, siccum. *Yellow,* flāvum. *Light,* lĕve. *Worthless,* vile.

strātum. *A bed.* See lectus.

strĕpĭtus, ûs. *A rattling noise.*—EP. *Hoarse,* raucus. *Loud,* clārus, ingens. *Distant,* longinquus. See sonus.

strīdor, ōris, masc. *A creaking noise.*—EP. *Shrill,* ăcūtus. See sonus.

strix, strĭgis, fem. *A screech-owl.*—EP. *Hoarse,* rauca. *Shrill,* ăcūta. *Flying or crying by night,* nocturna. *Ill-omened,* obscœna, sĭnistra, măla, infausta.

strŏphium. *A girdle.* See zona.

structūra. *Structure.*—EP. *Strong,* firma, vălĭda. *Ingenious,* sŏlers, callĭda, ingĕniōsa. *Lasting,* mansūra. *Surviving its makers or its inhabitants, etc.,* sŭperstes –ĭtis. *Marble,* marmŏrea. *Adamantine,* ădămantĭna.

strues. *A heap.*—EP. *Collected,* congesta, coacta. *Large,* magna, ingens. *High,* alta, ardua.

stŭdĭum. 1. *Zeal, eagerness.*—2. *A pursuit.*—EP. 1. *Fervent,* fervĭdum, fervens, igneum, ardens. *Active,* ācre, impĭgrum. *Unwearied,* indefessum. *Anxious,* sollĭcĭtum, anxium. *Friendly,* ămīcum.—2. *Praiseworthy,* laudābĭle. *Customary,* sŏlĭtum, consuetum, assuetum. *Ancient, precious,* priscum, vĕtus –ĕris. *Learned,* doctum.

stultĭtia. *Folly.*—EP. *Mad, ignorant of the future,* dēmens. *Rash, incautious,* incauta, præceps –ĭpĭtis, tĕmĕrāria. *Sad,* tristis, mĭsĕra, mĭsĕrābĭlis. *Talkative,* lŏquax, garrŭla.

stŭpor, ōris, masc. *Stupor, amazement.*—EP. *Silent,* tăcĭtus. *Sudden,* sūbĭtus, rĕpentīnus. *Great,* magnus, ingens. *Helpless, bewildered,* ĭnops –ōpis, āmens. *Frightened,* tĭmĭdus, terrĭtus, conterrĭtus.

stuppa. *Tow.*—EP. *Light,* lĕvis.

sturnus. *A starling.*—EP. *Chattering,* lŏquax, garrŭlus. *Kept in a cage,* clausus. *Brown,* fuscus. *Learned,* doctus.

Styx, Stўgis, fem. *The Styx.*—EP. *Of hell,* Tartārea, inferna. *Black, lurid,* ātra, nĭgra, lūrĭda. *Slow, lazy,* segnis, ĭners. *By which the Gods may not swear falsely,* imperjūrāta. *Hateful,* invīsa, ŏdiōsa, ĭnămābĭlis. *Horrid,* horrĭda, dīra. See Orcus.

suasor, ōris, masc. *An adviser.*—EP. *Prudent, wise,* prudens, săpiens, săgax. *Cautious,* cautus. *Friendly,* ămīcus. *Useful,* ūtĭlis.

suavium. *A kiss.* See osculum.

sūber –ĕris, masc. *The cork-tree.*—EP. *Light,* lĕvis. *Productive,* fēcundus, fērax. *Soft,* mollis.

subsellium. *A seat.* See sedes.

subsĭdium. *Aid, a reinforcement.*—EP. *Useful,* ūtĭle. *Saving,* sălūtare. *Friendly,* ămīcum. *Wished for,* optātum, exoptātum. *Desirable,* optābĭle, grātum. *Seasonable,* tempestīvum. *Present,* præsens. *Ready,* părātum. *Quick in coming,* promptum.

subtēmen, ĭnis, neut. *The woof.*—EP. *Soft,* molle. *Embroidered,* pictum. *Variegated,* vărium. *Purple, etc.,* purpūreum, etc.

successor, ōris, masc. *A successor.*—EP. *Eager,* cŭpĭdus. *Late,* sērus. *New,*

G 2

84　　SUC—SUS

nŏvus. *Related*, cognātus. *Expected*, exspectātus. *About to be*, fŭtūrus. See hæres.

successus, ûs. *Success.*—EP. *Joyful, prosperous*, fēlix –ĭcis, faustus. *Deserved*, mĕrĭtus, dignus. *Wished for*, optātus. *Hoped*, spērātus. *Late*, sērus. *Unexpected*, ĭnŏpīnus, nēcŏpīnus. *Despaired of*, despērātus. *Pleasing*, grātus, jūcundus.

succĭnum. *Amber.*—EP. *Bright*, lūcĭdum, fulgens. *Yellow*, flāvum, aureum, crŏceum. *Dropping*, stillans. *Arabian*, Ărăbum, Ărābium, Săbæum.

succus. *Juice.*—EP. *Fat*, pinguis. *Sweet*, dulcis. *Abundant*, largus. *Poured forth*, effūsus.

sûdor, ōris, masc. *Sweat.*—EP. *Bursting forth*, ērumpens. *Salt*, salsus. *Wet*, ūdus, hūmĭdus, mădĭdus. *Abundant*, largus. *Poured forth*, effūsus, prŏfūsus. *Hard-working*, ŏpĕrōsus. *Cold*, frĭgĭdus, gēlĭdus. *Liquid*, lĭquĭdus. *Continual*, assĭduus. See labor.

suffrāgium. *A vote.*—EP. *Given*, dătum. *Willing*, lĭbens. *Unanimous*, ūnănĭmum or ūnănĭme, concors –dis. *Fortunate*, fēlix –ĭcis, faustum. *Joyful*, lætum. *Eager*, cŭpĭdum. *Friendly*, ămīcum. *Welcome*, grātum.

suffŭgium. *A refuge.*—EP. *Safe*, tūtum. *Distant*, longinquum, rĕmōtum. *Known, usual*, nōtum, sŏlĭtum, consuetum, assuetum. *Secret, retired*, arcanum, lătens, ignōtum. *Wished for*, optātum. *Desirable, acceptable*, grātum, optăbĭle, ămābĭle, ămœnum.

sulcus. *A furrow.*—EP. *Straight*, rectus. *Deep*, altus, prŏfundus. *Fertile, making land fertile*, fertĭlis, fērax, fēcundus. *Long*, longus. *Marked out*, signātus.

sulfur, ŭris. *Sulphur.*—EP. *Yellow*, lūteum, flāvum. *Feeding fire*, flammĭfĕrum. *Strong-smelling*, grăveŏlens.

summa. *The sum or chief aggregate of anything.*—EP. *Extreme*, ultĭma. *Greatest*, maxĭma.

sumptus, ûs. *Expense.*—EP. *Abundant*, amplus, largus. *Profuse*, prŏdĭgus, prŏfūsus. *Lavished*, effūsus. *Excessive*, nĭmius. *Foolish*, āmens, insānus, *Unrestrained*, effrænus, dēfrænatus. *Wicked*, imprŏbus.

sŭpellex, ectĭlis, fem. *Household furniture.*—EP. *Rich*, dīves –ĭtis, ŏpŭlenta. *Slendid*, splendĭda, magnĭfĭca. *Golden*, aurea. *Collected*, congesta. *Ordinary, cheap*, vīlis, hŭmĭlis. *Old, old-fashioned*, antīqua, prisca, vĕtus –eris.

sŭpĕrātor, ōris, masc. *A conqueror.* See victor.

sŭperbia. *Pride.*—EP. *Foolish*, stulta, āmens. *Undeserved*, immĕrĭta. *Vain, empty*, vānus, ĭnānis. *Exulting*, exultans, læta. *Hateful*, invīsa, ĭnāmābĭlis, ingrāta. *Short-lived*, brĕvis, cădūca. *Mischievous*, damnōsa, măla, pernĭciōsa. *Swelling*, tŭmĭda, tŭmens. *Fastidious*, fastĭdiōsa, fastōsa.

sŭpercĭlium. 1. *An eyebrow.*—2. *The brow of a hill.*—EP. 1. *Gentle*, mīte. *Arched*, curvātum. *Beautiful*, pulchrum.—2. *High*, altum. See collis.

sŭperstītio, ōnis, fem. *Superstition.*—EP. *Foul*, fœda, turpis. *Silly*, insāna, āmens. *Cruel*, sæva, immītis, barbāra, fēra. *Ignorant, vain*, ignāra, vāna, ĭnānis.

supplĭcium. *Punishment.* See pœna.

sūra. *The calf of the leg.*—EP. *Swelling*, tŭmĭda, tŭmens. *Strong*, vălĭda.

surcŭlus. *A young shoot.*—EP. *Soft*, mollis, tĕner –ĕri. *Green*, vĭrĭdis, vĭrĭdens. *Swelling*, tŭmens, tŭmĭdus, turgens, turgescens, turgĭdus. *Rising*, surgens, exsurgens.

sus, suis, masc. fem. *A pig.*—EP. *Dirty*, immundus, fœdus, turpis. *Mischievous*, damnōsus, nŏcens, noxius. *Strong-smelling*, grăveŏlens. *With hard feet*, cornĭpes –ĕdis.

susceptum. *An undertaking.*—EP. *Great*, grande, magnum. *New*, nŏvum. *Unaccustomed*, insŏlĭtum, ĭnassuetum. *Brave, bold*, forte, audax. See conatus.

suspectus, ûs. *A looking up, respect.*—EP. *Due*, mĕrĭtus, dignus. *Customary*, sŏlĭtus, consuetus. See reverentia.

suspendium. *A hanging.*—EP. *Cruel*, sævum, crūdēle. *Miserable*, triste, mĭsĕrum, mĭsĕrābĭle. *Fatal*, fātāle. See Gradus.

suspīrātus, ûs, suspīrium. *A sigh.*—EP. *Sad*, triste, mæstus, lūgŭbris. *Repeated*, crēber –bri, rĕpĕtītus. *Anxious*, anxius, sollĭcĭtus. *Broken*, fractus. *Deep*, altus. *Impeding the voice*, impĕdiens vōcem.

SUS—TEG 85

sŭsurrus. *A whisper.*—EP. *Gentle,* lēnis, mollis.

sylva. *A wood.*—EP. *Thick,* densa. *Old,* vĕtus –ĕris, vĕtusta, antīqua. *Leafy,* frondea, frondōsa, frondens. *Green,* vĭrĭdis, vĭrĭdans, vĭrens. *Shady,* umbrōsa, ŏpāca. *Sacred,* sācra, sācrāta. *Of oak, of beech, etc.,* rōbŏrea, făgĭnea, etc. *Not cut down,* incædua, invĭŏlāta. *Dark,* tĕnĕbrōsa, ātra. *Pathless,* invia. *Silent,* tăcĭta, sĭlens. *Secret, full of secret places,* sēcrēta. *Inhospitable,* ĭnhospĭta.

sylvĭcŏla, æ, masc. *One who lives in the woods.*—EP. *Hardy,* dūrus. *Uncivilised,* rūdis, incultus. *Solitary,* sōlus.

T.

Tăbella, tăbŭla. 1. *A board, a plank.*—2. *A tablet, writing, picture.* 1. *Little,* parva. *Thin,* tĕnuis. *Of oak, beech, pine, etc.,* querna, făgĭnea, pĭnea, etc. *Cut,* secta.—2. *Written,* scripta. *Faithful,* fīda, fīdēlis. *To be kept,* servanda. *Mindful, keeping things in remembrance,* mĕmor –ŏris.

tăberna. 1. *A cottage.*—2. *A shop, a tavern.*—EP. 1. See casa.—2. *Rich,* dīves ĭtis. *Luxurious,* lauta, pinguis.

tābes. *Wasting away, that which causes wasting.*—EP. *Cruel,* crūdēlis, sæva, fĕra. *Destructive,* exĭtiōsa, exītiālis. *Slow,* lenta.

tăbŭlāria, um, plur. neut. *Archives.*—EP. *Ancient,* prisca, antīqua, vĕtĕra, vĕtusta. *Original,* prīma. *Sacred,* sācra, sācrāta. *Faithful,* fīda, fīdēlis. *Preserved,* servata. *Handed down,* trādĭta. *Lasting,* mansūra.

tăbŭlātum. *A storey of a house, a deck.*—EP. *High,* altum, arduum. *Solid,* sŏlĭdum. *Strong,* vălĭdum. *Of oak,* rōbŏreum.

tābum. *Gore.* See cruor.

tăcĭturnĭtas. *Silence.* See silentium.

tactus, ûs. *Touch.*—EP. *Gentle,* lēnis, mollis. *Sudden,* sŭbĭtus, rĕpentīnus. *Cold,* frĭgĭdus, gĕlĭdus.

tæda. *A torch, esp. a marriage torch.*—EP. *Made of pine,* pĭnea. *Anointed with pitch, sulphur, etc.,* cērāta, uncta, sulfŭrea. *Lighted,* accensa. *Shining, burning,* ignea, ardens, lūcens, collūcens, mĭcans. *Nuptial,* nuptiālis, jŭgālis. *Festive,* festa.

tædium. *Weariness.*—EP. *Long,* longum, diŭturnum. *Sad,* triste, ægrum. *Proud,* sŭperbum. *Intolerable,* intŏlĕrābĭle.

tænia. *A fillet.* See vitta.

talpa, æ, masc. *A mole.*—EP. *Blind,* cæcus.

tālus. 1. *An ancle.*—2. *A die.*—EP. 1. *Slender,* grăcĭlis. *Round,* tĕres –ĕtis, *Lightly moving,* lĕvia, ăgĭlis.—2. See alea.

tăpes, ētis, masc. **tăpētum.** *Tapestry, a carpet, etc.*—EP. *Embroidered,* pictus, vărius. *Embroidered with gold,* aurātus, ĭnaurātus. *Rich,* dīves –ĭtis. *Splendid,* splendĭdus, pulcher –chri. *Heavy,* grăvis.

Tartărus. *Hell.* See Orcus.

taurus. *A bull.*—EP. *Horned,* cornĭger –ĕri. *With horny feet,* cornĭpes –ēdis. *Strong,* rōbustus, vălĭdus, fortis. *Patient,* pătiens. *Fierce,* fĕrox, fĕrus, sævus. *Pugnacious,* pugnax. *Slow,* tardus, pĭger –gri. See bos.

taxus, i, fem. *A yew-tree.*—EP. *Poisonous,* vĕnēnāta. *Mischievous,* nŏcens, damnōsa, noxia. *Corsican,* Cymæa. *Flexible,* flexĭlis, flexĭbĭlis, lenta.

tectum. 1. *A roof.*—2. *A house.*—EP. 1. *Lofty,* altum, celsum, arduum. *Proud,* sŭperbum. *With fine ceiling,* lăqueātum. *Thatched,* strāmĭneum. *Lowly,* hŭmĭle.—2. See domus.

tĕges, ĕtis, fem. *A mat.*—EP. *Of rushes,* scirpea. *Of rope,* stuppea. *On the ground,* hŭmĭlis. *Valueless,* vīlis. *Dirty,* sordĭda, fœda. *Trodden in,* calcāta.

tĕgĭmen, tĕgŭmen, tegmen, ĭnis, neut. *A covering.*—EP. *Thick,* densum. *Safe,* tūtum. *Inviolable,* invĭŏlābĭle, invĭŏlātum. *Known, usual,* nōtum, sŏlĭtum, consuetum. *Shady,* umbrōsum, ŏpācum.

tĕgŭla. *A tile.*—EP. *Baked,* coctĭlis. *Red,* rŭbra. *Hard,* dūra. *Fatal (to Pyrrhus),* fātālis.

G 3

86 TEL—TES

tēla. 1. *A web.*—2. *A loom.*—EP. 1. *Thin,* tĕnuis.—2. *Continually at work,* assĭdua.

tellus, ūris, fem. *The Earth.* See terra.

tēlum. *A dart, any weapon.*—EP. *Missile,* missĭle. *Sent, shot,* ēmissum, intortum. *Iron,* ferreum, ferrātum. *Sharp,* ācūtum. *Bright,* cōruscum, mĭcans, fulgens. *Hard,* durum. *Fatal,* fatāle, fătĭferum. *Causing wounds,* vulnĭficum. *Piercing,* pĕnĕtrābĭle. *Rapid,* răpĭdum, vĕlox. *Flying,* vŏlātĭle. *Hostile,* ĭnĭmĭcum, adversum, hostĭle. *Blood-stained,* cruentum, sanguĭneum.

tēmo, ōnis, masc. *The pole of a carriage.*—EP. *Fitted,* aptātus. *Ashen,* fraxĭneus. *Long,* longus.

tempĕries, ĕi, fem. *Temperature.*—EP. *Equal, or favourable,* æqua. *Gentle,* mītis. *Pleasant,* grāta, jūcunda, ămœna. *Severe,* sĕvĕra. *Cold,* frĭgĭda, gĕlĭda. *Inhospitable,* ĭnhospĭta.

tempestas. *A storm.*—EP. *Horrid, terrible,* horrĭda, dīra, terrĭbĭlis. *Cruel,* fierce, sæva, fĕra. *Violent,* vĭŏlenta, fŭrĭōsa. See procella.

templum. *A temple.*—EP. *Sacred,* sācrum, săcrātum, sanctum. *High,* altum, arduum, sūblīme. *Marble,* marmŏreum. *Of white marble,* album, nĭveum, candĭdum. *Golden, ornamented with gold,* aureum, aurātum. *Noble,* nōbĭle. *Rich,* dīves -ĭtis, lŏcŭples -ētis, ŏpŭlentum. *Receiving offerings of frankincense,* thūreum. *Smoking with sacrifice,* fūmans. *National,* pātrium. *Ancient,* vĕtus -ĕris, vĕtustum, priscum, antīquum. *Dedicated,* dĭcātum. *Venerable,* vĕnĕrābĭle, vĕnĕrandum, vĕrendum. *Inviolable,* invĭŏlābĭle. *Magnificent,* magnĭfĭcum, splendĭdum. *Divine,* dīvīnum. *Everlasting,* æternum.

tempus, ŏris, neut. 1. *Time.*—2. *The temples of the head.*—EP. 1. *Quick,* răpĭdum, vĕlox. *Passing,* vŏlātĭle. *Passing quickly, or brief,* brĕve. *Long,* longum. *Past,* prætĕrĭtum, exactum. *Future,* fūtūrum, ventūrum. *Irrevocable,* irrĕvŏcābĭle. *Devouring,* ĕdax. *Cruel,* crūdēle, immīte.—2. See caput.

tĕnĕbræ, arum, plur. fem. *Darkness.*—EP. *Dense,* densæ. *Black,* ătræ, nĭgræ. *Brought over the earth,* obductæ. *Nocturnal,* nocturnæ. *Silent,* sĭlentes, tăcĭtæ. See caligo.

tĕnor, ōris, masc. *Tenor, course.*—EP. *Unvaried,* ūnus, gen. -ĭus, æquus, immōtus. *Tranquil,* tranquillus, plăcĭdus. See cursus.

tentāmen, ĭnis, neut. **tentāmentum.** *A trial, an experiment upon.*—EP. *Uncertain,* incertum, dŭbium. *Ambitious,* ambĭtĭosum. *New,* nŏvum, insŏlĭtum, ĭnassuetum. *Difficult,* diffĭcĭle, dūrum. *Great, important,* magnum, grăve. *Bold,* audax, forte.

tentātor, ōris, masc. *One who makes an attempt upon.*—EP. *Bold,* audax. *Unaccustomed,* rŭdis, insŏlĭtus, ĭnassuetus. *Rash,* præceps -ĭpĭtis, tĕmĕrārius.

tentōrium. *A tent.*—EP. *White,* nĭveum, candĭdum, album, albens. *Spreading,* extentum, pătens. *Large,* amplum, magnum, longum.

tĕpor, ōris, masc. *Warmth.*—EP. *Pleasant,* grātus, ămœna, jūcundus, ămābĭlis. *Of summer,* æstīvus. See calor.

tĕrĕbinthus, fem. *The turpentine tree.*—EP. *Sticky,* ¡tĕnax. *Strong-smelling,* grăvĕŏlens. *Orician, of Epirus,* Ōrĭcia.

tĕrēdo, ĭnis, fem. *A woodworm.*—EP. *Devouring,* ĕdax. *Secret,* cæca, occulta, lătens.

tergum. *A back.*—EP. *Broad,* lātum. *Flying,* fŭgax. *Cowardly,* imbelle, tĭmĭdum. *Unarmed,* ĭnerme.

tergus, ŏris, neut. *A hide.*—EP. *Shaggy,* villōsum, hirsūtum. *Strong,* vālĭdum. See pellis.

termes, ĭtis, masc. *An olive branch.* See ramus.

termĭnus. *A boundary.*—EP. *Fixed,* certus, pŏsĭtus. *Narrow,* angustus, arctus. *Ancient,* vĕtus -ĕris, priscus, antīquus. *Marked out,* sīgnātus.

terra. 1. *The earth.*—2. *Land.*—3. *A country.*—EP. 1. *Fertile,* fertĭlis, fēcunda, fĕrax, pinguis, læta.—2. *Dry,* sicca, ārĭda. *Wished for,* optāte. *Safe,* tūta.—3. *Powerful,* pŏtens. *Wide,* lāta. See regio, gens.

terror, ōris, masc. *Terror.* See timor.

tesqua, ōrum, plur. neut. *Uncultivated places.*—EP. *Desolate,* dēserta, sōla. *Inhospitable,* ĭnhospĭta. *Dangerous,* pĕrīcŭlōsa. *Pathless, out of the way,* dēvia, āvia. *Inaccessible,* ĭnaccessa. *Distant,* longinqua, rĕmōta. *Unknown,* ignōta. *Foreign,* pĕrĕgrīna.

TES—TIN 87

tessĕra. 1. *A die.*—2. *A watchword.*—EP. 1. See alea.—2. *Warlike,* bellĭca. *Known,* nōta. *Unknown,* ignōta.

testa. *A shell.* See concha.

testāmentum. *A will.*—EP. *Last,* ultĭmum, extrēmum, nŏvissĭmum. *Just,* justum, æquum. *Of one's father,* pātrium, pāternum.

testis, is, masc. fem. *A witness.*—EP. *True,* vērus, vērax. *False,* falsus. *Perjured,* perjūrus. *Knowing the truth,* conscius.

testūdo, ĭnis, fem. 1. *A tortoise.*—2. *Tortoiseshell.*—3. *A locking of shields together to form a sort of penthouse.*—4. *An arch, or vaulted roof.*—EP. 1. *Slow,* tarda, pĭgra.—2. *Hard,* dūra. *Variegated,* vāria, picta. *Beautiful,* pulchra, dĕcōra.—3. *Safe,* tūta. *Strong,* vălĭda, firma. *Advancing,* ingrĕdiens, incē-dens.—4. *Concave,* căva, concăva, convexa. *High,* alta, ardua.

textor, ōris, masc. **textrix, īcis,** fem. *A weaver.*—EP. *Diligent,* sēdŭlus. *Skilful,* pĕrītus, doctus, callĭdus.

textum. *Anything woven, a cloth.*—EP. *Rich,* dīves -ĭtis. *Beautiful,* pulchrum, dĕcōrum. *Embroidered,* vārium, pictum. *Simple,* simplex -ĭcis, rŭde.

textūra. *Texture.* See above.

thălămus. *A bedchamber, a bed ; esp. the marriage bed.* See lectus, conju-gium.

theātrum. *A theatre.*—EP. *Large,* magnum, ingens, spătiōsum. *Hollow,* căvum, concăvum. *Festive,* festum. *Joyful,* lætum. *Full of people,* frĕquens, plē-num. *Beautiful,* pulchrum, dĕcōrum. *Marble,* marmŏreum. *Applauding,* plaudens.

thēsaurus. *A treasure.*—EP. *Great,* magnus, ingens. *Rich,* dīves -ĭtis, lŏcŭ-ples -ētis, ŏpŭlentus. *Collected,* congestus, coactus. *Stored up,* condĭtus, sē-pŏsĭtus, rĕpŏstus. *Inviolate,* intĕger -gri, illæsus, inviŏlātus. *Safe,* tutus. *Of gold, of silver,* aureus, argenteus.

thŏlus. *A dome.*—EP. *Convex, concave,* căvus, concăvus, convexus. *High,* altus, arduus, sŭblīmis. *Gilt,* aureus, aurātus, inaurātus. *Painted,* pictus.

thŏrax, ācis, masc. *A breastplate.* See lorica.

thus, thūris, neut. *Frankincense, incense.*—EP. *Fragrant,* ŏdōrum, ŏdōrātum, frāgrans. *Sacred,* săcrum, sanctum. *Pious, offered by pious people,* pium. (*So*) *Suppliant,* supplex -ĭcis. *Votive,* vōtīvum. *Arabian,* Ărăbum, Ărăbium, Săbæum.

thȳmum. *Thyme.*—EP. *Fragrant,* frāgrans, ŏdōrum, suaveŏlens. *Pleasant,* grātum, jūcundum, ămœnum. *Growing low,* hŭmĭle.

thyrsus. *The wand of Bacchus and the Bacchanals, wreathed with ivy leaves.*—EP. *Sacred,* săcer -cri, săcrātus, sanctus. *Causing frenzy,* ămens, fŭriōsus. *Leafy,* frondens, frondeus. *Crowned,* cŏrōnātus. *Green,* vĭrĭdis. *Waved,* ăgĭtātus. *Sacred to Bacchus,* Bacchĭcus, Bacchēus, Bacchēus.

tiăra, and tiăras, æ, masc. *A turban.*—EP. *Eastern, Persian,* ͑Eōus, Persĭcus. *Effeminate,* mollis.

tībia. *A flute.*—EP. *Tuneful,* cănōra, dulcis, argūta, līquĭda. *Blown, played upon,* inflăta. *Sacred to Apollo,* Ăpollĭnea, Ăpollĭnāris, Phœbēa, Phœbēia. *Phrygian,* Phrȳgia, Bĕrĕcynthia. *Bored,* tĕrĕbrāta. *Light,* lēvis.

tībĭcen, ĭnis, masc., **tībĭcĭna.** *A flute-player.*—EP. *Tuneful,* dulcis, vōcālis. *Skilful,* doctus, pĕrītus, callĭdus, sōlers. *Untiring,* indēfessus.

tĭgillum, tignum. *A beam.*—EP. *Of oak, of ash, etc.,* quernum, fraxĭneum, etc. *Put together (of more than one),* compŏsĭtum. *Strong,* vălĭdum, firmum. *Cut,* sectum.

tigris, is, and **ĭdis,** masc., more usu. fem. *A tiger.*—EP. *Gætulian, Hyrcanian, etc,* Gætūla, Hyrcāna, Armĕnia, Lĭbўca, Gangetĭca, etc. *Furious,* răbĭda, fŭriōsa. *Untamed,* indŏmĭta. *Ravening,* răpax, vŏrax. *Cruel,* sæva, fĕra, immītis. *Striped,* măcŭlōsa, vāria.

tīlia. *A linden tree.*—EP. *Smooth,* lævis. *Soft,* mollis. See arbor.

tĭmor. *Fear.*—EP. *Unmanly,* imbellis, fœmĭneus. *Base,* turpis, indĕcōrus. *Helpless,* ĭnops -ōpis. *Apt to flee,* fŭgax. *Cold,* frĭgĭdus, gĕlĭdus. *Pale,* pal-lĭdus. *Trembling,* trĕmens, trĕmŭlus. *Doubtful,* dŭbius, incertus. *Anxious,* sollĭcĭtus, anxius. *Untimely,* intempestīvus. See the Gradus.

tĭnea. *A moth.*—EP. *Devouring,* ĕdax. *Mischievous,* nŏcens, damnōsa, per-nĭciōsa. *Concealed,* abdĭta, cæca, latens. *Silent,* tăcĭta.

tinnītus, ūs. *A clanging, a tinkling.*—EP. *Hoarse,* raucus. *Brazen, i. e. from*

G 4

88 TIR—TRA

brazen instruments, æreus, ærātus, ahēnus, ahēneus. *Loud*, clārus. *Distant*, longinquus, rēmōtus.

tīro, ōnis, masc. *A beginner.* — EP. *Inexperienced*, rŭdis, ĭnexpertus. *New*, nŏvus. *Young*, jŭvēnis. *Unaccustomed*, insŏlītus, ĭnassuetus.

tītŭlus. *A title.*—EP. *Well-known*, nōtus. *Proud*, sŭperbus. *Ancient*, vĕtus –ĕris, antīquus, priscus. *Memorable*, mĕmŏrābĭlis. *Illustrious*, illustris, cĕlĕber –bris.

tōfus. *Sandstone.*—EP. *Soft*, mollis. *Yellow*, flāvus. *Rough*, scāber –bri.

tŏga. *A gown.* — EP. *Long*, longa. *Dignified*, augusta. *Purple, white, etc.*, purpūrea, candĭda, alba, etc. *Embroidered*, picta. *Indicating manhood*, vĭrīlis. *Indicating peace*, pācīfica, tranquilla.

tŏmus. *A volume.* See liber.

tŏnĭtrus, ûs, neut. only used in gen. and abl. sing., plur. tonĭtrua, neut. *Thunder.* — EP. *Sounding in heaven*, cœleste, æthĕrium. *Terrible*, terrĭbĭle, dīrum, horrĭdum, mĕtuendum, tĭmendum. *Ominous*, præsāgum, prænuntium. *Of good omen*, fēlix –īcis, lævum. *Of bad omen*, infēlix, sĭnistrum. *Angry*, īrācundum, īrātum. *Destructive*, fātāle, exītiāle, exītiōsum. *Supreme*, sŭpremum, summum. *Powerful*, pŏtens.

tonsor, ōris. *A barber.*—EP. *Talkative*, lŏquax, garrŭlus.

tormentum.—1. *An engine for hurling stones, etc.*—2. *Torture.*—3. *Stimulus.*— EP.—1. *Huge*, ingens, vastum. *Fatal*, fātāle, exītiōsum, exītiāle, lētīfĕrum. *Warlike*, bellĭcum. *Applied*, admōtum.—1, 2. *Cruel*, sævum, fĕrum, crūdēle. 2. *Intolerable*, intŏlĕrābĭle. *Long*, longum, diūturnum.—3. *Sharp*, acre. See stimulus.

tornus. *A turning-lathe.* — EP. *Quick*, cĕler –ĕris, răpĭdus. *Cleverly used*, pĕrītus, callĭdus. *Going round*, vŏlūbĭlis.

torpor, ōris, masc. *Insensibility.*—EP. *Lifeless*, exānĭmis, exsanguis. *Inactive*, ĭners, pĭger –gri, segnis. *Silent*, tacĭtus, sĭlens. *Frightened*, terrĭtus, conterrĭtus, păvĭdus.

torquis, is, masc. fem. *A chain, esp. as an ornament.* — EP. *Golden*, aureus, aurātus, ĭnaurātus. *Jewelled*, gemmens, gemmans. *Splendid*, splendĭdus. *Stripped off*, dīreptus.

torrens, tis, masc. *A torrent.*—EP. *Violent*, vĭŏlentus. *Rapid*, răpĭdus, vēlox. *Descending from the mountains*, montānus. *Brawling*, raucus, strĕpens. *Rocky*, saxōsus, lăpĭdōsus. *Carrying things away*, răpax. *Unrestrained*, effrænus, dēfrænātus. *Foaming*, spūmeus, spūmōsus, spūmans.

torris, is, masc. *A firebrand.*—EP. *Burning*, flāgrans, ardens, igneus. *Lighted*, accensus. *Smeared with pitch*, pĭceus. *Smoking*, fūmans, fūmōsus, fūmĭdus, fūmĭfer –ĕri. *Destructive*, exītiōsus, exītiālis, nŏcens.

tortor, ōris, masc. *A tormentor.*—EP. *Cruel*, sævus, fĕrus, immītis. *Superstitious*, rēlĭgiōsus. *Mistaken*, errans, perversus.

tortus, ûs. *A twisting.*—EP. *Crooked*, sĭnuōsus, oblīquus, curvus, rĕcurvus. *Flexible*, flexĭlis.

tŏrus. 1. *A bed.*—2. *A muscle.*—EP. 1. See lectus.—2. *Strong*, vălĭdus, fortis. *Swelling*, tŭmĭdus, tŭmens. *Exerted*, intentus.

toxĭcum. *Poison.* See venenum.

trabs, trăbes, fem. *A beam.* See tigellum.

tractus, ûs. 1. *A dragging or drawing.*—2. *A tract of country.*—EP. 1. *Long*, longus. *Straight*, rectus. *Cruel*, sævus, fĕrus, sĕvērus, immītis. *Winding*, curvus, sĭnuōsus.—2. See regio.

trăgœdia. *Tragedy.*—EP. *Attic*, Cĕcrōpia. *Sacred*, sācra. *Dignified*, grăvis, sĕvēra, grandis. *Sad*, tristis, lūgŭbris. *Wearing a buskin*, cōthurnāta. *Stern-looking*, torva. *Fierce*, sæva, vĭŏlenta.

trăgœdus. *A tragedian.* — EP. *Learned*, doctus. *Illustrious*, inclўtus, clārus, insignis.

trăhea. *A sledge.*—EP. *Heavy*, grăvis. *Gliding easily*, lūbrĭca, făcĭlis. *Wintry*, *used in winter*, hўberna, hyēmālis, brūmālis.

trămes, ĭtis, masc. *A path.* See via.

transfŭga, æ, masc. *A deserter.*—EP. *Cowardly*, tĭmĭdus, imbellis. *Frightened*, terrĭtus, conterrĭtus. *Base*, turpis, infāmis. *Treacherous*, perfĭdus, infīdus.

transĭtio, ōnis, fem., **transĭtus, ûs**, masc. *A passage.*—EP. *Easy*, făcĭlis.

TRA—TUB 89

Rapid, răpĭdus, cĕler –ĕris, vēlox. *Granted*, dătus. *Short*, brĕvis. *Long*, longus. *Slow*, tardus.

transtrum. *A seat for rowers.*—EP. *Hard*, dūrum. *Numerous*, frĕquens, densum, plūrĭmum. *Of deal*, pīneum.

trăpētum. *An oil-press.*—EP. *Fat*, pingue. *Full*, plēnum.

trĕmor, ōris, masc. *A trembling.*—EP. *Timid*, păvĭdus, tĭmĭdus, imbellis. *Sudden*, sŭbĭtus, rĕpentīnus. *Making pale*, pallĭdus. *Making silent*, tăcĭtus. *Aged (of man)*, sĕnĭlis, *(of a woman)* ănīlis.

trĭbŭlum. *A threshing-machine.*—EP. *Rapid*, răpĭdum. *Going round*, vŏlŭbĭle. *Heavy*, grăve. *Iron*, ferreum.

trĭbŭlus. *A burr.*—EP. *Prickly*, spīnōsus, ăcūtus. *Sticking*, tĕnax.

trĭbūnal, ālis. *A tribunal.*—EP. *Just*, justum, æquum, prŏbum. *Venerable*, vĕnĕrăbĭle, vĕrendum. *Dignified*, augustum, grăve. *Wise*, acute, săpiens, argūtum.

trĭbūnus. *A tribune.*—EP. *Powerful*, pŏtens. *Sacred*, sanctus, săcer –cri. *Seditious*, sēdĭtiōsus, implăcĭdus.

trĭbus, ûs. *A tribe.*—EP. *Ancient*, antīqua, prisca. *Of one's father*, pătria, păterna. *Powerful*, pŏtens. *Rich*, ŏpŭlenta, dīves –ĭtis, lŏcŭples –ĕtis.

trĭbūtum. *Tribute.*—EP. *Servile*, servīle, servum. *Due*, dēbĭtum. *Exacted*, exactum. *Paid*, dătum. *Yearly*, annuum. *Ancient*, antīquum, vĕtus –ĕris, priscum. *Agreed upon*, compŏsĭtum, pactum.

trĭdens, entis, masc. *A trident.*—EP. *Powerful*, pŏtens. *Of Neptune*, Neptūnus. *Ruling the sea*, æquŏreus. *Great*, magnus. *Sacred*, săcer –cri.

triennium. 1. *A space of three years.*—2. *A triennial festival.*—EP. 1. *Long*, longum. *Slow to pass*, tardum.—2. *Regularly recurring*, sŏlenne. *Sacred*, săcrum, săcrātum. *Known*, *customary*, nōtum, sŏlĭtum, consuetum. *Wished for*, optātum. *Festive*, festum. *Well attended*, frĕquens.

trĭpŭdium. *A dance.* See chorea.

trĭpūs –ŏdis, masc. *A tripod.*—EP. *Sacred*, săcer –cri, sanctus. *Prophetic*, fătĭdĭcus. See oraculum.

trĭrēmis. *A trireme.* See navis.

tristĭtia. *Sadness.*—EP. *Tearful*, lăcrўmōsa, flēbĭlis. *Querulous*, quĕrŭla. *Melancholy*, ægra. *Miserable*, mĭsĕra, mĭsĕrăbĭlis. *Deserved*, mĕrĭta. *Long*, longa, diūturna. *Perpetual*, perpĕtua, æterna. *Likely to survive its cause*, sŭperstes –ĭtis.

trĭtĭcum. *Wheat.*—EP. *White*, album, nĭveum, candĭdum. *Yellow*, flăvum. *Nutritious*, almum. *Sacred to Ceres*, Cĕreāle.

trĭtūra. *Threshing.*—EP. *Seasonable*, tempestīva. *Autumnal*, aŭtumnālis. *Abundant*, larga, grăvis.

trĭvium. *A place where three roads meet.* See via.

triumphus. *A triumph.*—EP. *Victorious*, victor. *Joyful*, *happy*, fēlix –īcis, lætus. *Glorious*, clārus, ēgrĕgius, insignis. *Won*, rĕportātus. *Blood-stained*, cruentus, sanguĭneus, sanguĭnōlentus. *Sad*, tristis, flēbĭlis, lăcrўmōsus. *Deserved*, mĕrĭtus. *Wished for*, optātus. *Future*, fŭtūrus, ventūrus. *Easy*, făcĭlis. *(Of the procession) Splendid*, splendĭdus, magnĭfĭcus. *Golden*, aureus. *Long*, longus. See Gradus.

Trōja. *Troy.*—EP. *Reigned over by Laomedon, or Dardanus*, Lăŏmĕdontia, Lăŏmĕdontēa, Dardănia. *Built by Neptune*, Neptūnia. *Sacred*, săcra, săcrāta. *Overthrown*, ēversa, dŏmĭta. See Gradus.

trŏpæum. *A trophy.*—EP. *Warlike*, bellĭcum. *Victorious*, victrix –īcis. *Raised*, exstructum. *Noble*, nŏbĭle. *Lasting*, mansūrum. *Likely to survive the victors*, sŭperstes –ĭtis. *Uneffaceable*, indēlēbile. *Blood-stained*, cruentum, sanguĭneum, sanguĭnolentum. *Proud*, sŭperbum. *Illustrious*, clarum, insigne. *Conspicuous*, conspĭcuum. *Memorable*, mĕmŏrăbĭle. *Deserved*, mĕrĭtum.

truncus. *A trunk.*—EP. *Solid*, sŏlĭdus. *(Of a man) Lifeless*, exănĭmis, or exănĭmus, exanguis. *Unrecognised*, ignōtus. *Miserable*, mĭser –ĕri, mĭsĕrăbĭlis, flēbĭlis, tristis.

tūba. *A trumpet.*—EP. *Brazen*, ærea, ahēna. *Hoarse*, rauca. *Warlike*, bellĭca, Māvortia. *Loud*, clāra, sŏnax, sŏnōra. *Threatening*, mĭnax. *Terrible*, fierce, terrĭbĭlis, dīra, sæva, fĕra. *Distant*, longinqua, rĕmōta. *Hostile*, hostĭca, hostĭlia.

tūbĭcen, ĭnis, masc. *A trumpeter.*—EP. *Warlike*, bellĭcus. See above.

90 TUG—VAL

tŭgŭrium. *A cottage.* See casa.

tŭmor, ōris, masc. *Swelling.*—EP. *Great,* magnus, ingens. *Rising up,* exstans, exsurgens.

tŭmultus, ûs. *A tumult.*—EP. *Great,* magnus, ingens. *Sudden,* sŭbĭtus, rĕpentīnus. *Disorderly,* turbĭdus, implăcĭdus, inquiĕtus. *Seditious,* sēdĭtiōsus. *Of the people,* pŏpŭlāris. *Violent,* viŏlentus. *Insane,* insānus, vēsānus, fŭriōsus.

tŭmŭlus. 1. *A mound.*—2. *A tomb.*—EP. *Small,* parvus, exĭguus. *Raised,* ēdĭtus. *Conspicuous,* conspĭcuus, conspĭciendus.—2. See sepulchrum.

tŭnĭca. *A tunic.*—EP. *Purple, white, etc.,* purpŭrea, nĭvea, candĭda, alba. *Embroidered,* picta, vāria. *Fine,* tĕnuis. *Splendid, rich,* splendĭda, dīves –ĭtis. *Long,* longa.

turba. *A crowd.*—EP. *Great,* magna, ingens. *Collected,* coacta. *Admiring,* marvelling, mīrans, attŏnĭta. *Silent,* tăcĭta. *Noisy, hoarse,* clāmōsa, rauca. *Numerous,* frĕquens.

turbo, ĭnis, masc. *A whirlwind.*––EP. *Rapid,* răpĭdus, vēlox. *Violent,* viŏlentus. *Stormy,* prŏcellōsus, ventōsus. *Sudden,* sŭbĭtus, rĕpentīnus. *Mischievous,* damnōsus, nŏcens.

turdus. *A thrush.*—EP. *Tuneful,* dulcis, cănōrus, vŏcālis. *Brown,* fuscus. *Greedy,* ĕdax, ăvĭdus.

turma. *A troop of horse.*—EP. *Armed,* armāta. *To be feared,* mĕtuenda. *Rapid,* răpĭda, vēlox. *Fearless,* impăvĭda, imperterrĭta. See eques.

turris, is, fem. *A tower.*—EP. *Brazen,* ærea, ærāta, ahēna, ahēnea. *Adamantine,* ădămantīna. *Strong,* vălĭda, fortis. *Threatening,* mĭnax. *High,* alta, ardua, āĕria. *Conspicuous,* conspĭcua.

turtur, ŭris, masc. *A turtle dove.*––EP. *Dark-coloured,* nĭger –gri. *Faithful,* fīdus, fĭdēlis. See columba.

tussis, is, fem. *A cough.*—EP. *Causing panting,* ănhēla. *Sick, making sick, etc.,* ægra.

tūtāmen, ĭnis, neut. **tŭtēla.** *Defence, protection.*—EP. *Strong,* vălĭda, fortis, firma. *Assured,* certa. *Constant,* constans. *Faithful,* fĭda, fĭdēlis. *Fearless,* impăvĭda. *Divine,* dīvīna. *Powerful,* pŏtens. *Fitting,* apta.

tūtor, ōris, masc. *A protector.* See above.

tympănum. *A drum.*—EP. *Noisy, hoarse,* clāmōsum, raucum. *Phrygian,* Phrўgium, Bĕrĕcynthium.

tўrannis, ĭdis, fem. *Tyranny.* See below.

tўrannus. *A tyrant.*—EP. *Cruel,* crūdēlis, sævus, fērus, immītis. *Barbarian, foreign,* barbărus, pĕrĕgrīnus. *Lawless, unjust,* injustus, inīquus, imprŏbus. *Powerful,* pŏtens. *Hated,* invīsus, ŏdiōsus.

V.

Vacca. *A cow.*—EP. *White,* candĭda, alba. *Giving milk,* lactea. See bos.

vădum. *A ford, a shoal.*—EP. *Easily passed,* făcĭle. *Sandy,* ărēnōsum. *Shallow,* brĕve. *Muddy,* līmōsum. *Known,* nōtum.

vāgīna. *A scabbard.*—EP. *Embossed,* cælāta. *Golden,* aurea. *Shining,* splendĭda, nĭtens, fulgens. *Ivory,* ĕburna, ĕburnea.

vāgītus, ûs. *The cry of a child.*—EP. *Weak,* imbellis. *Helpless,* ĭnops –ŏpis. *Tender,* tĕner –ĕri. *Childish,* puĕrīlis.

vălētūdo, ĭnis, fem. *Health.*—EP. *Sound,* sāna. *Pleasant,* grāta. *Wished for,* optāta.

vallis, is, fem. *A valley.*—EP. *Deep, low,* alta, prŏfunda, rēducta. *Shady,* ŏpāca, umbrōsa. *Green,* vīrĭdis. *Grassy,* grāmĭnea. *Mossy,* muscōsa. *Hollow,* căva, concăva. *Cool,* gĕlĭda, frĭgĭda. *Between mountains or rocks,* montāna, saxōsa. *Woody,* nĕmōrōsa. *Winding,* curva, rĕcurva, incurva, sĭnuōsa. *Trackless,* āvia.

vallum. *A rampart.*—EP. *High,* altum, celsum. *Bristling with defences,* horrens, horrĭdum. *Strong,* forte. *Inaccessible,* inaccessum. *Safe,* tūtum. *Impregnable,* inexpugnābĭle, invictum.

VAL—VEN 91

vallus. *A stake.* See palus.

valvæ, i, fem. *Folding doors.* See porta.

vannus, i, fem. *A winnowing machine.*—EP. *Swift,* răpĭda. *Revolving,* vŏlūbĭlis. *Belonging to a farmer,* ăgrestis, rustĭca.

vāpor, ōris, masc. *Vapour, steam, etc.*—EP. *Moist,* ūdus, hūmĭdus, mădĭdus. *Dropping,* stillans, stillātus. *Rising,* surgens, exsurgens, ŏriens.

vas, vāsis, neut. *A vessel.*—EP. *Of gold, silver, etc.,* aureum, aurātum, argenteum, etc. *Of wood, beech, maple, etc.,* quernum, ăcernum, etc.

vastātor, ōris, masc. *A ravager.*—EP. *Cruel,* sævus, fĕrus, fĕrox, crūdēlis, immītis. *Rapacious,* răpax, ăvĭdus. *Successful,* lætus. *Hostile,* hostĭlis, hostīcus. *Foreign,* externus. *Terrible,* terrĭbĭlis, mĕtuendus, tĭmendus.

vātes, is, masc. fem. 1. *A prophet.*—2. *A poet.*—EP. 1, 2. *Divine,* dīvīnus. *Sacred,* săcer –cri, sanctus. *Pious,* pius.—1. *Foreknowing,* præscius, prōvĭdus, præsāgus. *Foretelling,* fătĭdĭcus, fătĭcănus. *Truthful,* vērus, vērax. *Skilful, wise,* pērītus, doctus, săpiens. *Consulted,* consultus, rŏgātus. *Frantic,* fūriōsus, āmens, insānus.—2. *Tuneful,* argūtus, līquĭdus, dulcis, cănōrus. *Mindful,* mĕmor –ŏris. *Undying,* immortālis. 1, 2. *Worshipping Apollo, protected by Apollo,* Ăpollĭneus. See poeta.

ūber, ĕris, neut. *An udder.*—EP. *Full,* plēnum, grăvĭdum, distentum. *Milky,* acteum.

vēcordia. *Folly.* See stultitia.

vectigal, ālis, neut. *Revenue.*—EP. *Ample,* magnum, amplum. *Annual,* annuum. *Royal,* rēgium.

vectis, is, masc. *A lever, a bar.*—EP. *Strong,* vălĭdus, fortis. *Iron,* ferreus, ferratus. *Oaken,* rŏbŏreus.

vectŏr, ōris, masc. 1. *One who carries.*—2. *One who is carried, a passenger, a rider, etc.*—EP. *Strong,* vălĭdus, fortis. *Patient,* pătiens. *Swift,* răpĭdus, cĕler –ĕris. *Slow,* tardus.—2. *Safe,* tūtus, incŏlŭmis.

vēlāmen, ĭnis, neut. *A covering, a veil.*—EP. *Thin, delicate,* tĕnue. *Modest,* pūdĭcum, mŏdestum. *White,* nĭveum, candĭdum.

vēles, ĭtis, masc. *A light-armed soldier.*—EP. *Light,* lĕvis. *Active,* ăgĭlis, ăcer –cris, impĭger –gri. *Quick,* cĕler –ĕris, răpĭdus. *Sudden,* rĕpentīnus, sŭbĭtus.

vellus, ĕris, neut. *A fleece.*—EP. *Shaggy,* hirsūtum. *Soft,* molle. *Thin,* tĕnue. *Light,* lĕve. *White,* candĭdum, candens, album. *Golden (of the golden fleece),* aureum, fulvum.

vēlum.—1. *A sail.*—2. *A curtain.* — EP. 1, 2. *White,* candĭdum, candens, album, nĭveum. *Stretched out,* extentum. *Hanging loose,* fluĭtans.—1. *Filled by the wind so as to belly out, swelling,* sĭnuosum, concăvum, turgĭdum, tŭmĭdum, tŭmens, plēnum. *Swift,* răpĭdum, cĭtum, vēlox. *Having a prosperous voyage,* fēlix, sĕcundum. *High,* altum, arduum.—2. *Embroidered,* pictum, vărium. *Embroidered with gold,* aureum, aurātum, inauratum. *Purple,* purpūreum. See the Gradus.

vēna. *A vein.*—EP. *Rosy,* rŏsea. *Full,* plēna.

vēnābŭlum. *A hunting-spear.*—EP. *Iron,* ferreum. *Barbed,* hămātum. *Thrown,* jactum, conjectum.

vēnātor, ōris, masc., fem. **venatrix,** īcis. *A hunter.*—EP. *Hardy,* dūrus, rŏbustus. *Light,* lĕvis. *Active, eager,* ăgĭlis, ăcer –cris, impĭger –gri. *Swift,* răpĭdus, cĕler –ĕris, vēlox. *Skilful,* pērītus. *Successful,* lætus, fēlix –īcis. *Following his sport in the winter,* hybernus. See below.

vēnātus, ūs. *Hunting.* — EP. *Long,* longus. *Unwearied,* indēfessus. *Rash,* tĕmērārius, incautus. See above.

vēnēfĭca. *A witch.* See saga.

vēnēfĭcium. *Witchcraft.* — EP. *Impious,* impium, nĕfandum, scĕlĕrātum. *Thessalian,* Thessălum, Thessălĭcum. *Practised by old women,* ănīle. *Magical,* măgĭcum. *Fatal,* fătăle, fătĭferum.

vēnēnum. *Poison.* — EP. *Mixed,* mistum, commistum. *Administered,* dătum. *Liquid,* līquĭdum. *Deadly,* fătăle, fătĭfĕrum. *Noxious,* noxium. *Hateful,* invĭsum, triste. *Wicked (referring to those who give it),* impium, scĕlĕrātum. *Colchian (from Medea),* Colchum, Colchĭcum. *Spanish,* Ĭbērum. *Black,* ātrum, nĭgrum. *Bitter,* ămārum.

vēnĕrātor, ōris, masc. *A worshipper.* See cultor.

92   VEN—VIA

věnia.—1. *Leave.*—2. *Pardon.* — EP. 1, 2. *Easily granted,* făcĭlis. *Kind,* bŏna, běnigna.—2. *Merciful,* clēmens. *Deserved,* mērĭta, dēbĭta.

venter, tris, masc. *The belly.*—EP. *Greedy,* ăvĭdus. *Full,* plēnus, sătur –ŭri.

ventus. *The wind.* — EP. *Stormy,* prŏcellōsus. turbĭdus, inquiētus, irrēquiētus, implăcĭdus. *Adverse,* adversus, ĭnĭquus. *Fair,* sĕcundus, æquus, fĕrens. *Wanton, changeable,* prŏtervus, vărius, mōbĭlis, lĕvis, mūtăbĭlis. *Shifting,* dŭbius, incertus. *Rising,* surgens, (*of many winds*) coortus. *Cold,* frīgĭdus, gĕlĭdus, ēgĕlĭdus. *Gentle,* lēnis, mollis. *Roaring, hoarse,* obstrēpens, raucus. See Notus, Boreas, Zephyrus. See the Gradus.

Věnus, ěris. *Venus.*—EP. *Idalian, Paphian, Cyprian, etc.* (*from places where she was worshipped*), Ĭdălia, Păphia, Cўpria. *Born of the sea,* mărīna, æquŏrea. *Beautiful,* candĭda, pulchra, formōsa, dēcōra. *Winning,* blanda. *Lovely,* ămăbĭlis. *Kind, friendly,* bŏna, běnigna, ămīca. *Wanton, playful,* lascīva, prŏterva. *Admirable,* aurea, ēgrēgia. See the Gradus.

věnustas. *Beauty.*—EP. *Fair,* candĭda, ēburnea. *Chaste, modest,* casta, pŭdīca, pŭdībunda. *Excellent,* ēgrēgia, præstans. See forma.

vēpres, is, masc. fem. *A briar.*—EP. *Prickly,* spīnōsus, ăcūtus. *Bristling,* horrĭdus, horrens, hirsūtus.

ver, věris, neut. *Spring.* — EP. *Fresh,* nŏvum. *Opening the year,* prīmum. *Fertile,* fertĭle, fēcundum, běnignum. *Purple, with purple flowers,* purpūreum. *Green,* vĭrĭde, vĭrĭdans. *Showery,* imbrĭfĕrum, plŭvium. *Mild,* mīte. *Flowery,* flōreum, flōrens. *Returning,* rĕdiens. *Revolving,* rĕvŏlŭbĭle.

verber, ěris, neut.—1. *A whip.*—2. *A blow.*—EP. 1, 2. *Cruel,* sævum, fĕrum, crūdēle.—1. *Bloody,* cruentum, sanguĭneum. *Twisted, plaited,* tortum.—2. *Repeated,* crēbrum, rěpětĭtum.

verbum. *A word.*—EP. *Irrevocable,* irrĕvŏcābĭle. *Uttered,* ēmissum. *Rash,* incautum, imprūdens. *Suppliant,* supplex –ĭcis. *Proud,* sŭperbum. *Vain,* vānum, irrĭtum, ĭnāne.

vērĭtas. *Truth.*—EP. *Fair,* candĭda. *Simple,* simplex –ĭcis. *Naked,* nūda. *Sacred,* săcra, sancta, dīvīna. *Golden,* aurea. See fides.

verna, æ, masc. *A slave.* See servus.

verres. *A boar.* See sus.

versus, ûs. *A verse.*—EP. *Rhythmical,* nŭmĕrōsus. *Learned,* doctus. See carmen.

vertex, ĭcis, masc. *A summit.*—EP. *High,* altus, arduus. See cacumen.

vertīgo, ĭnis, fem. *Giddiness.*—EP. *Causing dimness,* hěbes –ětis. *Causing silence,* tăcĭta. *Helpless,* ĭnops –ŏpis. *Ready to fall,* instăbĭlis, cădūca, incerta.

věru. *A spit.*—EP. *Iron,* ferreum, ferrātum. *Sharp,* ăcūtum.

vespa. *A wasp.*—EP. *Fierce,* fĕra, sæva. *Poisonous,* věnēnĭfĕra. *Little,* parva, exĭgua. *Winged,* ālāta, vŏlātĭlis.

vesper, ěris, masc., **vespěrus.** *Evening.*—EP. *Rosy,* rŏseus. *Golden,* aureus. *Cool,* frīgĭdus, gĕlĭdus. *Late,* sērus. *Shady,* umbrōsus. *Damp,* ūdus, hūmĭdus. See nox.

vestĭbŭlum. *A vestibule.*—EP. *First* (i. e. *the first thing one comes to*), prīmum. See aula.

vestigium. *A footstep, a trace.*—EP. *Conspicuous,* conspĭcuum, conspĭciendum, mănĭfestum. *Imperceptible,* cæcum, abdĭtum. *Silent,* tăcĭtum. *Fresh,* nŏvum, rěcens.

vestīmentum, vestis, is, fem. *A garment.*—EP. *Delicate,* těnuia. *Beautiful, becoming,* pulchra, dēcōra, dĕcens, apta. *Feminine,* fēmĭnea, mŭliēbria. *Embroidered,* picta, văria, lăbōrāta. *Put on,* superjecta, indūta, impŏsĭta. *Laid aside,* pŏsĭta, exūta.

věteraus. *Lethargy.*—EP. *Indolent,* ĭners, sēgnis. *Heavy,* grăvis. *Lifeless,* sēmiănĭmis and –us. *Silent,* tăcĭtus.

větustas. 1. *Antiquity.*—2. *Old age.*—EP. 1. *Distant,* longinqua, rěmōta. *Original,* prīma, ultīma. *Venerable,* věněrăbĭlis, věněranda.—2. See senectus.

vexillum. *A standard.*—EP. *Warlike,* bellĭcum, Māvortium. *Unfurled,* passum, pătens. *National,* pătrum. *Victorious,* victrix –īcis.

via. *A way* (*in any sense*).—EP. *New,* nŏva. *Old,* větus –ěris, prisca, antīqua. *Known,* nōta. *Usual,* sŏlĭta, consueta, assueta. *Much travelled or used,* trīta.

VIA—VIO 93

Paved, strāta. *Easy*, făcĭlis. *Short or easy*, brěvis. *Open or easy*, pătens. *Long*, longa.

viātor, ōris, masc. *A traveller.*—EP. *Weary*, fessus, dēfessus. *Wandering*, vāgus, errābundus. *Uncertain of his way*, dūbius, incertus. *Foreign*, pĕrĕgrīnus, externus. *Dusty*, pulvĕreus, pulvĕrŭlentus. *Unknown*, ignōtus.

vicīnia. *Neighbourhood, a being near.*—EP. *Well-known*, nōta. *Long*, longa.

vĭcis (see Gradus for cases). *Vicissitude.*—EP. *Various*, văria. *Alternating*, alterna. *Rapid*, răpĭda. *Fortunate*, fēlix –īcis, fausta. *Unfortunate*, infēlix, īnīqua. *Sudden*, sŭbĭta. *Unexpected*, īnōpīna, nĕcōpīna.

victīma. *A victim.*—EP. *Slain*, cæsa. *Offered*, ŏblāta, dāta. *Sacred*, sācra, sācrāta. *Crowned*, cŏrōnāta, vittāta. *Suppliant*, i. e. *offered by a suppliant*, supplex –īcis. *Of good omen*, fēlix –īcis, fausta.

victor, ōris, masc. *A conqueror.*—EP. *Proud*, sŭperbus. *Triumphant*, triumphans, ŏvans. *Illustrious*, clārus, præclārus, inclȳtus, insignis. *Powerful*, pŏtens. *Terrible*, terrĭbĭlis mĕtuendus. *Cruel*, sævus, fĕrus, immītis. *Blood-stained*, *blood-thirsty*, cruentus, sanguĭneus, sanguĭnōlentus. *Merciful*, mītis. See Gradus.

victōria. *Victory.*—EP. *Joyful*, læta, fēlix –īcis. *Genial*, alma. *Wished for*, *hoped for*, optāta, spērāta. *Assured*, certa. *Granted*, dāta. *Enjoyed*, pŏtīta. *Present*, præsens. *Future*, fūtūra. *Ancient*, prisca, vĕtus –ĕris, vĕtusta, antīqua.

victus, ûs. *Food.* See cibus.

vīcus. *A street.*—EP. *Broad*, lātus, spătiōsus. *Marble*, marmōreus. *Smoky*, fūmans, fūmōsus, fūmĭfĭcus.

vĭgil, ĭlis, masc. *A sentinel.*—EP. *Placed*, pŏsĭtus. *Careful*, cautus. *By night*, nocturnus. *Anxious*, anxius, sollĭcĭtus. *Fearless*, impăvĭdus. *By himself*, sōlus gen. –īus. *Sleepless*, insomnis.

vĭgĭlantia. *Vigilance.*—EP. *Anxious*, anxia, sollĭcĭta. *Sleepless*, insomnis. *Continual*, perpĕtua, assīdua. *Unwearied*, indēfessa.

vĭgor, ōris, masc. *Strength.* See vis.

villa. *A country house.*—EP. *Rustic*, rustĭca. *Simple*, simplex –īcis. *Happy*, fēlix –īcis. *Safe*, tūta. *Quiet*, tranquilla, plăcĭda. *Retired*, rĕducta, rĕmōta.

villĭcus. *A steward, a bailiff.*—EP. *Trusty*, fīdus, fĭdēlis. *Careful*, cautus, prūdens.

villus. *Coarse hair.*—EP. *Shaggy*, hirsūtus, hirtus. *Thick*, densus.

vīmen, ĭnis, neut. *A twig.*—EP. *Light*, lĕve. *Flexible*, flexĭlis, flexĭbĭle, lentum.

vinculum, sync. **vinclûm.** *A chain.*—EP. *Iron*, ferreum, ădămantīnum. *Hard*, dūrum. *Holding fast*, tĕnax. *Placed on a person*, impŏsĭtum, sync. impostum, conjectum. *Made by a smith*, făbrīle. *Slow*, *making one slow*, tardum. *Unloosened*, irrĕsŏlūta.

vindēmia. *The gathering of grapes.*—EP. *Seasonable*, mātūra, tempestīva. See uva.

vindēmiātor, **vindemĭtor**, **vīnĭtor**, ōris, masc. *A vine-dresser.*—EP. *Skilful*, pĕrītus, callĭdus, sōlers. *Anxious*, anxius, sollĭcĭtus. *Hardy*, dūrus, rōbustus.

vindex, ĭcis, masc. fem. *An avenger.* See ultor.

vindicta. *Revenge.*—EP. *Cruel*, sæva, fĕrox, crūdēlis, inmītis. *Bloody*, cruenta, sanguĭnea, sanguĭnōlenta. *Deserved*, mĕrĭta, dēbĭta, justa, digna. *Late*, sēra. *Instant*, instans, præsens. *Future*, fūtūra, ventūra. *Sure*, certa. *Inevitable*, ĭnēluctābĭlis.

vīnea, **vīnētum.** *A vineyard.*—EP. *Sunny*, ăprīca. *On a hill*, montāna. *Fertile*, fertĭlis, fēcunda, fĕrox. *Purple*, purpūrea. *Sacred to Bacchus*, Bacchĭca, Bacchēia. *Making glad*, læta.

vīnum. *Wine.*—EP. *Rosy*, rŏseum. *Making glad*, lætum. *Poured out*, effūsum. *Falernian*, *Cæcuban*, etc. (*the chief vintages of ancient Italy*), Fălernum, Cæcŭbum, Sētīnum, Chĭum. See Gradus.

vĭŏla. *A violet.*—EP. *Black*, nīgra. *Purple*, purpūrea. *Growing low*, hŭmĭlis. *Sweet*, dulcis, frăgrans, suavĕŏlens.

vĭŏlārium. *A bed of violets.* See above.

vĭŏlātor, ōris, masc. *A violator.*—EP. *Ruthless*, *cruel*, immītis, sævus, fĕrus, fĕrox. *Rapacious*, răpax, ăvĭdus. *Hostile*, infensus, hostīlis. *Furious*, fūrens, fūriōsus.

94 VIO—ULT

violentia. *Violence.*—EP. *Cruel,* sæva, fēra, aspēra. *Unbridled,* effræna, infrænis. *Swelling,* tŭmĭda. *Proud,* sŭperba. *Hostile,* infensa, hostĭlis.

vīpĕra. *A viper.*—EP. *Concealed,* lătens, abdĭta. *Poisonous,* vĕnĕnĭfĕra. *Hissing,* sĭbĭla. *Black,* ātra, nĭgra. *Swelling,* tŭmĭda, tŭmens. *Malignant,* măla, măligna.

vir, vĭri. *A man.*—2. *A husband.*—EP. 1. *Brave,* fortis, impăvĭdus. *Wise,* săpiens. *Illustrious,* clărus, inclўtus.—2. See maritus.

vĭrētum. *A garden.* See hortus.

virga. *A rod, a thin stick.*—EP. *Slight,* tĕnuis. *Light,* lēvis.

virgĭnĭtas. *Virginity.*—EP. *Sacred,* săcra, săcrāta, sancta. *Pious,* pia. *Perpetual,* perpētua. See below.

virgo, ĭnis, fem. *A virgin.*—EP. *Pure, chaste,* casta, pūra, prŏba. *Modest,* pŭdīca, pŭdībunda, vĕrēcunda. *Inviolate,* intĕmĕrāta, intacta. *Unmarried,* innūba, innupta. *Youthful,* jŭvĕnis. *Beautiful,* pulchra, candĭda. *Noble,* nŏbĭlis, gĕnĕrōsa.

virgultum. *A twig.*—EP. *Tender,* tĕnĕrum, molle. *Flexible,* lentum, flexĭle. *Green,* vĭride.

virtus, ūtis, fem. 1. *Valour.*—2. *Virtue.*—EP. 1, 2. *Fearless,* fortis, ănĭmōsus, impăvĭda. *Unalterable,* constans, immōbĭlis, firma. *Genuine,* vēra. *Ancient,* prisca, vĕtus -ĕris, vĕtusta, antīqua. *Celebrated,* clāra, inclўta. *Admirable,* ēgrēgia, insignis. *To be imitated,* ĭmĭtābĭlis, ĭmĭtanda. *Noble,* gĕnĕrōsa, nŏbĭlis. *Hereditary,* pātria, pāterna, ăvīta. 2. *Pure, honest,* pūra, prŏba. *Inviolate, incorruptible,* inviŏlāta, illæsa, intēgra, incorrupta.

vīrus, i, neut. *Poison.* See venenum.

vis, in plur. vīres, fem. 1. *Strength.*—2. *Violence.*—EP. 1. *Great,* magna, ingens. *Irresistible,* invicta. *Victorious,* victrix -īcis. *Fearless,* impăvĭda.— 1, 2. *Cruel,* sæva, fēra, immītis, crūdēlis.—2. *Sudden,* sŭbĭta, rĕpentīna. *Unexpected,* ĭnōpīna, ĭnexspectāta.

viscum. 1. *Misletoe.*—2. *Bird-lime.*—EP. 1. *Shining,* nĭtĭdum. *Grey,* glaucum. —2. *Tenacious,* tĕnax.

viscus, ĕris, neut. *The entrails.*—EP. *Inmost,* intĭmum, īmum. *Tender,* tĕnĕrum.

vīsum. *A sight, any thing seen.* See spectācŭlum.

vīsus, ūs. 1. *Sight.*—2. *A sight.*—EP. 1. *Acute,* ăcūtus. *Dim,* hĕbes -ĕtis.— 2. See spectaculum.

vīta. *Life.*—EP. *Mortal,* mortālis. *Brief,* brĕvis, frăgĭlis, cădūca. *Of uncertain duration,* dŭbia, incerta. *Full of anxiety,* anxia, sollĭcĭta. *Long,* longa, diūturna. *Happy,* fēlix -īcis, beāta. *Sad,* mĭsĕra, tristis.

vītis, is, fem. *A vine.*—EP. *Sacred to Bacchus,* Bacchĭca, Bacchēia, Bacchēa. *Purple,* purpŭrea. *Bearing clusters of grapes,* răcēmĭfĕra. *Bending,* lenta. *Productive,* fēcunda, fertĭlis. *Leafy,* pampīnea, frondōsa. *Sweet,* dulcis. *Sunny,* ăprīca.

vītĭsător, ōris, masc. *A vine-planter.* See vindemiator.

vĭtĭum. *A fault, vice.*—EP. *Base,* turpe, fœdum. *Shameful,* prŏbrōsum. *Wicked,* impium, scĕlĕrātum. *Incurable, irremediable,* immĕdĭcābĭle. *Indelible,* indēlēbĭle. *Inexcusable,* ĭnexcūsābĭle. *Ancient,* priscum, vĕtus -ĕris, antīquum.

vĭtrum. *Glass.*—EP. *Bright,* splendĭdum, lūcĭdum, fulgens. *Transparent,* pellūcĭdum. *Brittle,* frăgĭle.

vitta. *A fillet.*—EP. *Sacred,* săcra, săcrāta. *White,* alba, candĭda, albens. *Fatal (as put on a victim before sacrifice),* fătālis. *Worn by suppliants,* supplex -ĭcis.

vĭtŭla, vĭtŭlus. *A heifer or steer.*—EP. *Playful, wanton,* lascīvus, prōtervus. *Horned,* cornĭger -ĕri. See bos.

ūlīgo, ĭnis, fem. *The moisture of the earth.*—EP. *Damp,* mădĭda, hūmĭda. *Fertilising,* fertĭlis, læta, pinguis.

ulmus, fem. *An elm.*—EP. *Tall,* alta, ardua, prōcēra, ăĕria. *Hard,* dūra. *Leafy,* frondea, frondōsa. See arbor.

ulna. *An arm.* See brachium.

ultor, oris, masc., fem. ultrix, īcis. *An avenger.*—EP. *Sure,* certus. *Inevitable,* ĭnēvĭtābĭlis. *Fierce, pitiless,* sævus, fĕrus, fĕrox, immītis, crūdēlis. *Angry,* īrātus, īrācundus. *Impetuous,* ācer -cris. *Vigorous,* strēnuus, impĭger -gri.

ULV—URB 95

Present, præsens. *Impending*, instans. *Future*, fŭtūrus, ventūrus. *Late*, sērus. *Threatening*, mĭnax. *Deserved*, mĕrĭtus, dēbĭtus.

ulva. *Sedge.*—EP. *Growing by a river*, flŭmĭnea, flŭviālis. *By a marsh*, pălustris. *Worthless*, vīlis, ĭnūtĭlis.

ŭlŭla. *An owl.* See noctua.

ŭlŭlātus, ûs. *A howling or shrieking.*—EP. *Sad*, tristis, mœstus, mĭser –ĕri. *Timid*, păvĭdus. *Loud*, clāmōsis raucus. *Sudden*, sŭbĭtus. *Heard by night*, noc urnus. *Querulous, plaintive*, quĕrŭlus, flēbĭlis.

umbo, ōnis. *The boss on a shield.* See clypeus.

umbra. 1. *Shade.*—2. *A shadow or shade of a dead man, the shades below.*— EP. 1. *Cool*, frĭgĭda, gĕlĭda. *Leafy*, frondea, frondens, frondōsa. *Of a tree*, arbŏrea. *In a grove*, nĕmŏrōsa, nĕmŏrālis. *Known*, nōta. *Wished for*, optāta. *Sweet*, dulcis, amœna, grāta, jūcunda. *Spreading*, pătŭla. *Safe*, tūta, incŏlŭmis. *Green*, vĭrĭdis, vĭrĭdans. *Hospitable*, hospĭta. *Thick*, densa (see tenebræ).— 2. *Pale*, pallĭda. *Lifeless*, exănĭmis, exănĭma. *Happy*, fēlix –īcis, beāta. *Dear*, cāra, dīlecta. *Regretted*, dēsīdĕrāta. *Infernal*, infernа, Stўgia. See Orcus, Manes.

uncus. *A hook.*—EP. *Iron*, ferreus, ferrātus, ădămantīnus. *Barbed*, hāmātus. *Sharp*, ăcūtus. *Holding fast*, tĕnax.

unda. *A wave.*—EP. *Salt*, salsa. *Of the sea*, æquŏrea, mărīna. *Swelling*, tŭmĭda, tŭmens. *Foaming*, spūmea, spūmans, spūmōsa. *Refluent, ebbing and flowing*, rēflua, rēfluens. *Devouring*, ăvĭda, vŏrax. *Roaring, hoarse*, rauca. *Raging*, fŭriōsa, frĕmens. *Shining*, lŭcĭda, nĭtens. *Rising*, surgens.

unguentum. *Ointment.*—EP. *Fat*, pingue. *Sweet, fragrant*, dulce, frāgrans, ŏdōrum, ŏdōrātum. *Eastern, Assyrian, etc.*, ˜Eōum, Assўrium. *Costly*, prĕtiōsum, cārum, *Brought*, allātum.

unguis, is, masc. *A nail, a claw.*—EP. *Hard*, dūrus, rĭgĭdus. *Hooked*, uncus, ăduncus, rĕduncus. *Threatening*, mĭnax. *Hostile*, infensus, hostĭlis. *Cruel, pitiless*, fĕrus, sævus, immītis. *Rapacious*, răpax, ăvĭdus. *Tenacious*, tĕnax.

ungŭla. *A hoof.*—EP. *Solid*, sŏlĭda. *Hard*, dūra. *Resounding*, rĕsŏna. *Shod, armed*, armāta, ferrāta. *Rapid*, răpĭda, cĭta.

vŏcăbŭlum. *A name.* See nomen.

vŏcātus, ûs. *An invitation.*—EP. *Friendly*, ămīcus, bĕnignus. *Sudden*, sŭbĭtus. *Welcome*, grātus, acceptus. *Desired*, optātus. *Late*, sērus.

vŏlātus, ûs. *Flight.*—EP. *On high*, altus, arduus, sŭblīmis. *Rapid*, răpĭdus, præpes –ĕtis, cĭtus, cĕler –ĕris. *Dense*, densus.

vŏlŭcris. *A bird.* See avis.

vŏlūmen, ĭnis, neut. 1. *A revolution.* 2. *A book.*—EP. 1. *Continual*, assĭduum, crēbrum. *Winding*, sĭnuōsum. 2. See liber.

vŏluntas. *Will, wish.*—EP. *Free*, lībĕra. See cupido.

vŏluptas. *Pleasure.*—EP. *Delightful*, grāta, ămœna, jūcunda. *Short*, brĕvis. *New*, nŏva. *Sudden*, sŭbĭta. *Unusual*, insŏlĭta, ĭnassueta. *Luxurious*, luxŭriōsa. *Simple*, simplex –ĭcis. *Pure*, pūra. *Honourable*, prŏba, digna. *Deserved*, mĕrĭta. *Promised*, prŏmissa, pollĭcĭta. *Future*, fŭtūra. *Assured*, certa. *Genuine*, vēra.

vōmer, ĕris, masc. *A ploughshare.* See aratrum.

vŏrāgo, ĭnis, fem., **vortex, ĭcis,** masc. *A gulf, a whirlpool.*—EP. *Deep*, altus, prŏfundus. *Unseen*, cæcus, lātens. *Roaring*, frĕmens, raucus. *Devouring*, vŏrax, ăvĭdus. *Threatening*, mĭnax. *Fatal*, fātālis. *Raging*, turbĭneus, fŭriōsus, insānus.

vōtum.—1. *A prayer, a vow.*—2. *A wish.*—EP. 1, 2. *Pious*, pium. *Suppliant*, supplex –ĭcis. *Eager*, ăvĭdum. *Constant*, constans. *Continual*, assĭduum. *Repeated*, crēbrum, rĕpĕtītum. *Humble*, hŭmĭle. See preces.

vox, vōcis, fem.—1. *A voice, a sound.*—2. *A word.*—EP. 1. *Sweet*, dulcis, lĭquĭda, argūta, (*when singing*) cănōra. *Well known*, nōta. *Hoarse*, rauca. *Imperious*, impĕriōsa. *Loud*, magna, grandis.—2. See verbum.

ūpĭlio, ōnis, masc. *A shepherd.* See pastor.

urbs, bis, fem.—*A city.*—EP. *Ancient*, prisca, antīqua, vĕtus –ĕris, vĕtusta. *Sacred*, săcra, săcrāta, sancta. *Powerful*, pŏtens. *Great*, magna. *Proud*, sŭperba. *Splendid*, splendĭda, magnĭfĭca. *Celebrated*, clāra, inclўta. *Rich*, dīves –ĭtis, lŏcŭples –ētis, ŏpŭlenta. *With towers*, turrīt. *Strong*, vălĭda, fortis. *Impregnable*, ĭnexpugnābĭlis. *Invincible*, invicta, indŏmĭta. *Safe*, tuta. *Native (to an individual)*, pătria.

96   URN—ZON

urna. *An urn.*—EP. *Of earthenware*, fictĭlis. *Brittle*, frăgĭlis. *Small*, parva, exĭgua, arcta. *Funeral*, fērālis, fūnĕrea, fŭnĕbris. *The last*, ultĭma. *Sad*, *cause of tears*, tristis, flēbĭlis. *Brazen*, ahēna, ærea.

ursa, ursus. *A bear.*—EP. *Rough*, hirsūtus, hirtus, sētōsus. *Bristling*, horrĭdus, horrens. *Dwelling on mountains*, montānus. *Fierce*, fērox, fērus, sævus. *Terrible*, terrĭbĭlis, mĕtuendus.

urtĭca. *A nettle.*—EP. *Stinging*, ăcerba. *Worthless*, vīlis.

ūrus. *A buffalo.*—EP. *African*, Lĭbўcus, Gætŭlus. *Horned*, cornĭger –ĕri. *With hard feet*, cornĭpes –ĕdis. *Untameable*, indŏmĭtus. *Fierce*, fērus, fērox.

usus, ūs. 1. *Use.*—2. *Experience*, *skill.*—EP. 1. *Well-known*, *customary*, nōtus, sōlĭtus, consuetus. *Long*, longus. *Continual*, aseĭduus. *Ancient*, vĕtus –ĕris, antĭquus.—2. See experientia.

ŭtĕrus. *The womb.*—EP. *Fruitful*, fēcundus. *Pregnant*, grăvis, grăvĭdus. *Barren*, stĕrĭlis.

ūtĭlĭtas. *Usefulness.*—EP. *Great*, magna. *Proved*, spectāta. *Known*, nōta. *Lasting*, longa, mansūra. *Wished for*, optāta. *Genuine*, vēra. *Convenient*, commŏda, apta.

ūva. *A grape.*—EP. *Purple*, purpūrea, lĭvĭda. *Golden*, aurea. *Ripe*, mātūra. *Ripe in Autumn*, autumnālis. *Hanging*, pendens, dēpendens. *Generous*, gĕnĕrōsa. *Genial*, gĕniālia, alma.

vulgātor, ōris, masc. *One who makes known.*—EP. *Talkative*, garrŭlus, lŏquax.

vulgus, i, neut. *The common people.*—EP. *Low*, inconsiderable, vīle. *Ignoble*, ignōbĭle. *Fickle*, vărium, mōbĭle, mūtābĭle, lĕve, inconstans, infĭdum. *Ignorant*, ignārum.

vulnus, ĕris. *A wound.*—EP. *Fatal*, fātāle, fātĭfĕrum. *Bloody*, cruentum, sanguĭneum. *Dark*, ātrum, nĭgrum. *Sad*, *painful*, triste. *Ancient*, antĭquum, priscum, vĕtus –ĕris. *Deep*, altum. *Uniting*, *united*, colens. *Incurable*, immĕdĭcābĭle. *Inevitable*, inēvĭtābĭle. *Inconsolable (of a mental wound)*, inconsōlābĭle. *Sickening (esp. of a mortal wound)*, ægrum. *Glorious*, pulchrum, dĕcōrum.

vulpes, is, fem. *A fox.*—EP. *Crafty*, callĭda, astūta, dŏlōsa. *Red*, rūbra. *Treacherous*, perfĭda, infĭda.

vultur, ŭris, masc. *A vulture.*—EP. *Fierce*, fērox, fērus, sævus. *With hooked beak*, uncus, ăduncus, rēduncus. *Rapacious*, răpax. *Greedy*, ĕdax, ăvĭdus. *Flying swiftly*, præpes –ĕtis. *Living in the mountains*, *on the Alps*, *Caucasus*, etc., montānus, Alpīnus, Caucāsius.

vultus, ūs. *The countenance.* See facies.

uxor, ōris. *A wife.*—EP. *Chaste*, casta, pŭdĭca. *Faithful*, fĭda, fĭdēlis. *Loving*, ămans. *Lovely*, ămābĭlis, plăcens. *Beautiful*, pulchra, dĕcōra, candĭda, conspĭcienda, spectābĭlis. *Excellent*, ēgrēgia. *Agreeing with one*, concors –dis, ūnănĭma. *Dear*, căra, dīlecta. *Fruitful*, fēcunda.

Z.

Zĕphўrus. *The west wind.*—EP. *Gentle*, mītis, blandus. *Warm*, tĕpĭdus, tĕpens. *Blowing in summer*, æstīvus. *Hesperian*, Hespĕrius. *Happy (of good omen)*, fēlix –īcis, sĕcundus. *Genial*, almus.

zŏdĭăcus. *The zodiac.* See Gradus.

zōna. 1. *A belt.*—2. *A zone of the earth.*—EP. 1. *Of a virgin*, virgĭnea, *Chaste*, casta, pŭdĭca. *Embroidered*, picta, văria. *Embroidered with gold*, aurea, aurāta. *Round and smooth*, tēres –ĕtis. *Put in*, *or round a person*, indūta, circumfūsa.—2. *Habitable*, hăbĭtābĭlis. *Granted to men*, concessa. *Burning*, torrĭda. *Inhospitable*, ĭnhospĭta. *Frozen*, glăciālis, frīgĭda. *Northern*, Hўperbŏrea, Bŏreālis. *Forbidden*, vĕtĭta. *Inaccessible*, ĭnaccessa. *Pathless*, ăvia. *Distant*, longinqua, rĕmōta, ultĭma.

THE END.

LONDON: Printed by SPOTTISWOODE & Co., New-street-Square.

CPSIA information can be obtained
at www.ICGtesting.com
Printed in the USA
LVHW080558101022
730327LV00002B/68